FIVE HUNDRED TALES
TO TELL AGAIN

By the same Author

NELSON'S ENCYCLOPAEDIA
TALES OF TODAY
GOOD IN EVERYTHING
SHARE MY HARVEST
THE WONDERS OF YOUR HOUSE
AMERICAN ENGLAND
NEIGHBOURS
THE CHEERFUL DAY
ANOTHER CHEERFUL DAY
TALKING OUT OF DOORS
TALKING IN THE GARDEN
TALKING BY THE FIRE
THE SHINING HIGHWAY
NODDING WOLD
WINTER JOURNEY
UP HILL AND DOWN
GAY ADVENTURE
BRIGHT INTERLUDE
ALWAYS IT IS SPRING
CLOUD AND SUNSHINE
AND PASTURES NEW
FOLK TALES OF YORKSHIRE
TALES THEY TELL IN YORKSHIRE
THROUGH THE YEAR WITH H. L. GEE
THE PILGRIM
PLEASANT PEOPLE
THE FRIENDLY YEAR
THE DAILY ROUND
IMMORTAL FEW
THE SUNNY ROOM
H. L. GEE'S PLEASURE BOOK
etc.

The Friendly Series

ONE FINE DAY
CHANCE ACQUAINTANCES
ON MY WAY
AS IT HAPPENED

FIVE HUNDRED TALES TO TELL AGAIN

H. L. GEE

LONDON : THE EPWORTH PRESS

THE EPWORTH PRESS
(FRANK H. CUMBERS)
25-35 City Road, London, E.C.1

MELBOURNE CAPE TOWN
NEW YORK TORONTO

Published in 1955
Reprinted 1955

SET IN MONOTYPE IMPRINT AND PRINTED IN
GREAT BRITAIN BY THE CAMELOT PRESS LTD.,
LONDON AND SOUTHAMPTON

To
my friend
F. AUSTIN HYDE,
who has been telling short
stories a long time.

PREFACE

In making this collection of stories the compiler has had a twofold aim constantly in mind: To produce a book which, in addition to being a pleasure to read by the fire, is also a work of reference supplying a widely-felt need.

All the world loves stories, and here are 500 of them. Like the fairy music of Prospero's island, they give delight and hurt not, for nothing here is indelicate or cynical. Anecdotes of the famous —of kings and queens, statesmen, poets, musicians, artists, inventors, soldiers and sailors of many lands and every age—are side by side with stories of the common man. In these pages are tales of gods and goddesses and of everyday saints and heroes. We read of stirring events and of domestic incidents. There are epics of endurance in two world wars and there is an abundance of good humour. Nor is there any lack of stories which point to things spiritual. Turning these pages haphazardly we can hardly fail to find much that will encourage and cheer or touch a chord of sympathy or bring a smile or give inspiration.

500 Tales to Tell Again, then, is a book to open anywhere at any time—a pleasant, companionable book, an antidote to depression, a challenge to endeavour. Here's richness spiced with variety. Young folk glancing idly among these stories may perhaps find the imagination stirred; older folk—possibly a trifle disillusioned—may find something to rekindle faith in God and man.

But this compilation is not merely a book to while away an hour, it is—as already stated—a work of reference, for the addition of an unusually generous index enables us, if we choose, to use it as a tool.

These stories, legends, myths, parables, fables and anecdotes may all be told again. Each item illustrates a truth. The teacher will discover scores of tales illuminating history, biography, literature and science. To politicians, chairmen, after-dinner speakers, leaders of youth clubs, lecturers and others *500 Tales to Tell Again* may prove a rich source of illustrative material grave and gay.

A speaker will find that the index leads him with minimum

effort and maximum speed not only to tales illustrating such concrete subjects as cricket or music or Charles Lamb or Sir Winston Churchill or a well-known hymn but to such themes or abstractions as neighbourliness, patience, courage, forgiveness and prayer.

Often it is the human story which brings the truth home to us. The compiler believes that all these stories are worth telling. If worth telling once, surely they are worth telling again.

H. L. Gee

I

During the French Revolution, Jean Bon St André, a leader of the rising in Vendée, laughed in the face of a peasant and boasted: 'No more religion now! I'll have your steeples pulled down so that nothing will be left to remind you of your outworn superstitions.'

'Pull them down,' replied the peasant. '*You cannot help leaving us the stars.*'

2

One day in the reign of George the Third a woman was toiling in a harvest field near Weymouth. It was a sultry afternoon, and she was hot and tired as she plodded across the stubble, carrying heavy sheaves under her arms. Perhaps she was the least bit resentful, for she had not even a companion to talk to.

Presently she noticed that a man was leisurely approaching her. A gentleman, *indeed*—she could see *that* at a glance as he crossed the field to the corner where she was setting up stooks. A *fine* gentleman, surely. *And* a stranger. What could he want with her?

'My good woman,' murmured the fine gentleman, raising his hat as if she were a duchess and not a farm labourer's widow, 'tell me, how is it you are alone? I see horses tethered at the gate, and the rakes are thrown down here and there. Is anything afoot?'

'Oh, sir,' replied the woman, 'the rest have gone off to see the king.'

'Why, is he expected here today?'

'Yes, sir—so they say. Folk say he'll be driving along the road sometime this afternoon.'

'And wouldn't *you* like to see him going by?' asked the stranger.

'Indeed I would, sir. But I'm a widow, and I've five children to care for; and it's as much as a body can do to feed and clothe them without losing half a day's pay. No, sir, *I've* no time to go and see the king.'

The fine gentleman nodded. 'You are right, my good woman,' said he. 'Quite right.' Then he took out his purse, dropped two golden guineas into the astonished woman's hand, raised his hat as politely as before, and added: 'Oh, and when the others come back, tell them that as you couldn't go to see the king, the king came to see you.'

3

Speaking in Washington in 1943, Madame Chiang Kai-shek told this story:

A young Buddhist monk sitting outside his temple two thousand years ago looked very pious with his hands clasped. He was chanting Amita Buddha. Day after day he intoned these words, believing that he was thus acquiring grace.

One day the Father Prior of the temple sat beside him, and began rubbing a piece of brick against a stone. This went on day after day and week after week until, finally, the acolyte was overcome with curiosity, and burst out: 'Father Prior, what *are* you doing?'

'I'm trying to make a mirror,' replied the Father Prior.

'Why,' gasped the young monk, 'it's impossible to make a mirror of brick.'

'Yes,' was the reply, 'and it's just as impossible for you to acquire grace by doing nothing except chant Amita Buddha all day long.'

4

A young girl in a small German town had advertised a pianoforte recital, and below her name, as it appeared on the posters, was the information (quite untrue) that she was a pupil of Liszt.

The day before the recital the young pianist was suddenly terrified by the news that the great musician himself had arrived. For some months she had been masquerading as his pupil, but now her deception must be discovered, and all her hopes of making a living must inevitably be dashed.

Not knowing what to do, she finally decided to see the famous composer and tell him her story. In great agitation, therefore, she gained admittance to his room, and with tears streaming down her face and her hands clasped as she fell on her knees before him, she sobbed out her confession, explaining that she had been left an orphan, that she had no means of earning a livelihood other than her musical ability, and that she had pretended to be his pupil in order to win recognition.

Liszt looked at her with kindly eyes. 'You have done wrong,' he said; 'but we all make mistakes, and then the only thing left for us to do is to be sorry. I think you *are* sorry. Let me hear you play.'

Very timidly the girl obeyed, faltering at first, though she won confidence as she went on. She played marvellously, but Liszt corrected her in one or two points, and then said: 'My dear, I have now instructed you a little. You *are* a pupil of Liszt. You may go on with your concert; and as you tell me the programmes are not yet printed, you may add that the last item will be played, not by the pupil, but by the master.'

The Children's Newspaper.

5

Many years ago a Scottish nobleman happened to be dining in one of the stately homes of England. The room was magnificently furnished; the tableware was exquisite and the distinguished guests included some of the richest people in the land.

But the Scotsman was known to be poor.

Eventually Scotland became the topic of conversation; and one of the guests, pointing to an elaborate candelabrum in which dozens of candles were shining among richly ornamented silver foliage, declared that in all Scotland there was not one candlestick half so valuable.

To the amusement of the guests, the Scottish nobleman instantly replied that in his brother's castle in the Highlands were candlesticks worth far more than the superb candelabrum then above his head.

This wild boast was greeted with roars of laughter; but the Scotsman stuck to his word, there and then inviting anyone who cared to accept his brother's hospitality to see the candlesticks for themselves.

So it came about that some weeks later a dozen English people arrived at a dour castle overlooking a lonely glen. In due course they were piped to dinner in a bare hall with one long table. A chair was provided for each guest; and behind each chair stood a tall, broad, kilted Highlander holding a naked sword in one hand and a flaming torch in the other.

'Gentlemen,' said the poor but proud Scottish nobleman, 'behold the candlesticks!'

6

A Chinese teacher, a great admirer of Western civilization, secured a book giving the rules governing football. For weeks his pupils studied the rules until they could recite them perfectly. Then they went into a field and tried to play, but although they knew the rules by heart they were quite unable to play the game until an English schoolboy showed them (in half an hour) just what to do.

7

While at his Adirondack camp, J. P. Morgan, the American millionaire, one day decided suddenly to return to the city. Accordingly he telegraphed the president of the railroad that he wished the 10.24 to be stopped at Paul Smith's station. When he arrived, five minutes before the train, the station master was industriously checking figures.

'You got your orders to flag the train this morning?' J. P. Morgan asked crisply.

'No, I didn't get no orders to flag no train this morning.' The station master went on scribbling.

'You mean to say you're not going to flag this train?'

'Nope—not without orders.'

J. P. Morgan hurried into the station and emerged carrying a red flag. A whistle was heard up the track. The millionaire flourished the flag, and the train came to a stop.

'You'll hear about this,' J. P. Morgan told the station master as he boarded the train.

'Don't get excited,' was the reply. 'The 10.24 allus stops.'

JAMES BARNES: *From Then Till Now.*

8

Long ago, when the nave and transepts of a great cathedral were nearing completion, an unknown craftsman is said to have asked if he might share in the work. His was an unusual request. He would like, he told the master builder, to be allowed to fill one of the windows with coloured glass; and he pleaded so earnestly that when he added he would do it without payment, the master builder replied: 'Very well, we will see what you can do.'

To himself he said: 'After all, if this fellow proves hopeless at his job, we can easily knock *his* glass out, and get a skilled workman to do it again.'

So the unknown craftsman was left to go to work in his own way; and for months he laboured behind a screen, until at last the window was finished.

There came a day when what had been hidden was brought to light—a thing of indescribable beauty, for this window was richer in glorious colour than any of the other windows in the cathedral; so wonderful indeed that people came from far and near to see it.

'But where did you find all this exquisite glass?' asked the astonished and delighted master builder.

And the unknown craftsman is said to have replied: 'Sir, I picked it up here and there inside and outside the cathedral. *This window is made of fragments that had been thrown away as useless.*'

9

Aesop tells the story of two men walking along a road together and coming upon an axe lying in the way. They were friends, but the man who saw it picked it up, saying, 'Ah, I've found an axe. This *will* be useful.'

'Do not say I,' said the second man. 'Say *we* have found an axe, for we are friends, and are on the road together. Surely it is *our* axe, and we shall sell it and share the money?'

But the first man would not agree.

Now it happened that they had not gone far when the owner of the axe came running towards them. The moment he saw the first man carrying the axe he threatened to prosecute him. 'Oh, dear,' cried the poor fellow, 'we *are* in trouble now.'

'Do not say *we*,' said the second man. 'Say rather *you* are in trouble. You would not let me share the prize—you can hardly expect me to share the trouble.'

10

When Joe was a boy of twelve he was so shy that it took him a week to pluck up courage to ask old Mr Francis to lend his brace and bit.

'Brace and bit?' repeated Mr Francis, looking over the top of his steel-rimmed spectacles. 'What for?'

Joe hesitated at the door of the joiner's shop. 'Well,' he began.

'Speak up!' ordered Mr Francis. 'Speak up!'

Joe spoke up. 'It's this way, Mr Francis,' he explained. 'I'm trying to fix a shelf in our shed.'

'Shelf, eh? What for?'

'Well, one day, perhaps, I'll be able to buy a box . . . I'm saving up for one . . .'

'Box, Joe? What for, eh?'

'Oh, just so that if sometime I get a bit of wire-netting—perhaps on my birthday—and if I can fix the box on the shelf . . .'

'Yes, yes, but this wire-netting, Joe. What's *that* for?'

'Well, Mr Francis, I thought perhaps later this year, if I keep on saving up, I'll be able to buy a couple of rabbits. But first . . .'

'You want to borrow my brace and bit, eh? I see. Now listen, Joe. I'll lend you my brace and bit, if you promise to take care of it. You run along and get that shelf fixed. Then come back here. You'll find a box in the corner, *and* a bit of wire-netting. They're yours, Joe. And you'll need a pair of hinges for the door—forgotten *them*, hadn't you? Oh, and if you like to cycle over to Wykington tomorrow, my son there'll *give* you a couple of rabbits, if you tell him I say so.'

It all happened years ago, and Joe is now a married man with a schoolboy son who keeps rabbits; but he often says that, odd though it may sound, it was old Mr Francis who first gave him a hint of what the love of God is like.

11

John is a philosopher though not yet quite six.

His father died over a year ago. His mother, who has not a penny to spare, goes out to work five days a week, and John has to take his brother, Gordon—who is three years younger—to the Day Nursery every morning before going on to school. He is never home much before five in the afternoon, and even then he has to lend a hand with the chores. So life isn't easy for John.

Luckily, Mr Hopwood lives next door—a genial, middle aged gentleman who has always had a soft spot for John. He's a handy-man, and there is a shed at the bottom of his garden. It's amazing what comes out of that shed.

But the most amazing end product of Mr Hopwood's skill and devotion was a wheelbarrow. It was painted bright green outside and bright red inside; and Mr Hopwood, being a very wise man, arranged that it squeaked when trundled along the ground. One Saturday morning not long ago he presented that wheelbarrow to John, and John could hardly believe his eyes . . . or his ears. When Mr Hopwood went off to work he left John singing at the top of his voice—singing as he wheeled his squeaking wheelbarrow up and down the garden, the happiest boy in England.

But at dinnertime there was no singing. Mr Hopwood looked over the garden wall, and saw John standing on the path. His cheeks were stained with tears. 'Anything wrong?' inquired Mr Hopwood.

'It's the wheelbarrow,' replied John. 'Look! It was all *so* lovely; and then, *what* do you think? Gordon came out, and he's scratched every bit of it with a nail!'

'Well,' exclaimed Mr Hopwood. And then again, 'Well!'

For a moment man and boy stared at each other. Then John squared his shoulders. 'Oh, well,' he said tremulously, 'I've been *pushing* it nearly all the morning. I guess I'll have to *pull* it now!'

12

Early last century the good folk in a village near Falkirk were dispirited. Strictly religious as they were, they felt that the Lord's work was not progressing satisfactorily, and eventually an elder of the kirk went to see the old minister, and spoke to him very gravely. In his solemn way the elder said he thought there must be something wrong somewhere—perhaps in the minister's preaching, for a whole year had gone by and not one person had been added to the congregation. Well, strictly, there *had* been one addition, but one of no consequence, since it was merely a boy.

'It is true,' said the minister. 'It is true; but I have great hopes of that one.'

So the elder walked home sadly, but satisfied that he had

made his protest, and the minister went on with his work, perhaps doubting a little.

One day the boy called to see the minister, asking very timidly if there were any means of getting a better education. The minister, delighted, said he would do what he could.

That boy, the only convert made during the year, was to win a gracious place among the world's best men and women, for he was Robert Moffat, the great missionary.

13

Molière, the friend of all men, high and low, good and bad, knew what it was to be acquainted with poverty. He never forgot, in his own hour of triumph, how much the poor suffer.

Strolling in the country outside Paris one afternoon, he met a poor old man who was hobbling along the dusty road. Without as much as the least indication of what he was about to do, Molière overtook the old fellow, slipped a coin into his hand, smiled, and hurried on.

The old man, looking at his open palm, was astounded. Then he quickened his step. 'Monsieur,' he called, trembling and breathless, 'but Monsieur has no doubt made a mistake. This, Monsieur, is a piece of gold!'

'I intended it to be, my friend,' was the genial reply, 'and since you are so honest, why, here's another to go with it—and God bless you!'

14

In the early days of the settlers in North America news came that the Indians were on the war-path—in a real, not merely a figurative sense; and that they were making a big 'round-up' of the whites. Already they had destroyed many settlements, killing the settlers and burning their cabins; now they were advancing towards a settlement where, among others, lived a Quaker with his wife and two small children.

As soon as news of the danger reached the settlers, the men held a hurried consultation, deciding that, as they were not strong in numbers, there was only one course open to them, namely, to abandon the compound at once, and ride off to a fort some miles away, believing that they would there find other settlers, and that by using the fort as a base they might make a combined attack on the Redskins. Within an hour of this decision the settlement was deserted, the men riding off with their wives and children, and whatever valuables they could carry.

But the Quaker did not ride off. He remained in the settlement; first because he did not believe in fighting, and secondly because he *did* believe in friendship.

When every other cabin was deserted his own sheltered all he held most dear. When the settlement was strangely quiet there was the sound of childish laughter in his log-dwelling; and even this was unheard after sundown, for the little ones were put to bed. For an hour or two after dark the Quaker and his wife went on with their work by lamplight, and when all was finished they retired for the night, the Quaker, as his custom was, drawing in the latch-thong—the strip of leather which hung outside the door so that anyone might come in by pulling it down and so raising the latch.

After a time, however, he said, 'Wife, ought we not to have left the latch-thong *outside*? Surely God can protect us, if it be His will, without our fastening the door against our enemies?'

'Thou knowest,' she replied, simple, trusting Quaker that she was—though she could not have been human if there had been no anxiety in her heart.

So the Quaker opened the door, drew out the latch-thong, and left it hanging limply outside, ready for all who cared to come in. Then he went to bed.

He was roused, not by any sound, for the stillness was unbroken, but by a sense that all was not well. Going to the window he looked out, and there in the moonlight were dark forms gliding among the cabins. The Redskins had come. One glance was enough to show him that they were angry. They gesticulated wildly, and soon the silence was stabbed by rising voices and shouts and cries. The birds had flown! One by one the log-cabins were set on fire.

Stepping back into the room, the Quaker stood rigid, hardly daring to breathe. Suddenly two eyes appeared at the window; a face was pressed close against the glass. Other eyes looked in; there were shouts and yells and the pad of naked feet on the hard ground. He had been seen—he, and his wife, and children—and the Indians were running round the cabin. There was a momentary silence, then another cry. . . . The time had come.

With a whispered prayer on his lips and his arm round his wife, his back to his children that he might not see the sight he feared most of all, the Quaker stood erect.

But why did not the Indians rush the door at once? Why need they delay? The seconds went by like centuries. The end *must* come—would not God be merciful and let it come quickly?

How long he stood there waiting, the Quaker never knew, but there came a deathly silence—some trick was being planned, no doubt—and the tension became almost intolerable; after the frantic hubbub, the stillness was more ominous. He waited for death, prayed for it, longed for it, was ready and anxious to welcome it. At last, unable to bear the suspense any longer, he strode across the floor, wrenched open the door, flung it far back and stood as a target for a hundred arrows.

Not a Redskin was in sight. Far above the dark pines the moon looked down on the deserted settlement. At first the Quaker could not believe that deliverance had come, but presently he glanced up, and there, nodding faintly in the breeze, was a white feather in the thatched roof.

It was the Red Indians' sign of friendship.

15

Mark Twain tells us of a neighbour of his, a connoisseur of books, who knew less about the art of being friendly than he did about first editions. Once, Mark Twain asked if he might borrow a book, and the connoisseur replied: 'You may consult it in my library, but I cannot let you take it away.'

There came a day when the book-lover asked if he might borrow Mark Twain's lawn-mower, whereupon the humorist replied: 'Certainly, but you must use it in *my* garden.'

16

When a son was born to Napoleon all France was delighted, the people giving the Little King, as he was called, a wonderful golden cradle with a winged figure of Victory over the hood. The idol of France, he was a fascinating little fellow, and had everything the heart could wish for.

There is a quaint story of a day when Napoleon took him on his famous white horse, Marengo, for a military review in the

Champ de Mars. As the child was only three there was some anxiety as to whether he might cry when the trumpets sounded and the drums rolled, but he was very good indeed.

After all the pomp and ceremony, Napoleon asked him what he would like best as a reward for behaving so well.

It was a wonderful opportunity. The man whose armies were everywhere triumphant was ready to do a child's bidding. Had the Little King asked for a fortune he might have had it. If he had begged for something which kings alone can give, would not Napoleon have been able to supply it? But this small boy who had slept in a golden cradle made only a modest request, 'Please,' he whispered, 'may I go and paddle in the mud?'

17

A Leeds teacher took a class of slum children to Ilkley not long ago. The green fields thrilled the boys, who rolled among the grass, plunged through ferns, and sang and shouted. They talked excitedly. Forgetting the smoke of the city, they gave themselves up to the enjoyment of their sunny hour; but it was all over much too soon.

One incident impressed the teacher more than anything else. When the scholars were back in Leeds, a little fellow *kissed the bus.*

Yorkshire Post, 1937.

18

Imagination goes a long way. A charlady who does not approve of electric ovens has declared that the worst of them is that the food always tastes of electricity.

19

Once upon a time, in the early morning of the world, all the animals went to the chief tailor to have tails fitted.

Well, the Manx cat had not gone far when he saw a horse with a bushy tail, and he wished he had one like that, so he went back to the tail man and asked for a tail like a horse, and the tail man, though furious, gave him one. The little Manx cat was pleased with his bushy tail till some rabbits caught sight of him. They laughed so loudly that the Manx cat was very upset, so he slipped off his tail, and ran back to the tail man to ask for the three-inch tail he had had at first.

But when he got to the cave he saw a notice outside which said: *Gone away for ever.*

20

From America comes the story of a blind man who lived in a pleasant little house with a large garden. Being retired, he spent every spare moment in his garden, where—in spite of his handicap—he planted and weeded and kept his lawn smooth as a billiard table. Spring, summer and autumn, his garden was a picture of glowing colour.

'Say,' remarked a visitor to that town in New York State, 'what's the idea? You can't see a thing, can you?'

'Not a thing!'

'Well, then, why bother with the garden? What's the use of flowers if you don't know one colour from another?'

The blind man, standing by the wall, his bare arms folded, smiled at the stranger. 'Well,' said he, 'I guess it's this way: First, I've always liked gardening; and just because I'm blind don't seem a good excuse for giving it up—I kind of *feel* my way around. Second, if I can't *see* what's growing I can touch my flowers and shrubs—caressing 'em. Third, I can smell the fragrance I've helped to create. And fourth—well, I guess there's *you*.'

'Me? But you don't know *me*.'

'No, but I knew you'd be coming by one of these days; and if this bit of God's earth were a wilderness, you'd be disappointed. After all, just because what a feller does don't help *him* a lot is no reason for not doing it—'specially if it helps others a bit.'

'Guess I never thought of it that way,' admitted the visitor.

'And, of course,' added the blind gardener, smiling again, 'folk coming by stop and have a chat with me, same as you're doing now, and I reckon that means something to a blind man, you know.'

21

Indra, god of a Thousand Eyes, was one day walking in a beautiful forest near the city of Benares. Presently he came to a stricken tree, a sad spectacle amid the luxuriant foliage. Sitting on one of the boughs was a parrot, and Indra laughed when he saw it. 'Foolish bird,' he cried, 'why do you sit in the shade of decay when all around is beauty?'

'Oh, king,' the parrot answered, 'I was born under these leaves. I learnt to fly from these branches, and this tree sheltered me in my earliest days. Shall I now desert it because it is old and decayed?'

'Well spoken,' said Indra. 'I will reward you for your loyalty by granting any boon you ask.'

Without hesitation the parrot replied: 'I have only one request: Restore this tree.'

So Indra laid his hand on the stricken tree, which at once became full of life and loveliness.

22

You are to picture a tall, bearded man who looks rather grim as he sits at a desk in his study. He is working anxiously, for there is much to be done, and the task requires great concentration. The law of the house—as severe as the law of the Medes and Persians—is that he must never on any account be disturbed during the time set apart for his writing. *Never!*

You see him, then, sitting at his desk, frowning, toiling, engaged upon investigations of supreme importance until the study door opens an inch or two, very softly, and a chubby, rosy little face—the face of a boy of four—appears. Very gravely he addresses the distinguished scientist at the desk—this tall, bearded man who happens to be the boy's father.

'If you'll tum out and play wiv us, I'll give you sixpence,' says the small boy.

The stern man rises from his chair, frowns more terribly than ever, hesitates a moment, looks down at the eager, pleading face, and then, having put his pen on the desk, crosses the room on tiptoe, steals furtively out of the house, and follows the tempter into the garden, doing no more work all that morning.

He was Charles Darwin.

23

Bedale is one of the quietest little towns in Yorkshire, and there it was that Tom and Annie began to think of getting married soon after Tom had secured a good post in Leeds. Eventually they rented a house, and the two of them had a happy time furnishing it.

A day or two before the wedding they had a look round their new home, and were very pleased with it. 'There's only one thing worries me, Tom,' murmured Annie. 'You see, Leeds is such a great, noisy place. There's trams running half the night just outside our front door, and there's trains shunting at the back. I doubt, Tom, I'll not sleep over well the first night or two.'

Affectionately her lover put his arm about her. 'Noo then, lass,' he murmured gently, 'dean't fash thi sen. If it's ower noisy here i' Leeds, tha mun go back to thi muther's while you've getten used tiv it.'

24

A humble clerk in Whitehall had a bright idea one day. In his office were scores of ancient files crammed with out-dated and wholly worthless correspondence. Why not burn the lot, and thus make more room for recent letters? Greatly daring, the clerk ventured to suggest this, doing so in true bureaucratic style, for he submitted his proposal in the form of a chit which was duly sent to his immediate superior.

As that individual heartily agreed, he endorsed the chit, and forwarded it to *his* superior, who sent it to another department, where it was advanced to a yet higher authority. Thus the idea worked its way to the supreme authority and, in the fullness of time, the chit returned to the humble clerk.

'Your recommendation is approved,' declared the Big Chief. 'The files referred to in your communication of the 8th may be destroyed *provided that copies are made of all papers beforehand.*'

25

Once upon a time—for though a true tale it is charming enough to begin in this way—there was a little scullery-maid all alone and by herself halfway between two places, and weeping sadly. She was sitting on a box, and the box was very heavy, and so was the little maid's heart.

Presently a shabbily dressed man came up the hill, stopped when he saw the maid in tears, and asked very kindly what the matter might be.

The little maid answered all in one breath. 'Oh, dear, dear,' she said, 'I'm the new scullery-maid at Arundel Castle, and I've come by train today, and a porter at the station promised to carry my box all the way for me, but when he got as far as this he said, "How much are you going to give me, Miss?" and I said, "Sixpence," because it was all I had; and he said, "No good, Miss; make it a shilling," but I couldn't, you see, so he dropped the box, and here I am.'

'Well, well,' said the shabby man. 'I'll carry it for you.'

'Now that's real good of you,' murmured the little maid, smiling through her tears.

So the shabby man hoisted the heavy box on his shoulder, and the two walked towards Arundel Castle. To such questions as, 'What sort of a body is cook?' and, 'Do you know the butler?' and, 'Have they late dinner *every* night?' the shabby man answered to the best of his knowledge. Thus they came to the back door, or very near, when the little maid inquired suddenly, 'Are *you* something in the castle?'

'Well, yes,' murmured the shabby man vaguely.

The little maid looked him up and down before she said: 'I should think you're the odd man about the place, aren't you?'

The shabby man permitted himself to smile. 'I guess that just fits me,' he agreed.

There was a pause, and then the little maid added impulsively, 'Tell me what they call you.'

'Call me?' The shabby man seemed at a loss to know precisely *what* they called him. At last, aware that a pair of very searching eyes were scrutinizing him, he shuffled away, remarking, almost apologetically, 'Oh, they just call me *Norfolk*.'

Then the shabby man went round to the front door.

26

When a German in South Africa played on his violin Gluck's *Ach! Ich habe Sie verloren*, a group of uneducated Hottentot women listened spellbound, some weeping. Next day the air was being sung all over the native village.

27

Two girls employed in the soap works at Port Sunlight went on holiday to a famous Lancashire resort. One day they set out for a mystery drive by motor coach. This proved to be a run to Port Sunlight, and included the privilege of being shown over the soap works!

28

Even though we cannot see our way we may be sure that all will be well if we put our trust in God. So, at any rate, thought a boy lying in hospital in France.

We say a *boy*, for he was little more than that—a soldier who had not lived twenty years, and whose love of living no one could measure. Far from home and kith and kin, he was suffering day and night. His eyes were bandaged. One day a doctor removed the bandage, made an examination, shook his head, and whispered a word to a nurse.

Presently a chaplain came into the ward. 'Tell him the news,' pleaded the nurse. 'I can't—he's been so wonderfully brave and patient, the dear laddie.'

Feeling that this was the hardest task he had ever had, the chaplain sat by the bed. 'Son,' said he, 'I have to tell you that you'll never see again.'

For a time—for what seemed a *long* time—there was no reply, though the young soldier's lips twisted oddly. He was thinking, no doubt, of all the years ahead, if they were given to him, in which he would miss the things he loved so much—birds and flowers and trees, sunrise and sundown, the faces of dear ones. 'It isn't news, *really*,' he whispered huskily at last. 'I kind of guessed it, you know . . . though all along I hoped against hope. . . . Will you come again tomorrow, padre?'

The chaplain promised that he would; and, sure enough, next day he sat on the bed, and asked as cheerily as possible: 'Well, how do you feel about it *now*, son?'

'Oh, I'm all right *now*, padre,' was the reply. 'I've got my second wind, as you might say. You know the twenty-third Psalm? Well, there's a verse that just fits me if only you'll let me alter one word.' Then, quietly and calmly, almost happily, the boy went on: ' "Yea, though I walk through the valley of the shadow of *life*, I will fear no evil . . . *for Thou art with me*." '

29

A traveller in Holland who had heard much of Dutch pasties thought he would like to sample one. He therefore called the lady of the house at which he was staying and said, 'Madam, I should like to try a Dutch pasty. Will you be so good as to make one?'

'What!' she exclaimed. 'Make a Dutch pasty when I do not know if you have money enough to pay? Do you not know, sir, that it will cost thirty guilders?'

The traveller's friend explained that such an amount could be raised. 'For,' said he, 'my companion is an expert flute-player, and he can easily go out and make thirty guilders by playing.'

'Oh, indeed?' said the sceptical landlady. 'Is that so? Then I must hear him!'

Setting her arms akimbo, she stood before the visitor and demanded a tune on his flute. Taking up his instrument, the traveller played such sweet airs for her that she was enchanted by his performance. 'Ah, sir,' said she, 'there's no doubt you can play. You will easily raise the money. I will go now and make the Dutch pasty.'

So off she went, little dreaming that when she had called the tune it had been played for her by Frederick the Second of Prussia, then travelling incognito through Holland.

30

He married an admiral's daughter, and on his wedding day he wore the first V.C. ever pinned on a hero's coat. His name was Charles Davis Lucas, and he was mate of a paddle steamer, the *Hecla*, then commanded by Sir William Hall—whom everyone knew as Nemesis Hall, one of the sternest of all admirals in the British Navy.

The British were attacking the batteries on Aland Island, and there was hard and furious fighting that June day in 1854, when the *Hecla* was being fired on at five hundred yards. Almost every shot told; and there came a moment of horror when a shell landed on the deck, and skidded into a corner, the fuse still burning. In a matter of seconds the shell must explode. Instant death was inevitable—or so it seemed.

One man only was not paralysed with fear. He was Charles Davis Lucas, who ran forward, calmly picked up the shell, and hurled it into the sea.

In this way the mate saved the ship. Stern Nemesis Hall, looking on from the bridge, singled out the amazingly cool seaman for special mention; and it was for this act of courage that Charles Davis Lucas was awarded the first V.C. And since none but the brave deserve the fair we are glad he married the admiral's daughter—clear proof that there is romance in real life after all.

31

On one occasion two Leeds business men took advantage of the lunch hour to hurry to the Headingley Cricket Ground in order to watch a particularly interesting match—every match being particularly interesting, of course. Feeling hungry, one of the two whistled to a boy near the entrance to the Ground. 'Here, sonny,' said he, 'take this shilling, and bring us three meat pies from the shop at the corner—if you look sharp you can have one of them for yourself.'

Off went the lad like the wind, returning breathless within a minute or two. 'Eightpence change,' said the honest fellow.

'Here, what's the idea?' demanded the business man.

'It's your change,' the boy explained. 'They'd only *my* pie left.'

32

John Sebastian Bach was never rich, and in youth he was exceedingly poor. As a boy he often tramped as many as thirty miles a day to hear some famous organist, and on one occasion he had walked all the way to Hamburg, where he found himself without money, hungry, and a long way from home. In this forlorn state what should he do but linger before the window of an inn from which there came the delicious smell of cooking.

It was indeed a savoury smell, and poor Bach would have given anything (if he had had something) for a morsel of food, when suddenly the window opened and someone (he never knew who) threw him *two herrings*!

Bach thanked heaven for them. Then came a surprise: *There was a Danish ducat in each herring!*

33

It is related that the Russian general, Suwaroff, was one day approaching the French in Italy, when what might have proved an ugly incident occurred. His army, exhausted by the hardships of forced marches, hungry, discontented and desperate, was on the point of mutiny. They were far from home, having cut their way down to the Italian frontier and climbed the great St Gotthard Pass, a feat of endurance which would be difficult for an army today and was still more difficult in the eighteenth century.

At last the troops would go no further. Their own land hundreds of miles behind, unknown dangers before them, they refused to have the great mountain barrier between themselves and all hope of retreat.

It was then that Suwaroff's amazing power to obtain his own way was put to the test. He was one against thousands. All his plans rested on a single decision. Either he advanced and tried to win victory or he retreated and was for ever disgraced. Another general might have attempted to use rhetoric. Some might have bullied. Suwaroff did neither. Taking his stand at the head of his army, blaming no man for mutiny, he commanded a grave to be dug in the road. The soldiers watched sullenly. Was it for the first mutineer? Silence fell on the great company as the grave was dug deeper, the earth piled up at the sides. Then General Suwaroff strode to the edge, turned to his men, took off his uniform, and said, 'Soldiers, bury me here. I cannot survive the disgrace of abandoning the expedition.'

With that he sprang into the grave and lay down.

His deed, more than his words, impressed his men. They went on, proud to follow so fine a leader.

34

At a state banquet given by Frederick the Great of Prussia to his courtiers and noblemen, the monarch asked those present to explain why his revenues continued to diminish despite incoming taxes. An old general of the Hussars remarked dryly, 'I will show Your Majesty what happens to the money.'

Taking a piece of ice from a decanter, he lifted it high for inspection. Then he handed it to his neighbour, requesting him to pass it on from hand to hand to the King. By the time the piece of ice, originally as big as a man's fist, reached Frederick, it was about the size of a pea.

Christian Science Monitor.

35

Two travellers, Aesop tells us, agreed to stand by each other in danger. Suddenly a savage bear rushed on them. One traveller, forgetting his companion and his promises, immediately ran to a tree and climbed into its branches. The other, left to himself, felt that he had no chance of survival. Remembering, however, that a bear will not touch a dead body, he threw himself flat on his face and pretended to be dead.

The bear came up, sniffed at him all over, and at length, feeling satisfied there was no life in the body, walked off.

At this the coward descended from his hiding-place and asked, with a smile, what it was the bear had whispered. 'I noticed,' said he, 'that he put his mouth very close to your ear.'

'Why,' replied the other, 'he gave me this very good advice: never trust those who in the hour of trial refuse to stand by their friends.'

36

Once there was a clockmaker who made a little clock, and said to it: 'Now, little clock, I have made you strong enough to strike a million times.'

Then he wound up the clock, and put it on a shelf near a big grandfather clock; and the little fast-ticking clock said: 'I say, I say, what do you think? What *do* you think? I've got to strike a million times! I'll never do it—never, never, never. A million! Just *think of it*!'

And the grandfather clock solemnly replied: 'Do not *think* of it, little fellow. Think of something else. All you have to do is to strike one or seven or twelve, as the case may be . . . just keep on striking when the time comes, and so, bit by bit, without noticing it, you'll reach the million mark!'

And it was so!

37

A very old man and a very bright-eyed little girl were sitting in the twilight one evening. The man was the gentle yet dauntless

Quaker poet, John Greenleaf Whittier, who became blind in old age, but very greatly loved his home at Amesbury among the green hills of New Hampshire in America. His friend was a visitor, and the poet had unintentionally given her a difficult problem to solve.

'Read me something,' Whittier begged.

But the twilight had deepened, and there was not light enough for anyone to read. Not wishing to remind the old man of his blindness, the tender-hearted little maid pretended to read, though actually she recited part of Whittier's poem on the *Eternal Goodness*. After she had repeated the famous words:

> 'I know not where His islands lift
> Their fronded palms in air;
> I only know I cannot drift
> Beyond His love and care,'

the poet said, 'Dear child, what beautiful lines. Who wrote them?'

'Why, *you*, Mr Whittier,' the little girl replied.

'Did I?' said the old man slowly. 'Then God must have given them to me, for I could never have written such words without Him.'

38

There has come down to us a charming story of little Thomas Westwood who, as a boy, lived next door to Charles Lamb. Whenever one of the literary giants of the day looked in for a chat with 'Elia', Mary Lamb used to tap at Thomas's window as a signal that he might steal into the room and hear the immortals talking.

39

'Murderer! Coward! Liar!' someone once wrote to Sir Winston Churchill, enclosing savagely sarcastic verses.

'I am very sorry to receive your letter with the evidence it gives of your distress of mind,' replied Churchill. 'The fact that you do me the greatest injustice does not deprive you of my sympathy, since you have obviously suffered so much.'

HOWARD PHILIP: *The Psychologist*.

40

Once upon a time there was a little man whose name was Button Gwinnett. He was born at Down Hatherley, in Gloucestershire, his father being vicar for forty years. After trading in Wolverhampton, where he found his wife, Button sailed to America in 1765, became a respectable citizen of Savannah, in Georgia, kept a store there, bought goods wholesale, sold them retail, owned a plantation, did no one any harm, won a local reputation for honesty and all-round decency, and by some odd trick of fate found himself taking up a pen in 1776 to sign the *Declaration of Independence*. That was the peak of his career, for next year he fought a duel and got himself killed. So ends the story, one might imagine; but the fact is that the story really only begins at this point.

For very soon after the *Declaration of Independence* had become history, the signatures appended to it began to be regarded as precious in the eyes of autograph hunters. The fifty-five men who had signed the document were looked upon as the Fathers of the United States, and letters or bills or business transactions bearing their signatures became increasingly valuable. As the years went by the signatures of fifty-four of the 'fathers' were snapped up readily at a fair rate of exchange, but before long Button Gwinnett's signature began to soar in price.

Oddly enough, having been unimportant all his life, having attended few public meetings, and having signed very few documents of note, his signature became the rarest of all the fifty-five. Had he been, say, Mayor of New York, autograph hunters might have come upon five hundred documents signed by him; being only Mr Gwinnett, a modest planter, few of his signatures came to light, and people who wanted to boast that they had a complete 'set of the fathers' were quickly compelled to pay a higher price for a scrap of paper with Button Gwinnett's scrawl on it than for any others. Such is the irony of fate that within fifteen years of the *Declaration of Independence*, autograph collectors were paying £500 for Button Gwinnett's signature, and in later years the price jumped to over £10,000.

One day, when the price was high, someone in Wolverhampton, in England, happened to be looking through old files, and came by chance upon three of Button Gwinnett's signatures. The little English shopkeeper, it seems, had attended some minor committee, signed the minutes, and by doing so had subsequently caused a flutter in two continents, his three strokes of the pen being bought up at fabulous prices by American collectors.

Is not all this an unexpected illustration of the truth of Shakespeare's dictum that some are born great, some achieve greatness, and some have greatness thrust upon them?

41

The proprietor of a grocer's shop in a remote village kept a commercial traveller waiting. His one assistant was a girl who, standing on a stool, reached down a can of peas, and in doing so dislodged others, one of which crashed on the commercial traveller's head. Luckily he was wearing a hard black hat. It was knocked over his eyes.

To be thus ill-used while waiting patiently for orders was bad enough, but the commercial traveller's humiliation was complete when the proprietor snapped, 'Hey, be careful, Miss. That might have been a customer!'

42

During the gold-rush in Colorado an astute mining engineer offered two ignorant men forty thousand dollars for their claim. The sum was reasonable, but the owners of the claim declared they would sell out for nothing less than a hundred thousand dollars.

'Very well,' said the engineer. 'Come to my hotel tomorrow morning.'

The two ignorant men arrived at the appointed time, and the mining engineer immediately untied a canvas bag, and with a fine flourish poured out before their hungry eyes a cascade of twenty thousand dollars. 'It's yours if you care to do a deal,' he urged.

Without more ado the men exclaimed: 'Done . . . Make out the deed!'

43

Henri was a Frenchman, and Michael a stray dog who struck up a friendship with Henri and stayed behind in the rear trenches during World War I whenever an advance was made. Every time the soldiers returned, Michael scanned all the faces anxiously till the one face he knew and loved appeared. Then all was well.

So it went on time after time.

One day the soldiers returned, but Michael did not find Henri's face. He waited till the last man was in. Then he dashed out from the camp, racing under heavy fire to the derelict no-man's-land. Presently he returned carrying a glove—Henri's glove, and a search-party went out to look for their fallen comrade. At last they stumbled on him, but he was stiff and cold, and there was no time to bring back a dead man. In spite of whinings from the stray dog, the party ran for cover.

All next day a battle raged in that area, and in the evening a shadow advanced to the French lines. A sentry who was about to shoot, put down his rifle when he saw it was only Michael.

But Michael was not alone. He had been dragging something, and was breathless with exertion. Someone went out and found what looked like a bundle of rags, torn shreds of clothing, and in them, Henri, wounded, ill, *but still alive.*

What is more, Henri lived to pat Michael on the head many times after that.

44

This is the true story of a patchwork quilt which helped to spread the gospel.

It was made by a poor old woman who attended a church in England which some years before had been proud to see one of its Sunday-school teachers go out to Africa as a missionary. Full of enthusiasm, the young man dreamed of the time when he would be able to build a little chapel; and one day it seemed as if his dream were coming true, for the native chief of that district declared that he was willing to sell a piece of land. Unfortunately, however, the missionary could not pay the high price demanded, so he wrote to the church of his boyhood, told the people of his chance, and begged them to help.

They did. Organizing a sale of work, the ladies sewed week after week. All their embroidery, pillow-slips, baby clothes, tablecloths and other gifts were exquisite, with one exception—a patchwork quilt, its squares sewn together with coarse thread, its vivid colours crude and ill-matched.

Most of the articles were disposed of at the sale, though (as had been expected) no one bought the patchwork quilt. It had been kind of the old woman to make it, but it was good for nothing.

What, then, should be done with it? They could not give it away; it was too ugly. They dare not burn it lest the old woman should hear of it and be grieved. At last someone suggested that the oddments left over from the sale should be tied up in the patchwork quilt, and the parcel sent to the missionary in Africa. It was a happy solution to an embarrassing problem.

The money which had been raised was mailed with a letter saying a parcel was on its way; but although the sum was considerable it was not even half enough to pay for the plot of land. Hoping against hope, the missionary called on the chief and tried to bargain with him, only to find that the fellow refused to lower his price.

It was a sad young missionary who unpacked the parcel of goods from his home church when it arrived some weeks later. The dainty garments he knew would sell for a few handfuls of meal or bunches of fruit, no more; as for the patchwork quilt, he wondered what in the world the ladies at home had been thinking about to send it to a country where the greatest difficulty of all was to keep cool.

One day he announced his sale, the natives flocking to see what they could buy. The chief was among them. He had no eyes for the garments which had been made by well-to-do ladies with clever fingers. He was not interested in lace and silk. The exquisite embroidery meant nothing to him. The one thing upon which he set his heart was the gaudy quilt with its dazzling patches of green and blue and yellow and crimson. What the ladies at home had despised he coveted the moment he saw it. The quilt fascinated him. He fingered it. He threw it over his broad black shoulders. He strutted about in it. At last he asked if he might buy it.

The missionary, hiding a smile, said it had been made far across the sea; there was no other like it.

'If you will give me this marvellous garment,' declared the chief, 'I will let you have the piece of land you want.'

A bargain was struck at once. The chief was delighted, the missionary thankful; and when, a little later, his story of what the patchwork quilt had done reached his home town, a poor old woman's heart was filled with joy because the work of her loving fingers had been so richly blessed.

45

A poor fisherman happened one day to find a copper bottle in his net after fishing in the Arabian Sea. The copper bottle had a queer seal. When the fisherman had broken it and had pulled out the cork, he was amazed to see a cloud of black smoke rise into the air, gather itself into a fantastic shape, and become a horrible genie. 'Mercy, sire, mercy,' cried the spirit. 'Forgiveness I plead, forgiveness, O great and mighty Solomon, king of the wide lands, monarch . . .'

'Just a minute,' said the fisherman, 'there's some mistake. Who do you take *me* for?'

'King Solomon,' replied the dreadful spirit.

'Bless us,' exclaimed the fisherman. 'Solomon died long ago.'

'Then,' said the genie, 'I will rush through the earth slaying and destroying, for I have long been a prisoner, and now I thirst for revenge. And, what is more, I'll begin with *you*.'

The genie was raising his long arms as he spoke, but the fisherman, frightened almost out of his wits, said hurriedly: 'Yes, very good. Do as you like, kill as many as you like—but even if you hurl the mountains into the sea, I'll never believe anybody *your* size came out of this bottle! Never!'

'You don't believe it?' asked the angry genie. 'You don't think I'm powerful enough to do *that*? I'll show you!'

He did. Condensing in the twinkling of an eye, he returned to the copper bottle. 'Well, who would have thought it?' murmured the fisherman to himself, neatly replacing the cork and throwing the bottle back into the sea.

46

'I wonder at your patience,' said Susannah Wesley's husband to her on one occasion. 'You have told that child the same thing twenty times.'

The wise mother of John and Charles Wesley answered with rare philosophy: 'Had I satisfied myself by saying it only nineteen times, I should have lost all my labour.'

47

'George,' ordered the small boy's mother, 'how *could* you tell your aunt she is stupid? Go and say you are sorry.'

Reluctantly George obeyed. 'Please, Aunt,' he mumbled, 'I'm sorry you are stupid.'

48

A story told of Alexander the Great is one of few which remind us that, after all, he was only a man. No one knew more about fighting than he did, and no one ever conquered nations as he did, but he did not know everything. Painting was one of the subjects of which he was deplorably ignorant.

Calling on an artist one day, Alexander watched him at work, and presently began trying to air his little knowledge of art. At last the artist turned to him and said, 'Noble prince, do you not see that even the boy who cleans up the studio is laughing at you?'

Alexander was not angry. Accepting the merited rebuke, he went on conquering nations instead of pretending to be an authority on painting.

49

At Spennithorne, in Yorkshire, is the grave of little Thomas Beckwith who was only ten when they laid him to rest in 1844. After he had passed on they opened his desk and found his copybook, in which the last words he ever wrote were: *I hope to make good progress in my learning*.

50

Once upon a time there was a Sicilian boy who had neither mother nor father, and was so poor that he had to work three years before he had saved enough money to buy himself a good meal. Determined to give himself a treat, the lad was on his way to spend his earnings, when up came an old beggar who said, 'I am very hungry.'

At once the boy replied, 'Here, take my wages and buy some food. I'll go back and work another three years.'

'You are as generous as you are simple,' said the old beggar.

As he spoke he changed into a bright spirit. 'I give you three wishes,' he declared.

'Thank you very much,' the lad replied. 'Please give me a gun that never misses, speech so that no one can refuse me anything, and a violin which will make people dance.'

So the spirit gave the lad his wishes.

Now, the first thing the boy did was to shoot a pheasant with his magic gun. Out came the farmer, who was very angry; but when he heard the violin he danced till he offered the boy a thousand crowns if only he would stop playing.

No sooner had the young musician got his money than the farmer told the magistrates he had been robbed, so the boy was quickly arrested, tried, and taken to the market place, where he was to be hanged. With the rope round his neck, the boy asked the magistrates to let him play one last tune on his violin—and as no one could refuse, the violin was brought.

The fun started at once, for as soon as the boy began to play, the magistrates, the hangman, the farmer, and everyone in the square began dancing—and they kept on dancing hour after hour till they had no shoes on their feet and were ready to drop. Very glad they were to let the musician go free.

So, back to his own village the lad went, taking his gun, his fiddle and his thousand crowns with him; and as nobody could resist his honeyed speech, he married the prettiest girl and lived happily ever after.

51

Dr Jones of Ohio never possessed much money, for he had a bad habit of writing 'Paid' against accounts which, in fact, had never been paid; and he had a still worse habit of putting himself at the disposal of anyone who needed him by day or night.

His surgery was a little room on the second floor, and his old horse pulled a ramshackle buggy. The doctor's medical knowledge was perhaps old-fashioned, but his kindness and patience were boundless, and his smile (so folks said) was as good as his medicine, or even better.

For nearly fifty years Dr Jones healed and helped and cheered and guided till one day he was found with his head on his arms. He was dead in that little room of his up a flight of stairs.

Folk clubbed together to give the doctor a decent burial,

though they could not afford to erect a stone to his memory. They laid him to rest, thought kindly of him, and turned away sorrowfully—all except the new doctor who had been tremendously impressed by the way in which the old doctor had lived to serve.

He it was who took down the doctor's sign—a board with faded gilt letters. This he placed reverently on the new grave to serve as a tombstone. It said simply:

DR JONES
UPSTAIRS

52

Emanuel Swedenborg, born at Stockholm in 1688, died in London in 1772. One of the most extraordinary men of his time, he was distinguished as a scientific and religious writer, and today his immense number of books are regarded as something like an epitome of knowledge.

The philosopher Kant tells us with circumstantial detail how he was present at a dinner party given by Swedenborg; and how, during the meal, Swedenborg became restless. Then, greatly perturbed, he rose from the table and looked out of the window. His friends asked what was the matter, and he told them quite definitely that there was a fire blazing in Stockholm, and that it was near his own house and was advancing towards it. For an hour or so he was in an agony of mind, but presently he returned to his friends saying, 'All is well. The fire has been put out.'

All this would not be wonderful if we did not know that Swedenborg was over two hundred miles from Stockholm that evening—and that afterwards every detail he had described proved to be correct.

53

Little Slowcomb's bowling is in a rare tangle against Eleven of the Constabulary. The parson, who is captain, consults his forces in the middle of the wicket while P. C. Vokes (not out 57) mops his brow. As a last resort, the parson asks Huggins, his gardener, to 'send up a few'. Huggins takes the ball, rolls up his sleeves, and as he does so, good intentions light a fire in his bosom. Huggins has never yet been seen to bowl, and, indeed, does not quite yet know himself whether he can bowl. But the parson, wishful to set a cunning field, asks, 'Fast, slow or medium, Huggins?'

And Huggins ponders for just a second, then replies, 'Well, sir, I can't 'zactly say yet a while; I s'all leave it to natur'.'

NEVILLE CARDUS: *The Summer Game.*

54

George Clifford, Lord of Skipton, was always seeking adventure on the high seas, loving excitement so much that he fitted out ships at his own expense, and went sailing off to the Spanish Main, keeping a sharp look-out for treasure galleons, and attacking them with supreme skill and irresistible good humour. The more the merrier for him, and he would any day run away from an inferior squadron in the hope of engaging superior numbers.

Having brought home gold for England, he sailed in the old *Elizabeth Bonaventure*, and was the first to pour shot into the Armada. Being first to fire at the enemy, he was first to run out of ammunition; and so, as he could do no more than laugh at the dons, he clapped all sail on the top-gallants, and beat his way up the Channel, hurrying to Tilbury with news.

They say he was taken at once into the presence of our first Elizabeth, and that he found her sitting under an oak in a walled garden. A gay sea-dog was George Clifford, the sailor earl with a mischievous twinkle in his eye. 'Your Majesty,' said he, 'it hath pleased God to scatter your enemies.'

Elizabeth, agitated, thankful and proud, rose to her feet. As she did so she dropped her glove, which the Yorkshireman picked up and was handing back when she said (strangely like a woman and very unlike a queen for once), 'Keep it, sir, in memory of this hour.'

That he did keep it we know, for in the National Portrait Gallery we may see George Clifford of Skipton with Elizabeth's glove on his hat.

55

An elephant and a mouse crossed a wooden bridge. When they were safely over, the mouse exclaimed: 'My, didn't we make it shake?'

56

Aboard a liner bound for Southampton, Sinclair Lewis, the American novelist, paced the deck in step with a friend. Presently he happened to notice a woman reading, and was thrilled to observe that she had one of his own books on her knee. In an eager and excited whisper Lewis said to his friend, 'Look, she's reading one of *my* books! That's fame! Here am I, Sinclair Lewis, and here is an obviously intellectual woman *absorbed* in something . . .'

At that moment, however, the passenger tossed the book overboard.

57

In Yorkshire they tell a story of a farmer who, meeting a friend at the cattle market, asked for a loan of ten pounds. 'I'll pay you back next market day,' he promised.

He kept his word; but a few months later he again asked his friend to lend him ten pounds. 'No, no,' was the answer. 'You took me in last time; I'll not be taken in again.'

'Took you in?' the farmer repeated in amazement. 'Why, I paid every penny the day I said I would.'

'Aye, I know that,' his friend retorted. 'So you did. *But I never thought you would!*'

58

There was much excitement in the Indian city, for the Rajah was expected.

Early in the morning of the great day, a beggar made his way to the street along which the procession was to pass. Many people were there already—a good-humoured crowd quite ready to throw a handful of rice into his wooden bowl. 'These people give me rice,' muttered the beggar as he elbowed his way to the front row of sightseers, 'but if only I'm lucky enough to catch the Rajah's eye, *he* will give me gold.'

At last, when the sun was overhead and tens of thousands of men and women and children lined the street, the cheering began. Presently the Rajah himself came riding by on a huge elephant.

'My bowl! My bowl! See my bowl!' shouted the beggar. 'Of your charity, give me something!'

The elephant was halted. The Rajah looked down. 'Give *me* something,' said he.

But how *could* a penniless beggar give anything to a Rajah rich beyond all telling? Angry, disappointed, frustrated, the beggar picked out a single grain of rice, and handed it with a bad grace to one of the Rajah's attendants.

The gorgeous procession moved on, but while others cheered, the beggar wept in the dust until, peering into his bowl, he found there a piece of gold the size of a grain of rice.

'Fool, fool that I am,' he cried. '*Why did I not give all I had?*'

59

I expect to pass through this world but once. Any good thing, therefore, that I can do, or any kindness I can show to any human being, let me do it now. Let me not defer it or neglect it, for I shall not pass this way again.

Probably no quotation is more familiar, yet no one knows who said it first. It has been attributed to many writers, but it seems almost certain that it comes from a Quaker of whom the world has heard too little.

He was Stephen Grellet, an American of French birth who passed on in 1855 after living a beautiful and useful life.

One day there came to Stephen the conviction that he must speak to men in a distant lumber camp. A voice said, *Preach*, and Stephen obeyed.

It was a long ride through the forests. Day after day he followed the path, always sure in his own mind that he was being divinely guided to the place where God had a piece of work for him to do. He knew he was near the clearing before he came in sight of it, for he had seen it all in vision.

Hurrying forward, eager to give his message, he expected to hear the sound of axes and saws, and to see smoke curling up against the tall trees. But no sound disturbed the peace; there was no smoke, for the clearing was deserted. A few huts where the lumberjacks had slept weeks before stood empty, and not a man was in sight. The long shed where all had dined was there, much as Stephen had pictured it, but weeds were already growing up between the wooden tables and benches. He had come far to preach, and there was no one to listen.

Had he come to the wrong camp? He could not believe it.

Had the voice been mocking him? It had never done so before. Had he misunderstood? There, in the clearing, Stephen Grellet waited patiently to know what he should do, and in the stillness of the woods came the same voice with the same message. It said, *Preach!*

That was all the guidance he needed. Striding across the clearing, he tied his horse to a tree, entered the communal dining-shed, and preached.

At first the thought kept coming to him that he was making a fool of himself, but he had been disciplined by years of obedience, and bit by bit he forgot the empty benches, preaching as if to a great congregation. He told those wooden seats that wrong doing and wrong thinking build up a wall between man and God, and that only repentance can break down the wall and bring peace and joy.

When he had finished he rode home through the woods. He had preached to nobody—but he had obeyed the inner voice.

Long years after, when this queer experience was almost forgotten, business brought Stephen to London; and one sunny spring morning the old Quaker, with the massive figure and the gentle face shaded by a broad-brimmed hat, was crossing London Bridge when someone seized him roughly by the arm, exclaiming: 'So *there* you are! I've found you at last, have I?'

'Friend,' said Stephen, surprised at this unexpected challenge, 'I think thou art mistaken.'

'Mistaken?' exclaimed the other, a big man with a bronzed face and powerful hands. 'Mistaken, when I've sought you in two continents? No, sir, I'm not mistaken. I know the face and figure—and now that you have spoken, I recognize the voice, sir. And I remember the sermon!'

'Hast thou heard me preach, friend?' asked Stephen.

'I have,' said the other, looking steadily at him. 'I heard you preach when you thought you were preaching to nobody. You preached at our old clearing in the woods. I was foreman of the gang that had moved on, and when I went back to the old camp for something I'd left behind, you were preaching to empty benches. At first I thought you were mad; then I found you were sane and sincere. I listened because I could not help it. I was miserable for weeks until I found a Bible. The men jeered, but I kept on reading it; and somehow I seemed to find my way to the light—and I gave the men no peace till *they* found it, too. One sunset we all got down on our knees and prayed that we might live more finely. Three of the men are missionaries now, and since then I've always wanted to meet you and tell you that you never preached more powerfully than on that day when you thought you were preaching to nobody.'

60

'Where shall we bury you?' asked the friends of Socrates as he was about to drink the cup of hemlock.

'Anywhere you like,' he replied, *'if you can catch me.'*

61

As a letter writer, Mr Gladstone was obliged to confine himself to the urgent matters of the moment. 'With him', wrote Lord Morley, 'the pen was no instrument of diversion.' Among the tens of thousands of his letters which I have seen, it would be difficult to select more than a few score in a lighter vein. From the few I should like to quote one.

During the Committee stage of the Home Rule Bill in the winter of 1893, when the House of Commons was working at fever heat, a little boy, seven years old, wrote this letter, on pencilled lines and in a large round hand, to the Prime Minister:

DEAR MR GLADSTONE,—I am very sorry we cannot go to Ireland for Christmas as you have only given Father four days' holiday. And I hope you will give him some more after this letter.

Yours sincerely,
GEORGE SYDNEY HERBERT.

The boy's father, afterwards the fourteenth Earl of Pembroke, was a member of the Opposition ranks, and Mr Gladstone may have known young George Herbert personally, for he had been on terms of great friendship with the Pembroke family. But it is still remarkable and revealing that, amid all the turmoil of the longest session on record, the Prime Minister should have found time to send this reply—and by return of post:

MY DEAR BOY,—It is very sad. I feel for you. As you cannot

go to Ireland, so I cannot get home, to my only home, at Christmas. And you, I hope, will have many, very many, very happy Christmases: but I, having had eighty-three already, feel I am taking one of my last chances.

Can anything be done? Not by me. But I think your Father could do something, if he thought it right to ask some ten or dozen of his friends whether they could abate a little the number and length of their speeches. For they are so fond of him that I believe they would then do it. But I could not expect them to do it for my asking. If they did it for him, there is no saying whether it would enable you to go to Ireland.

With best wishes for Christmas, Easter, and all other times.

Ever yours,

W. E. GLADSTONE.

A. TILNEY BASSETT broadcasting (January 1952) on *Gleanings from Gladstone's Papers*.

62

Once more Billy was near the bottom of the class. 'I came home with Mr Roberts tonight,' said his father. 'He told me that Alan was top again.'

'Yes, Dad,' said Billy. 'But you must remember what brainy people Mr and Mrs Roberts are.'

63

Some years ago a woman in Leeds needed a washer for a tap, so she inquired at several shops, but was unable to get what she wanted. Happening to pass palatial showrooms where gleaming cars stood in magnificent array, she plucked up courage to ask a salesman if they happened to have the kind of thing for which she was looking.

As it happened, the manager heard what she said. Coming forward he explained that it was unlikely they would be able to find a washer of that kind. 'But,' he added, 'we can make one.' So, while the woman looked at some of the cars, the washer was made. 'There's no charge,' said the manager, when the woman offered to pay.

Off she went with her washer, and the incident was quickly forgotten. Eight years later, however, when her husband needed a motor-lorry for his business, he remembered that washer. Among all the motor specialists in the city, he decided to go to the firm where he knew that courtesy and consideration had been shown to his wife over a very trifling matter.

64

'And this,' said the German guide, pointing to an old-fashioned instrument, 'is Beethoven's piano, the very one on which he composed many of his most famous works.'

A party of tourists was being conducted round the musician's home at Bonn. One relic after another had been viewed, and now they were being shown the greatest treasure of all. 'Did Beethoven *really* play this instrument?' asked a girl, rather disdainfully. Obviously her opinion of the old piano was not very high.

'He did,' replied the guide. 'It is one of our priceless possessions.' Plainly he reverenced the name of Beethoven, for his eyes lit up when he spoke of the great composer.

The light died suddenly, however, as the girl who had asked the question sat down at the piano and began playing a popular foxtrot. Turning from the instrument, she said lightly, 'I suppose you get lots of tourists playing this piano?'

'We certainly get many visitors,' replied the guide coldly. 'Only last year I had the honour of conducting the great Paderewski through these rooms.'

'And did *he* play the piano?'

'No. He considered himself unworthy even to lay a finger on it.'

65

Rudyard Kipling's mother consulted Sir William Hunter, the historian of British India, as to what she and her husband were to make of their son.

'Send him to me,' said Hunter. Having had a long talk with Rudyard, he wrote to the mother: 'Make nothing of the boy; he will make himself.'

66

At York they tell the story of Colonel Morris, a Royalist of Charles Stuart's day, who, having been basely betrayed, was imprisoned with his friend Blackburn. Both were condemned to death, but one night they contrived to climb through the window of their cell, and lower themselves down the wall. Morris got down safely, but his friend Blackburn fell and broke his leg. For one there was no chance of escape, for the other a good prospect of freedom; but Morris refused to save his own skin. He remained with his friend, dying with him on the scaffold a day or two later.

67

Two young people hiking along a road twenty miles north of Stirling halted for a chat with an old man who was leaning over a gate. 'Glad you use your legs instead of running around in a motor-car,' observed the old man.

'Oh, it's great fun,' Doris told him. 'Dulce and I adore hiking. We did the Kelso district last year, and the west coast the year before. It's fine exploring Scotland and getting to know all there is to know!'

'Aye, to be sure, to be sure,' was the slow reply. 'But it's a big job. By the way, I'm something of an explorer myself.'

'Indeed?' Dulce raised her delicately pencilled eyebrows. 'I say, that's really interesting. What parts of Scotland have *you* been in?'

The lined face relaxed a moment. 'Well,' said the old man, 'I've tramped around these parts in summer and autumn and winter, and I've seen it all in spring. I've been on the braeside at dawn and sunset, and I've walked near the burn by moonlight. I've searched for flowers in the dells, and have kept making discoveries; and I've watched the play of light and shadow across the hills. Off an on, ye ken, it's taken me just about eighty years to get a kind of nodding acquaintance with the district, a sort of preliminary look round, as you might say. Maybe one day, when I've a bit of time to spare, I'll begin examining it all in detail.'

There was a rare smile about his lips as he added: 'And after *that* I'll maybe go further afield . . . but it'll take a long time to get to know all Scotland. And even that,' he added, 'is child's play compared with exploring the height and breadth and length and depth of the love of God.'

68

In the Louvre is a picture in which Murillo shows us the interior of a convent kitchen where the work is being done by beautiful white-winged angels instead of mortals in old garments. One shining spirit is serenely putting a kettle on the fire, another is lifting a pail of water with truly heavenly grace. There is one angel reaching plates from the kitchen dresser; and there is even a little happy cherub running about and getting in the way while trying to help.

Surely all this reminds us that heaven is about us in our kitchen, and that God may help us with the most menial and humdrum tasks.

69

Strength of limb is a fine thing, of course, but quickness of thought is often more advantageous. Generations have heard this story of how the wren became king of the birds, and no doubt many a moral has been appended.

We are told that one day all the birds of the air came together to choose a king. The peacock declared that the most beautiful deserved the honour. The owl was for choosing the most solemn of birds; the lark suggested that the finest singer should be king; the parrot said that obviously they needed the bird which talked most; the swallow was of the opinion that their king should be swift in flight.

But the eagle, blustering a great deal, loudly proclaimed that the most powerful should be king, and that the true test was the height to which a bird could fly. 'Whoever rises highest, let *him* be king,' said he, and as he was the strongest, the rest were compelled very reluctantly to let him have his way.

Up they flew, therefore, climbing as high as they could, the eagle out-soaring them all. But when he was about to descend from his dizzy height, behold, to the amazement of all who watched, a little wren leapt from his back, and climbed still higher.

So the wren was crowned king, for everyone said that he had flown higher than all the others—and that he must also have brains to have thought of such a clever ruse.

70

Duncan, lying off the Texel with his own flagship, the *Venerable*, and only one other vessel, heard that the whole Dutch fleet was putting to sea. He told Captain Hotham to anchor alongside of him in the narrowest part of the channel, and fight his vessel till she sank.

I have taken the depth of the water, added he, *and when the 'Venerable' goes down, my flag will still fly.*

ROBERT LOUIS STEVENSON.

71

While digging among the ruins of Pompeii a few years ago, workmen came across something curious and pathetic.

All of us, of course, have heard of the tragic fate of the famous Roman city overwhelmed and completely destroyed by an eruption of Vesuvius in A.D. 79. It had long been a pleasure resort for wealthy Romans, and it was gay to the end. That end came suddenly—the solid ground trembled; noon grew dark as midnight; sulphurous fumes drifted through the streets, and a rain of hot ashes never ceased until houses and temples and theatres and baths were buried. Where there had been singing and laughter was silence, a silence unbroken for nearly a score of centuries.

Of about 20,000 inhabitants, some 2,000 lost their lives, among them a woman who loved finery above all else. As the deadly rain of fire came down, she decided to run to the harbour and escape by ship. That was wise, but this rich and beautiful woman stayed behind just long enough to collect as much jewellery as she could carry. Snatching up her rings, she hastily thrust them on her fingers. There was no time to hunt for a box or a bag in which to cram her ornaments, so she picked up as many as she could hold, and rushed into the street, clutching her pearls and diamonds, her rubies and sapphires, her gold brooches and her ear-rings—a wealth of finery that would be valued at thousands of pounds today.

But she delayed too long. The poisonous fumes overcame her as she ran; and with all her trinkets she stumbled, fell, and died clutching the things she prized so much.

There, under the ashes of Pompeii, she lay; and when the

excavators found her she was still lovely, and her hands were still laden with jewels.

72

In *A Labrador Doctor*, Sir William Grenfell tells of a Glasgow professor who once mixed kerosene, mustard and castor-oil in a cup, dipped his finger in, sucked it, and then calmly handed the cup round his class of students. Each student obediently dipped a finger in the cup and sucked it, all making ugly faces, for the concoction was unspeakably horrid.

When the cup was at last returned to the professor he shook his head sadly. 'Ah, gentlemen,' he said, 'I'm afraid you didn't use your powers of observation. The finger I dipped into the cup was not the one I afterwards put into my mouth.'

73

Once upon a time, says Aesop, there was a merry cobbler who used to sing at his work from morning till night. Across the road lived a very rich and very miserable man who hated to hear the cobbler singing, so one day he went into the cobbler's shop and said, 'How much do you earn in a year?'

'Oh,' said the cobbler, 'about fifty crowns, but I am perfectly happy.'

Then the rich man held out a bag and said, 'Friend, here are one hundred crowns, you're welcome to them.'

The cobbler could hardly believe his ears. Delighted at his extreme good fortune, he kept counting out the money, wondering what he should do with such a large sum. He had no time to sing. The next day he feared that he might lose his wealth; and, as days went by, he grew so anxious lest his neighbours should know of it, and lest a thief should steal his money, that he never had one happy moment. Always he was wondering if his money were safe; and before many weeks he who had been the happiest of men became one of the most wretched—so fearful and so anxious that he never sang again.

74

Little Derek was having his first experience of school. 'And how do you like going to school?' asked his aunt.

'Well, I like going and I like coming back,' said Derek; 'but I'm not so sure about the time in between.'

75

The scene is London. The time, between five and six one evening some years ago. Already the tide of traffic has turned, and is flowing out towards the suburbs; and here, standing at the pavement edge, in one of the busiest streets, a poor old broken-down musician of sorts is playing his violin for all he is worth.

Not that he is worth much, for the greasy cap near his feet has no more than two pennies in it; and, if the truth must be told, people tend to hurry by rather than pause to fumble for a coin. Still, the old man fiddles away, though his right arm aches, and the fingers of his left hand have long since lost whatever skill they once possessed.

But now a tall man of commanding appearance strides along the crowded pavement—a man with grey eyes, sensitive mouth, handsome features. He stands a moment, the eyes closed as if with pain. Then the lips twist whimsically. 'Excuse me,' he says in a gentle voice known to countless admirers, 'may *I* play a tune on your violin, my friend?'

'Why, yes, sir, yes.'

So there in the busy London thoroughfare the stranger takes the cheap violin and the well-worn bow, and a moment later there come throbbing on the evening air the rich tones of a light musical favourite. It rises above the roar of the traffic and beats into the ears of city men and women in haste to catch bus or train. They pause, stare, smile, respond irresistibly to the wink of the kindly and famous violinist, and with sudden and unexpected delight halt to listen. Then, as if to show that they, too, can emulate his own bravado, they throw coins into the cap—no coppers, now, however, but sixpences and shillings and even half-crowns, the old decrepit musician looking on in utter astonishment.

So, for a few minutes, the master musician plays the old fiddle before handing it back with a friendly grin as he bids its owner good luck.

76

His lordship, having thrown open his picture gallery to visitors, had left the gardener in charge. A visitor stood admiringly

in front of a portrait. 'Is that an Old Master?' he inquired.
'No, sir,' replied the gardener. 'An old missus.'

77

Once a week the road-sweeper came by with his brush. He was a friendly old fellow; and Miss Gidding, at The Hollies, got into the habit all that summer of taking him a glass of lemonade and a slice of cake. He thanked her shyly, and that was all.

But one evening there came a knock at the back door of The Hollies. The road-sweeper was there, a cauliflower in one hand, a bunch of sweet peas in the other. He seemed embarrassed as he said, 'I've brought you these here, Ma'am—for your kindness.'

'Oh, but you shouldn't,' exclaimed Miss Gidding. 'It was nothing.'

And then the road-sweeper said an odd thing. 'Well, no,' he agreed, 'may be it wasn't much, really, Ma'am. *But it was more than anybody else did.*'

78

Aesop tells us that there were four bulls which were great friends. They went everywhere together, fed together, and lay down to rest together, always keeping so close to each other that if any danger were near they could all face it at once.

Now, there was a lion which had determined to have them, but he could never get at them singly. He was a match for any one alone, but not for all four at once. However, he used to watch for his opportunity, and when one lagged the least bit behind the others as they grazed, he would slink up and whisper that the other bulls had been saying unkind things about him. This he did so often that at last the four friends became uneasy. Each thought the other three were plotting against him. Finally, as there was no trust among them, they went off by themselves, their friendship broken.

This was what the lion wanted. One by one he killed them, and made four good meals.

79

In the turbulent days of the American War of Independence there was a simple, God-fearing, and greatly-loved old preacher named Peter Miller who was proud to number George Washington among his friends. And his friends were many, for he had a genius, this Baptist minister, for sharing the joys and sorrows of others.

But although Peter Miller was loved and admired, he had one inveterate enemy, a thoroughly despicable fellow named Wittman. Stung, perhaps, by the other's popularity, Wittman did all in his power to abuse the Baptist minister, and to bring his name into disrepute. This enmity persisted until one day Wittman was arrested for treason. Found guilty at his trial, he was sentenced to death.

'And a good thing, too,' said many, when they heard the news.

But when Peter Miller heard the news he said: 'I must go and see my friend, George Washington!'

Being too poor to own a horse, he walked all the way to Philadelphia—seventy miles along rough roads; and when he arrived he sought out George Washington and pleaded for Wittman's life.

'I'm sorry, Peter,' replied Washington. 'I'm very sorry, but I can do nothing. Justice must take its normal course.'

'But you could pardon him,' urged Peter Miller.

Slowly Washington shook his head. 'No,' he said. 'I would do much for you, Peter—but I cannot save your friend's life.'

'My friend?' echoed the white-haired preacher. 'My friend! Why, he's the bitterest enemy I have—and always has been. But I willingly forgive him, and I'd like to win his friendship.'

George Washington thought a moment. Then he said quietly: 'So you've walked seventy miles to plead for an enemy, Peter? He is pardoned.'

80

At Islington, a village at the edge of Dartmoor, and far above the sea, was a churchyard gate in an arch with a room over it. We do not know how many times the careless woman of Islington passed through the lychgate, but one day as she went that way she was in haste, so she flung the gate open, *and let it bang behind her*.

She began hurrying across the churchyard. Suddenly she stopped short in utter consternation. There was a creaking sound; then—as she turned—she saw the most astonishing sight in the story of Islington. The walls of the lychgate trembled and bowed; the upper room, at that time used as a village school, fell with a roar, slates scattering everywhere, bricks and mortar tumbling in heaps as the floor gave way. One scholar took shelter in the chimney. Four went head-first into the churchyard. Another child was buried under a heap of stones in the street, and the schoolmaster himself came down quicker than usual. The wonder was that no one was really seriously hurt.

Never bang gates!

81

John Gray, a Methodist local preacher, never failed to thank God for something, no matter how bad times might be. One Sunday he battled through wind and sleet to his appointment at a village chapel, the small congregation wondering what he could be glad about in such weather.

'O, Lord,' John prayed fervently, 'this here's a wretched day, and no mistake—but we thank Thee, Lord, that *every* day isn't as bad.'

82

In old China, where for countless centuries it was the ambition of every family to have at least one clever student who should do well at the examinations, there was, says a legend, a boy who was sent to school with a view to his becoming a learned man. When he was only three years old his father died, and his mother began to work hard day and night so that the lad might have the best education possible.

As soon as he was old enough the boy went to school, and had a good master. He learnt many things and enjoyed his lessons; but after a year or two he grew tired, and wished he had not to work so hard. At last, going home one day when he ought to have been in school, he announced that he was not returning. Instantly his mother picked up a knife and slashed at a piece of cloth she had been weaving in colours. The boy—knowing she had been working on the cloth for months, and that it was to have been sold for a large sum of money—was amazed. 'My son,' said his mother, 'you are not half as grieved over the ruin of this piece of cloth as I am over the ruin of my hopes for you.'

So impressed was her son by this that he went back to school determined to work hard and grow up to be a clever man—which he did.

83

There was born in 1725, in London, a man who, as a lad, went to sea, later became an infidel, was flogged as a deserter from the Navy, suffered cruelly at the hands of a brutal slave dealer in Sierra Leone, spent a terrible night aboard a waterlogged vessel, death staring him in the face all the time, and for four years was master of a slave ship. Miraculously he was converted, and in later life he had the poet, Cowper, as his neighbour.

This sinner turned saint enriched English literature and the world's religious experience by writing such glorious hymns as, *How sweet the name of Jesus sounds*, and *Glorious things of thee are spoken*.

He was John Newton, who died in 1807.

84

A story is told of an American musician who learned that we give only when the gift really does cost something.

While touring in Spain he was shown hospitality by a grandee who, though much impoverished, had a noble house filled with the faded splendour of more glorious days. Among many treasures were a number of flags that had been carried in battle long centuries before; and these—all of them of embroidered silk—were of particular interest to the visitor.

While the American was the guest of the grandee he delighted his host by playing to him for hours; and soon after his return home he was very greatly surprised to receive from Spain one of the embroidered flags he had so much admired. It was the grandee's way of expressing his appreciation.

Now the musician was perfectly well aware that his interest in the flag was merely that of a collector's appreciation of anything old. He liked it for its colour. He valued it because it had survived several centuries. But that was all. It meant nothing more than that to him, whereas to the Spanish grandee it was a personal as well as a precious belonging, a link with the spacious days his proud family had once enjoyed. Realizing all this, the musician wrote a letter warmly thanking his host, and explaining that he felt overwhelmed by the generosity which had been shown. The flag meant more to the sender than it could ever mean to anyone else—and therefore he was returning it.

So the old flag crossed the Atlantic again; but a few weeks later it was back in America once more; and with it a note from the proud grandee: 'Sir, I shall never forget how wonderfully you entertained us here—how can I ever thank you unless I give something which means much to me?'

85

Two farm labourers met in the East Riding of Yorkshire. 'Well, George,' exclaimed the first. 'Ah nivver thowt ti meet thoo soa far from wark.'

'Ah'll tell thoo what it is,' replied the other. 'Ah've left mi job.'

'Left? Whativver for?'

'It's this way. A while sin we'd an auld coo died on t'farm, and for weeks efter we'd nowt ti eat but beef. Then an auld sheep died, and we'd nowt ti eat but mutton.' The labourer passed his hand across his forehead. 'Noo t' owd woman's died,' he went on desperately, '*so Ah've left*!'

86

Silly old gentleman, always pottering about in his garden, or—worse still—talking to people over the fence. Pity he hadn't something better to do. Anyhow, Mrs Reid—*young* Mrs Reid—hadn't given him many chances to waste *her* time while he made stupid jokes about the weather.

She hung the washing on the line in a businesslike way; and when Mr Next-Door (as she styled him) looked up from his weeding and beamed at her, she tossed her head and kept her chin tilted.

'Might be wet if it rains,' observed the silly old gentleman.

'Funny!' snapped Mrs Reid, removing a peg from her mouth, and feeling very much like throwing the clothes-basket at the idiot grinning over the fence.

Anyhow, she got the line filled with washing. She fed and dressed the baby. She did herself up (as she said), and glanced at the sky, and took a risk. Pushing the pram, she went into town

—calling at the grocer's where she was delayed no end of time. And while she was there, *down came the rain.*

Mrs Reid was breathless when she arrived home—breathless and very angry; but she was still more breathless and very much angrier when she discovered that the washing had gone . . . every garment, every peg, and even the line itself.

While she was still staring uncomprehendingly, a round and whiskery face appeared over the fence. 'Ah,' said that silly old gentleman next door, 'I was right. The rain *was* damp!'

'If you think you're being funny . . .' Mrs Reid began, her voice full of fury. Then she stopped.

'I knew you wouldn't want all the washing wet *again*,' said Mr Next-Door. 'So I took it in, and folded it, and I brought the line in as well. I'll bring 'em round in your clothes-basket, if you like. . . .'

Mrs Reid, *young* Mrs Reid, says now that Mr Next-Door is just the best neighbour anybody could wish to have!

87

In 1872 John Smith of New York State was told that he was too weak and sickly for the army. The man who told him died long ago, but it was not till the other day that John passed on at one hundred and five.

A newspaper in 1937.

88

A French legend tells us that long years ago a little juggler was well known in the towns and villages between the Marne and the Loire. Every summer he travelled along the roads, doing his tricks for a very few sous. His stock in trade was a worn square of carpet, some knives and plates, and six shining balls. His jokes were third-rate. His skill was mediocre. The manner in which he threw and caught his plates and knives was not at all wonderful, though he never failed to win applause with his last act, the climax of his one-man show. For this he stood on his head, and kept the six shining balls in the air with his feet. Afterwards he would spring to his toes, smile lovably at the crowd of onlookers, gather their coins in his battered hat, and push on to the next village.

So it went on; but he never earned enough to keep himself in comfort through the cold winter months. His body was thin; his clothes were shabby. Often he had not even a stable in which to shelter. It is not surprising, therefore, that one December morning he fainted, and was found lying in a ditch by a monk who gathered the juggler into his strong arms and carried him, as if he had been a babe, to the monastery.

There the juggler was taken care of, fed, nursed back to health and strength, and shown much kindness. Weeks became months, and the juggler was about to take the road again. But one thing troubled him. He could make no thankoffering to the Blessed Virgin.

The monks were able to sing and chant. The juggler knew no hymns or psalms. The monks could carve crucifixes and make stained glass windows, but the juggler had no such skill. The monks prayed long prayers, but the juggler knew no Latin. What, then, could he do?

One April evening, after supper and during the hour when the monks were allowed to converse in the refectory, he stole on tiptoe into the church, walked down the long aisle, mounted the steps in the chancel, and laid his tiny square of worn matting before the statue of the Blessed Virgin. The church was almost in darkness except for the yellow candle-light about the statue; and in that one pool of light the juggler, who loved much and was truly thankful, went through his small repertoire of tricks—throwing his knives, catching his plates, cracking his poor jokes, and finally standing on his head, keeping the six shining balls twirling in the candle-light.

As it happened, one of the monks on his way to the refectory caught sight of this tomfoolery. Horrified, he ran to the Abbot, who, accompanied by the angry brethren, rushed into the church just as the travelling showman was ending his programme. To think that this base fellow should reward them for their hospitality by desecrating their church! To think that this half-wit should dare to perform his outlandish tricks on consecrated ground and before the Blessed Virgin. . . . The Abbot and the monks were speechless with indignation.

It was at that moment that the miracle occurred. As the Abbot ran forward to curse the juggler, he looked up, pausing in amazement as the Blessed Virgin herself stepped down from her pedestal, touched the juggler with her right hand, and smiled as she gave him her blessing.

All the prayers and praises of the monks, all their matins, primes and evensongs, all their alms and sacrifices, had failed to earn a benediction like that; and so, lost in wonder and adoration, the trembling Abbot and the monks fell upon their knees, and begged mercy for their souls.

89

The story is told that at a dinner of the National Arts Club a Chickasaw Indian painter, Red Feather Colbert, was present in full tribal regalia, which included a magnificent necklace of teeth. One of the guests who asked about the necklace was told that the teeth were from alligators.

'Ah,' said the lady, 'I suppose they mean the same to you as pearls do to us.'

'Not quite,' was the reply. 'It doesn't take much of a man to take a pearl from an oyster.'

90

'Dear me, Johnny,' exclaimed the teacher, 'you look as if you haven't been washed for a week! Whatever would you say if *I* came to school looking like that?'

'Please, Miss,' murmured Johnny, 'I'd be too polite to mention it.'

91

In the sixteenth century there lived at Milton Abbas, in Dorset, a boy, John Tregonwell, who when only five had an astonishing adventure. He was in the care of his nurse, and together they walked across the lawns near the abbey, which still keeps its old tower. It was a lovely summer day, and perhaps we may forgive his nurse for turning a moment to look about her at the fair green world. Brief as that glance was, it was long enough for Master John to disappear.

When the nurse called there was no answer. She hurried this way and that, but could not find Master John. Then she ran to the half-ruined tower, panting anxiously up the dusty steps which brought her out of darkness into sunshine again. Her heart pounded furiously. Fear gave wings to her feet. There, above her head, Master John was leaning over the crumbling parapet, his hand stretched out to pluck a flower. Another instant, and she would have laid hold of him; but she was too late. Master John overbalanced, and fell sixty feet.

Do you wonder that the nurse dare not mount the last two or three steps? Do you wonder that she was too frightened and distressed and overcome with remorse to look down from that dizzy height on the broken body at the foot of the tower? She did what any girl would have done. She ran down the steps, knowing what she must find. Out of the gloom into the sunshine once more she sped, *there to find Master John calmly gathering daisies*. Greeting her with a smile, he showed her the flowers he had found. True, the daisies in the tiny hand soon withered, but the memory of them remained fresh in the nurse's mind to her last hour.

And the explanation of this mystery? Simply that Master John (as was the fashion in those days) wore stiff nankeen petticoats, his garments thus serving as a parachute. Lightly he had landed on the lawn, and then, with unconcern which is peculiar to childhood, had thought nothing of his providential descent, his one desire being to gather daisies as a gift for nurse.

92

Albrecht Dürer, the wonderful German artist, had an amazing mastery of line, crowding more brush-strokes into an inch, it is said, than any man before or after. One day Bellini, an old artist, called on him and asked if, as a great favour, he might see one of Dürer's brushes. Dürer gave him one, and Bellini examined it carefully. He tried it on his thumb-nail. To his surprise he found it was only an ordinary brush—an ordinary brush which Dürer used in an extraordinary way.

93

Granny loved much—but she did her duty; and so, when her granddaughter exclaimed one day, 'You wait till I'm queen,' she retorted severely: 'Before you become queen, my dear, you will have to learn to be a lady.'

'Yes, Granny,' murmured a very deflated Elizabeth—who then had quite a long time to wait for her Coronation.

94

Farinelli, perhaps the greatest male soprano the world has ever heard, took London by storm in 1734, and for twenty-five years remained the court singer in Spain, where he lived as one of the richest and most respected men in the land—and all for singing four songs a day!

There came to him one day his tailor with a wonderful new suit of clothes. When the clothes had been tried on and found perfect, the tailor stammered that if it would please the gentleman he wished for no payment; that, indeed, he would accept none, only a favour, a favour—and here the honest fellow trembled at his own temerity—which only a king should ask, not a poor tailor.

'Well?' asked Farinelli.

'Sir, would it be possible for me to hear *one* song? All the world is talking of your voice, sir, and I have longed to hear it.'

Then Farinelli took the tailor by the arm, and led him to his music room, where he sang first one song, then another, then half a dozen. Thus he continued for an hour, the tailor being charmed and amazed.

The recital over, the tailor was about to depart after numerous expressions of thanks when Farinelli held him back. 'Friend,' said he, 'I have done you a favour. It is only fair that you should do me one.' Then he took out his purse, and insisted on the tailor accepting almost twice the sum he would have charged for the clothes.

That was Farinelli every bit.

95

A father who had seven sons was distressed because they were always quarrelling. One day he desired them to come to his room. Then he laid before them seven sticks which were fastened together. 'Now,' said he, 'I will give a hundred crowns to the one who can break this bundle of sticks.' Each tried to the utmost of his strength, and each was obliged to confess that he could not break it.

'And yet,' said the father, 'there is no difficulty about it.' So saying, he untied the bundle, and broke one stick after the other with the greatest ease.

Then he said, 'As it is with these sticks, so it is with you.

As long as you hold together, you are a match for all your enemies; but if you quarrel and separate, it will happen to you as to these sticks which you see lying broken on the ground.'

96

On 25 November 1835, Andrew Carnegie was born at Dunfermline in Scotland. When a lad of thirteen he emigrated with his father and mother, who were driven to America by the Hungry Forties. Andrew began work at five shillings a week in Allegheny, where he was a bobbin-boy.

Then came the great day when he became a message-boy for the Pittsburgh Telegraph Office.

Andrew was nothing if not thorough, and in order to be able to deliver the telegrams (which were sent without addresses) he spent days learning the whereabouts of all the principal people in the district. For twelve months young Carnegie, the boy who was to become one of the world's richest men and greatest benefactors, ran with messages or sat watching the operators tapping out the Morse code. Every week he took home his earnings, well knowing they formed an important part of the family budget.

One day when it came to Andrew's turn to receive his wages, the manager pushed him to one side. Andrew stood trembling from head to foot. He saw the other boys receiving their money, and was sure that unwittingly he must have committed some offence. He was about to be 'fired'. What would happen at home?

At last the manager turned to Andrew. 'My lad,' he said, 'you are worth all the other boys put together, so I'm adding two dollars and twenty-five cents a week to your wages.'

Nothing in all Andrew Carnegie's long and amazingly successful life thrilled him more than that. It was so wonderful that he dare not trust himself to tell the family that night. At tea he handed his mother the usual sum, keeping back the thrilling news till breakfast next morning.

97

We know he was much loved and greatly admired. Born in 1759, Schiller grew up to be great in stature as well as in name, and was known far and wide for his knitted brows, hollow cheeks, and his tall figure which in later years became warped and twisted.

His play, *William Tell* (inspiration of Rossini's highly successful opera), has made his name a household word. Above all others, it has possessed the hearts of his own people, a people ready to criticize, but equally ready to praise whenever praise is merited.

There is something profoundly moving about that day when the great man, worn by suffering, perhaps a little embittered by the long struggle for fame, knew himself conqueror of the people's hearts. His *William Tell* was performed at Leipzig, and after the first act the audience burst into frantic applause. They called for Schiller. Trumpets gave a grand flourish, and the people cheered. At the close of the performance (badly done as it was) the audience rushed out to see the great man. A lane was made for him to pass along amid the cheering crowds. With head bowed—for success humiliates noble minds—he walked slowly, all eyes on him; and as he passed he heard mothers and fathers whispering to their children, 'Look! That is Schiller!'

It warmed his heart.

98

The world famous magician, Houdini, was a romantic lover all his married life. For over thirty years—busy as he was—he never once allowed a day to pass without writing a love-letter to his wife, often quite a long letter. When he was away he posted his 'love' every morning. When he was at home he had a happy trick of hiding love-letters in all sorts of out-of-the-way places. Finding them unexpectedly was one of the most delightful surprises his wife ever enjoyed; and even after his death his widow would now and then come upon a passionate expression of his adoration in a letter tucked away in some long-unopened drawer or among a pile of handkerchiefs in a cupboard.

99

While crossing the Atlantic in the latter half of last century, a small company of passengers gathered on deck to sing hymns. After they had sung, *Jesu, Lover of my soul*, one of the company turned to a man close by, and said, 'Excuse me, sir, but I can't help feeling I've heard your voice before. You seemed to be singing that hymn with great fervour—is it possible that I've heard you on some other occasion?'

'I do not know,' replied the second passenger, 'that we have ever met before, but I'll tell you why I sing this hymn as I do. It means much to me. Years ago, when a soldier in the Confederate Army during the American Civil War, I was told off one dark night to do sentry duty. Our camp was near a wood, and I knew the enemy to be close at hand. I don't mind confessing, sir, that I was terribly nervous. Eventually I began singing this hymn; and I shall never forget coming to the words:

Cover my defenceless head
With the shadow of Thy wing.

Somehow, at that moment, a feeling of security came over me, and I remained at my post without fear until dawn.'

'That is interesting,' said the first passenger, 'for I was a colonel in the Northern Army, and one night, camping near a wood, I took a dozen men to within a few yards of the enemy's lines. As you say, it was very dark, but we could just make out the figure of a man marching up and down. He was a sentry, and I whispered the command to take aim. At that moment, sir, he began singing:

Cover my defenceless head
With the shadow of Thy wing,

and I felt somehow that I simply could not give the order to fire. We all listened until he had finished singing the hymn. Then I whispered, "Lower rifles," and with my men I moved off to another sector.'

100

'How long did it take you to make that sermon?' asked a lady once, speaking rather excitedly to a well-known preacher.

'Oh,' was the unexpected reply, 'I should say about fifty years, on and off.'

101

A very old tale from India says there were once four foolish beggars, clothed in rags, who by chance met in a beggars' hut near a small village. All day they had been holding out bowls in the market place, begging charity of those who moved to and fro. As the sun was setting and the shadows were lengthening, they limped to the hut. There they sat round a very small fire of sticks, all of them discontented and suspicious.

Now it happened that the first beggar had nothing in his wooden bowl except a little meat. The second had his bowl half filled with vegetables. A few spices only lay at the bottom of the third beggar's bowl; and all that the fourth beggar had collected was four or five handfuls of rice.

So there in the hut, as twilight deepened, the four foolish beggars talked and grumbled until one suggested that if they put water in the pot hanging over the fire, and if each threw into it the contents of his own bowl, there would be broth enough for everyone.

The idea of enjoying a savoury supper was loudly acclaimed, and the pot having been filled, the beggars sat round eagerly.

But the first beggar, who thought himself a cunning fellow, realized that if the other three threw in spices, vegetables and rice, why, there would be no need for *him* to share his little store of meat. So, in the half-light he *pretended* to drop his meat in the pot, afterwards chuckling to think that he would enjoy a tasty supper, and still have his meat all for himself.

As it happened, the second beggar did the same with his vegetables; the third with his spices, and the fourth with his rice, each pretending to throw everything he had into the common pot, all hiding their food under their rags.

They say there was no end of quarrelling in the beggars' hut that night when the pot was lifted off the fire, and *nothing* was found in it except hot water.

102

'How dismal you look,' observed a bucket to his companion as they were going to the well.

'Ah,' replied the other, 'I was reflecting on the uselessness of our being filled, for though we always go away full, we always come back empty.'

'Dear me, how strange to look at it *that* way,' said the first bucket. 'I enjoy the thought that however empty we come, *we always go away full!*'

103

The Hull steamer *Flixton* was off Portland in the last months of World War I when the look-out saw a white line running along the surface of the water. Every man knew it meant death, for the white line was the wake of a torpedo, and the torpedo had been fired from a German submarine which was even then rising to the surface to witness the destruction of the British steamer.

Laden with enough explosive to send the *Flixton's* crew to glory in an instant, the torpedo raced through the water, so precisely aimed that it must have hit her amidships and a few feet below the water-line. Never was annihilation more nearly inevitable. It seemed that nothing in the world could prevent it—another five seconds, a mere fifty feet, and the ship would blow up, scattering metal and limb. If anything was impossible, it was that the torpedo would not shatter the *Flixton.*

Yet the impossible happened. Something went wrong with the mechanism. The torpedo rose strangely and unexpectedly out of the water; and, incredible as it must seem, it turned within a few yards of the ship, and began travelling back to the submarine from which it had been fired. A minute later a gigantic explosion sent a tower of water into the air.

The torpedo had done its work—but it had destroyed the German submarine instead of the British ship.

104

Only a few months after Victoria had become Queen, the Duke of Wellington visited her at Windsor on a solemn errand. A soldier had been court-martialled, and all that remained to be done was for Her Majesty to add her formal signature to the death warrant, a duty which at that time devolved on the reigning monarch.

Pen and ink were at hand. Placing the warrant on the table, the Duke—stern and determined—summarized the findings of the court and explained the normal procedure. But the Queen, young, gentle and sympathetic, shrank from the dreadful responsibility. 'Have you *nothing* to say for this poor fellow?' she asked.

'Nothing, Madam,' was the curt reply.
'Can you not think again?'
'It is useless.'
'But what has he done?'
'I have explained, Madam, that he has deserted the Army, not once only but three times.'
'I implore you to think again, Your Grace.'
The Duke could not fail to note the pleading in the young Queen's eyes and the tremor in her voice. He frowned, and for some moments there was silence in the room. 'Well, Your Majesty,' he said at last, 'there is nothing to be said for him as a soldier, but at the court-martial one witness spoke in praise of his private life.'
'Oh, thank you, *thank you*,' the Queen exclaimed. 'Thank you, Your Grace.' Then, snatching up the pen, she wrote *Pardoned* above the royal signature.

105

The German Emperor, Conrad the Third, ruled large dominions from 1138 to 1152, but his position on the throne was never secure, and most of his life was spent in fighting.
A tale told of him has to do with his siege of the castle of Weinsberge, where the troops of the Duke of Bavaria had held out for a long time, but could hold out no longer. The Duke—driven to the last extremity—was for surrendering, which in those days meant certain death, as no quarter was likely to be shown, but the Duchess begged that she might have permission to speak with the Emperor. Permission was granted. During a truce the Duchess—a very charming woman—not only informed the Emperor that the garrison was about to surrender, but implored him to have mercy on the womenfolk.
The Emperor (who had never dreamed of harming them) readily granted her petition; and when she further begged that she and the other women might be permitted to leave the castle in safety, each taking with her one thing she treasured, that request also was granted.
The Duchess then returned to the castle, and soon afterwards the gates opened, and out came the women, each with her husband on her back. It was a pretty trick, and even the grim Emperor could not forbear to smile.

106

One day in 1938 Dorothy Sparkes hunted for sevenpence and found a diamond.

She had been given sevenpence to spend at a garden party held at Kingstanding, near Birmingham, but unfortunately this girl of thirteen lost her money. She looked high and low for it; and it was while hunting in the grass that she saw something shining—a diamond which had been lost from the Lord Mayor's chain of office.

107

In 1942 a little boy was told that his father had been made a Brigadier-General. For some moments he was so completely overawed that he could not speak, but at last he asked wistfully, 'Mummy, would you mind if I still call him Daddy?'

108

Coming out of the operating theatre, Lord Lister, eminent surgeon and pioneer of antiseptics, was waylaid by a small girl, a patient in the hospital. Having performed a major operation, Lord Lister was tired. 'Please, Doctor,' begged the child, 'will you operate on my dolly?'

Busy man though he was, Lord Lister at once made a show of operating on the patient, afterwards carefully sewing up the incision so that the stuffing would not come out.

109

Perhaps the proudest moment in the life of Agesilaus, King of Sparta, was the occasion when he himself showed an important ambassador the sights of the city. Together they toured the capital, in those days the first city in Greece; and many things there were to surprise the ambassador.

At the end of the day the ambassador made bold to say, 'O king, I have seen your capital, but one thing astonishes me. You have no walls for defence, no gates, no great towers. Why is this?'

'Sir Ambassador,' replied Agesilaus, 'I fear you have not observed carefully. You shall go with us tomorrow, and we will show you the walls of Sparta.'

Next day the king and the ambassador drove out of the city and came to a plain where an army was drawn up in battle array. Said Agesilaus: 'There, Sir Ambassador, thou beholdest the walls of Sparta—ten thousand men, *and every man a brick*!'

110

It was in 1688 that James the Second issued his letter on the *Declaration for Liberty of Conscience*, a document which was to be read in all the churches. A copy of this royal mandate coming into the hands of the Mayor of Scarborough, a very pompous individual, that gentleman sent it to Noel Boteler, the vicar, commanding that it be read in the parish church the following Sunday, when Mr Mayor and the Corporation would attend divine service.

Now the vicar of Scarborough cared not a rap for James the Second or his letters, and when Sunday came round he conducted the service without a word about the *Declaration for Liberty of Conscience*. Suddenly, Mr Mayor, filled with righteous indignation, strode from his seat, and there, before the astonished congregation, laid hold of the parson and soundly caned him, after which Mr Mayor walked back to his seat and waited for the service to continue.

Many who were present did not like this action of the Mayor's, particularly some officers of the Castle. Meeting next day on the town bowling green, they determined to teach the Mayor a lesson. They sent for him, and when he refused to obey, one of them despatched a little company of soldiers, who brought Mr Mayor much against his will. He was, indeed, bubbling over with wrath at such a gross insult to civic dignity.

By this time a crowd had gathered on the green, and Mr Mayor began hectoring everybody. Meanwhile, someone produced a blanket and someone tripped up Mr Mayor—and in a trice that Scarborough worthy was flying sky-high and falling perilously near the ground; and thus, with little deportment, he went up and down and up and down to the delight and satisfaction of all who saw it.

111

The Baptist minister and his wife had been on holiday. At the first prayer meeting held after their return, a good brother got down on his knees, and said:

'Oh, Lord, we thank Thee for bringing back our beloved Pastor. We are glad to have him among us once again, and we praise Thee that Thou hast cared for him and for his wife, for Thou, O Lord, preservest man and beast.'

112

In 1936 Sir John Simon told the people of Kilmarnock about a London business man who, when King George V was ill, took a taxi to Buckingham Palace, and waited there an hour to read the latest bulletin. The taxi then went on to a London station. When it arrived, the business man was surprised to see that the taximeter registered only one shilling. 'Your meter's wrong,' he said. 'I've kept you waiting an hour.'

'Well,' said the taximan, 'what's wrong with the meter? *Isn't he my king as well as yours?*'

113

She has been sixty years a queen, but she is fast declining. Weary of pomp and circumstance, tired out with all the strain of being a queen and of having to go here and there and do this and that, she would gladly sit by the fire and just be an old woman.

Even her interest in politics and world affairs is diminishing, and almost pitifully she asks to be excused from the ordeal of seeing her ministers. Her secretaries, long accustomed to waiting her pleasure, are kept at a distance, for there is little she wishes to say now, and they are free to deal with her correspondence as they think fit. Her ladies-in-waiting read the newspaper to her, but (may we let the secret out?) she sometimes falls asleep before the column is finished. She is a great queen, but she is also a little old woman, very, very tired.

She makes a brave fight to the end, however; and here is a request that she will visit Netley Hospital. Shall she go? Can she possibly go to half the places where she is wanted? One of her secretaries will reply that Her Gracious Majesty is interested . . . and so forth, but regrets that she is indisposed at the moment . . . and so on.

No, she will go to Netley! She *wishes* to go.

So she is driven over to see two wounded soldiers. They are to receive the V.C., and as the door opens and Queen Victoria comes in very slowly, the order to rise is given. But Her Majesty (a woman surely) says, 'Certainly not!' The rest of the company may rise, of course, but not the two wounded men.

Then, without help from anyone (this in itself is unusual, for she is now accustomed to lean on a strong arm), she crosses the room, pins the decorations, says a few gracious words, and retires.

It is the last time she decorates a hero with the Victoria Cross, and it is also the only time that a soldier has remained seated in her presence.

114

'A hundred years ago,' said the teacher, 'there was no wireless; there were no aeroplanes, no cars, no buses, no cinema films, no television. Can you think of anything else of importance which did not exist last century?'

Tommy, the slowest boy in the class, put up his hand at once. 'Please, Miss, *me*,' he suggested brightly.

115

One day in 1835 two officers walking along a street in France stopped to look at a serious little boy busy sketching. He was no more than six, and the officers, coming up behind him, peeped over his shoulder. What they saw amazed them. There, to the very life, was a drum-major—a fellow standing only a few yards off.

The officers asked if they might have the sketch. The child handed it to them, and as soon as they returned to barracks they passed it round. 'Drawn by a child of six,' they declared.

'Impossible!' exclaimed the Colonel.

'But I tell you, we watched him doing it,' said one of the officers, warming as he spoke.

'Impossible,' repeated the Colonel. 'Anyhow, if it really did happen, bring the artist to me. If he can draw *me* as he drew that fellow, I'll pay for a dinner for everybody!'

So the officers searched for the child, and found him. He was marched into the officers' mess, made to sit on a chair at one end of a long table, and told to sketch the Colonel, while twenty officers or more stood round.

And sketch the Colonel he did—the outline of the face, the nose and eyes and chin and collar and hair, and, last of all, the cigar. No sooner did the Colonel see the portrait than he declared he would gladly pay for the dinner.

The child was John Everett Millais.

116

In the art gallery at Düsseldorf there was a picture of the Crucifixion by Stenburg, a masterpiece begun with little religious fervour and finished in a blaze of devotion. Below the picture were the words:

> All this I did for thee,
> What hast thou done for Me?

One day a wealthy young man drove into Düsseldorf, and while his horses were being groomed at the inn he wandered round the town, sight-seeing. He walked carelessly into the art gallery, paused before Stenburg's picture, and read the challenging lines.

It is said he stood there still as stone, not a few minutes only but for hours. Other visitors arrived and departed. The light faded. The curator, waiting to go home, became impatient, and at last tapped the nobleman on the shoulder. The two went out together.

Returning to the inn, the young man drove on to Paris—but he was a different young man, for he had dedicated himself to a new way of life, and was to become known the world over as the founder of Moravian Missions.

He was Zinzendorf.

117

'Say,' remarked one tramp to another, 'that fellow across the road is idle beyond words. He's been sitting there doing nothing for two hours!'

'Oh? How do you know?' asked the second tramp.

'Because *I've* been sitting here watching him!'

118

A visitor was one day looking round St Paul's Cathedral when the vast building was only half finished. Addressing one of the masons, the visitor said, 'What are *you* doing?'

'Cutting stone,' replied the mason without even looking up.

'And *you*?' the visitor inquired, speaking to another workman.

The labourer answered that he was earning so many shillings a week.

Then the visitor found a man carrying a block of stone. 'And what are *you* doing?' he inquired.

Looking up at the great forest of scaffolding, the workman replied proudly, 'Sir, I am helping to build a cathedral.'

119

It was a very happy household. There was Leopold, a fine musician, and vice-master in the Bishop's Chapel at Salzburg in Austria. There was his adoring wife. There was Marianne, a schoolgirl; and there was little Wolfgang, a child not quite four years old.

Marianne was learning to play the harpsichord, and day after day the handsome Leopold stood behind her as she practised in the drawing-room upstairs. How very patient and loving her father was—and how cleverly he showed Marianne how to play some particularly difficult piece. She was making progress—very good progress, and that was excellent, to be sure.

And there, almost lost in the big armchair, sat Wolfgang, little Wolfgang who had never to be told to keep quiet when Marianne was practising.

One evening, at sundown, Leopold patted Marianne's shoulder, saying she had done remarkably well. At that moment Wolfgang climbed on his father's knee and begged to be allowed to play the pretty piece Marianne had now mastered.

What a joke that was. Picking up his baby son, Leopold laughed, tapped the tiny nose, and said, 'Look at your small hands. Why, you cannot span the notes yet. You must wait, little man. You must wait!'

There was no end of fun during tea, and Marianne had to tell her mother about Wolfgang wanting to play one of the classics. When the meal was finished, Marianne helped to clear away the crockery while Leopold lit his pipe.

But the pipe went out. Leopold was on his feet. 'Listen, mother,' said he in awed tones, 'listen! Marianne is playing that piece better than ever!'

But Marianne was washing pots in the kitchen.

His wife following, Leopold crept upstairs, the lamp in one hand, his pipe in the other. He pushed open the drawing-room door, and there was little Wolfgang playing in the darkness. 'I love it so!' whispered the child.

It was the beginning of Mozart's life of melody.

120

'Eh, you're a bit early this morning, aren't you?' exclaimed Mrs Grindle, as the milkman opened the back door.

'Yes,' said the milkman.

Mrs Grindle was scraping potatoes at the kitchen sink. 'Eh,' she went on, 'I expect you was up nice and early on a sunny morning like this. Makes you glad to be alive when the sun shines, don't it?'

'Yes,' said the milkman.

'Two pints, same as usual. I feel on top of the world myself, as a matter of fact. But I didn't yesterday. Not a bit. That Mrs Owen, next door, don't half go off the deep end. You *can* spare two pints, can't you?'

'Yes,' said the milkman.

'That's nice of you. Eh, the way she went on soon after our Alice came home from school! She stood arms akimbo by the fence, and went on at me something awful. It didn't half upset me, and so uncalled for; said our Alice had been shouting at the top of her voice all across dinner time, and her head was like to burst, and the sooner I started keeping an eye on Alice the better for everybody. She said there was no living next door to some folk, and then she stamped in, and slammed the door. It gave me quite a turn—it would have upset anybody, wouldn't it?'

'Yes,' said the milkman.

'Minute she slammed that there door, thinks I to myself, "All right, my lady, I've finished with *you*, I have, for good and all. I'm through," that's what I said to myself. But after a bit, I kind of thought about it and remembered Mrs Owen had lost her husband in the war, and that she hasn't no children, and is a bag of nerves, poor soul . . . so, what d'ye think? Why, about nine I went round with a bit of fish I'd cooked for my old man; and she started crying, and axed me to forgive her. Eh, she was *that* sweet to Alice first thing this morning; made me feel on top of the world. You *do* when you've sort of done what's right, don't you?'

'Yes,' said the milkman.

121

One cannot help marvelling at the amazing courage men show in time of war. A story of the days when the French had nothing better to do than storm Minden, tells us that the town was strongly fortified and that its battery poured shot into the attacking party at such a rate that whole lines of soldiers were wiped out. It was a hail of death calculated to shatter the courage of the bravest. After repeated attacks the French advance regiment hesitated.

At that moment their commander, M. Perer, a grenadier of fine face and splendid courage, calmly rode out in front of the men, the lead spattering all about him. Moving slowly down the line without even a glance to the right where the guns were flaming, he produced his snuff-box, tapped it nonchalantly, took snuff gently, flicked off the dust with his fine cambric handkerchief, and said, smiling, 'Well, my dear boys, what is it? What *is* it? The cannon? Dear, dear, how very annoying. It kills, of course; oh yes, it kills—but march on and try to forget it. Come along, boys, come along!'

They went on—to victory.

122

We were admiring a handsome piece of furniture, and our host, smiling at his wife, said, 'It has a story all its own.'

His wife smiled too. 'The minute I saw the bureau in the auction rooms,' she explained, 'I knew it was just the thing for John, so I made up my mind to buy it. The room was crowded next day, and I found myself pushed to the front. Presently the bureau was put up for sale. The bids ran up from six pounds to eleven, after which there were only two of us bidding. I kept nodding to the auctioneer till at last it was knocked down to me at fifteen pounds.

'I didn't say anything to John, as I wanted the bureau to be a surprise. But I never expected to surprise him as much as I really did, for at tea that afternoon he said: "My dear, I happened to look in at the auction rooms this afternoon. I squeezed in at the door, and found them putting up a bureau I'd have been glad to buy. It fetched fifteen pounds, and I bid up to fourteen pounds ten. I'd have got it for twelve pounds if someone else hadn't kept on bidding. I'm sorry I let it go. It was a bargain even at fifteen pounds!" '

123

Little Pauline could not be persuaded to go to sleep, so her grandfather went up to her room, lay on top of the bed, and pretended he was very tired.

Pauline, aged three, snuggled up close and was very still; but a few minutes later she astonished everyone by appearing in the lounge, and saying calmly: 'There now, I've gotted granddad off to sleep at last.'

124

It was the first time the clergyman, newly-appointed to the parish, had called on Mr and Mrs John Turner, two middle-aged folk living in a furnished flat. They made him welcome, and were so friendly that within a few minutes their visitor felt quite at home as all three sat by the fire.

'We've known better times,' said Mrs Turner. 'But my husband had to retire early owing to heart trouble, and life hasn't been easy these last few years. John does a lot of the housework for me. You see, I'm almost blind, and my arthritis makes it hard for me to get about. And then, of course, it was a great sorrow when Richard was killed in the last year of the war; and we have a daughter—but she went off, and we just don't know where she is now. It nearly broke our hearts at the time.'

'Yes,' said John, 'Mary's right. We've had a lot of trouble; a lot of trouble. But then, though it may sound a bit odd, in one way we've never been happier. Somehow, our troubles have brought us closer together. We help each other, and we cheer each other—why, I often say, this last year or two has been one long honeymoon.'

'It's true,' Mary went on, smiling across at the husband she could hardly see. 'It's *wonderfully* true. And there's something else.'

'Well?' asked the clergyman encouragingly.

'Well,' she said softly, 'our troubles have done more than bring us closer together—they've thrown us back on God. He's been nearer to us in the dark days than ever He was when things were going well and life was easy; we seem now as if we're *always* conscious of His presence.'

125

One spring morning a shoe-box arrived by post in Manchester. When Mrs Milner opened it—wondering as she did so—she found inside, packed in damp moss, hundreds of primroses, and a little card with the words: 'Just a bit of sunshine from Devon to Lancashire.'

'Well,' she exclaimed to her husband, 'how *very* sweet of my sister. Why, they're just lovely! I'll arrange them in the black bowl, and put them in the hall.' Then she stood by the breakfast table, one finger on her cheek. 'No,' said she, 'I'll stand them in water, and this afternoon I'll take them to Mrs Fulwood—she needs a bit of cheering up.'

That is what Mrs Milner did. Mrs Fulwood, who had lost her husband earlier in the year, was very grateful. She said the primroses were the very spirit of spring, and that they would light up the room.

But an hour after her visitor had left, she gathered up the primroses, and hurried into one of the dingiest streets in the city. There she called to see Helen, a girl in her 'teens who has been a cripple for over ten years. 'I've brought you these primroses,' said Mrs Fulwood. 'They've come all the way from Devon. Aren't they just lovely?'

Helen said they were, and her eyes lit up as she touched them almost reverently. As soon as Mrs Fulwood had gone, however, Helen said to her mother: 'Mum, just pop in next door, will you, and give these to Mrs Duffield—she *loves* flowers, you know.'

So Helen's mother went round with the primroses. Mrs Duffield was thrilled with the unexpected gift, and kept looking at the primroses all that evening. But in the morning she put them in a brown paper bag, and took them with her when she went to do the rough work at Mrs Milner's. 'Eh, Ma'am,' she said as soon as she arrived, 'you've been that good to me, I've brought you these here primroses—they're from Devon, Ma'am; and aren't they just lovely?'

126

The guide had been showing a party round a famous picture gallery. When all the masterpieces had been seen, and the guide had talked himself hoarse explaining the function of art, the techniques of various painters, the motif of this composition and the subtleties of that, he concluded: 'And now, would anyone care to ask a question?'

After a long pause one of the ladies said timidly, 'If you please, what brand of polish do you use to keep the floors so bright?'

127

During World War I an Irish soldier, who had at one time been a comedian, got up a pantomime in a convalescent camp. He himself played a very energetic part in the production, and his antics and wisecracks caused roars of laughter among the audience of wounded men.

No one who saw and heard the comedian dreamed for a moment that after each exit he cowered in the wings, trembling from shell-shock and writhing in agony from a recent wound. Friends behind the scenes begged him not to go on the stage again, but each time his turn came he took a deep breath, and rushed back to raise one laugh after another.

128

From Italy comes this old tale:

The wall of a monastery church was to be enriched with a great painting, and a famous artist was commissioned to do the work. So high was the wall that much scaffolding was needed for him to reach every part of it, and there sprang up a host of poles and a great show of planks.

Then the artist came. He climbed the scaffolding and stood facing the wall, his hands behind him. All day he stood there, or moved a very little to the right or left. The next day he was still standing there. He never mixed a colour, never picked up a brush, and not a stroke of work did he attempt even on the third day. Always he stood there with his hands behind him.

At last the reverend Father spoke. 'My son,' he said, 'you do not seem to be making much progress with the painting.'

'Father,' the artist replied, 'the picture is now finished. *All that remains is to paint it on the wall.*'

129

'Out of my sight, insect!' roared a lion to a buzzing gad-fly. 'Trouble not your king when he would rest from the cares of state.'

'What!' cried the fly. 'Am I *so* contemptible in your sight? Do you think I'm afraid of *you*? Quick! Defend yourself!'

The lion, finding that the insect would not be brushed away, was obliged to accept the challenge; so to battle they went.

But the lion, according to Aesop, had no chance against his more nimble opponent, who stung him sharply on the neck. Foaming with rage and pain, the lion roared so terribly that all his subjects crept in silence to their caves and dens, but the little fly continued to sting his enemy on the nose and lip till the lion was almost mad with agony. He tore himself with his claws. He lashed his sides and beat the air with his tail, and at length, quite worn out, he sank to the ground.

Away flew the victorious fly, humming songs of triumph. But the conqueror had the misfortune to get entangled in a cobweb, where he was speedily dispatched by his old enemy, the spider.

130

In 1951 four hundred acres of moorland in the North Riding of Yorkshire were destroyed by fire *because somebody dropped a lighted match.*

131

Thomas Babington Macaulay, when only four, had an amazing vocabulary. Taking coffee in a great lady's house one day, he was severely scalded when a cup was upset. His hostess fussed a good deal. Putting her arms round Thomas, she tried to console him, using baby language, until the future historian astonished her by saying, 'Madam, I thank you, but the agony is now abated.'

One day early in 1941 two Britishers thought they would take a hand in winning the war. One was a wireless operator, the other a pilot whose plane, though sadly out of date and incapable of travelling more than sixty miles an hour, was doing good service for the Kenya Defence Force, particularly in conveying patients to hospital.

It happened that the pilot, tired of routine flying, looked round for an exciting experience. He longed for a thrill, and said so to his wireless operator, who was in need of a thrill, too, it seemed. They did not wish to shirk duty, but they *did* want to go the second mile which is accounted as service. It was not long before they were off.

First, the guilty pair sought for a forty-gallon oil-drum. Having found one, they filled it surreptitiously with high explosives. Then they calmly attached an improvised fuse, rolled their lethal weapon into the old plane, taxied along the fairway, and made off before anyone could shout, 'Stop!'

A draughty machine it was—full of creaks and ominous rattles; but it soared over the trees, headed north, and quickly reached the Italian frontier. Far away on the horizon loomed an enemy fort, their objective. It was all a madcap flight, unauthorized, unpremeditated, certainly unofficial—and there would be awkward questions afterwards. The risks were enormous, for the drum of explosives had been packed by amateurs, the plane was by no means reliable, and the fort was bristling with anti-aircraft guns. But anything is preferable to boredom. So the audacious pair flew on. Anti-aircraft fire crackled round them. More than one bursting shell shook the machine so violently that the wireless operator had to stand with his legs far apart and hold on to the drum of explosives in a desperate attempt to prevent the 'bomb' and the ramshackle plane going to glory together.

Once over the target, the machine turned back, dived to within a few hundred feet of the ground, and roared through a hail of shrapnel. Suddenly from the cockpit came the sharp order: 'Push her over, Jack!'

Jack pushed.

As the door of the plane swung open the drum rolled into space. A deathly silence ensued, followed by a thud when the improvised 'bomb' bounced near the door of the fort. For a moment Jack believed their errand had been in vain; but the two madmen had done their work better than they knew, for the drum exploded with a terrific roar, and when at last the smoke and dust drifted away, the pilot and his accomplice saw that they had wrecked the fort itself, and brought down every building near by.

Having finished the job they went home to tea.

H. L. GEE: *Tales of Today.*

133

It was ridiculous, of course, for every day His Holiness received hundreds of letters, many of them from very important people. What chance, then, was there of Pope Pius the Ninth taking any notice at all of a letter from a schoolboy? But this little chap in Rome had boundless faith; so, without a word to anyone, he dared to write to His Holiness. The sheet of paper was covered with blots, and the letter was full of spelling mistakes. He wrote to the Pope as he might have written to a brother or an uncle. He wanted 37 lira, he said, because his mother was ill, and there was medicine to buy, and they hadn't any money, and could the Pope help him?

One of the Pope's secretaries sent a letter inviting the schoolboy to the Vatican next day.

The little chap arrived punctually. Unintimidated by the splendour about him, he smiled at the Pope, and thanked him for the golden coin His Holiness put into his hand. 'But this is only twenty lira, and I need thirty-seven,' he pointed out.

'Ah, yes, yes,' replied Pope Pius. 'I had forgotten how much you had asked for. Here is another twenty lira.'

'But this is too much, and I have no change,' said the little fellow. Then, with a merry laugh: 'Never mind, I'll run round with the change tomorrow.'

'Do,' urged His Holiness.

So the small boy with the great faith called again at the Vatican, and was ushered once more into the Pope's presence. 'I've brought you the three lira,' he announced.

'Thank you,' replied His Holiness. 'But you are to keep it for yourself; and I want to tell you that I have been making a few inquiries. I will see to it that you receive a good education, and that your mother will never again be in want.'

134

Returning from an adventurous expedition to North America, Sir Humphrey Gilbert sailed, not in the larger of his two vessels, but in the smaller—the *Squirrel*—of only ten tons burthen, surely a frail barque in which to face the dangers of the great Atlantic?

His vessel foundered but, shortly before she went down, Sir Humphrey called out: 'Fear not. We are as near heaven by sea as by land.'

135

The platoon I joined in 1914, Number Eight in the 10th Duke of Wellington's, was a platoon with a character of its own.

Though there were some of us in it young and tender enough, the majority were rather older and grimmer than the run of men in the battalion; tough factory hands, some of them of Irish descent, not without previous military service, generally in the old militia.

When the battalion was swaggering along you could not get Eight Platoon to sing; it marched in grim disapproving silence. But there came a famous occasion when the rest of the battalion, exhausted and blindly limping along, had not a note left in it. Gone now were the boasts about returning to Tipperary, the loud inquiries about the Lady Friend. The battalion was whacked and dumb.

It was then that a strange sound was heard from the stumbling ranks of B Company, a sound never caught before; not very melodious, perhaps, nor light-hearted, but miraculous: *Number Eight Platoon was singing.*

J. B. PRIESTLEY: *English Journey*.

136

Once upon a time there was a boastful man who declared he did not care what people said. So three acquaintances plotted to humble him.

One morning, as the boastful man walked to business, one of his acquaintances met him and murmured sympathetically: 'I'm sorry to see you looking unwell this morning.'

'Nonsense,' said the boastful man. 'There's nothing wrong with me.'

Presently he met another acquaintance. 'Dear me,' the friend exclaimed, 'you look quite ill, old man. Are you *sure* you ought to be out?'

The boastful man smiled bravely. 'There's nothing very much the matter with me,' he replied.

A few minutes later he was met by his third acquaintance who took him quickly by the arm, saying anxiously, 'Try not to faint. I'll call a taxi. You're ill.'

So the boastful man, who had never felt better in his life, was hurried home; and it was not till some days later that he felt well enough to leave his bed.

137

The following authentic account of an incident on the high seas in World War I appeared first in Arthur Mee's *My Magazine*. The story was told to an American journalist by a British officer of high rank, and we believe the hero was awarded the V.C.

A white line ran across the grey sea, and an explosion shattered a trawler. One man alone escaped, a young lieutenant who found himself swimming among the wreckage.

Suddenly his feet struck something firm, and a moment later he found himself aboard a submarine—the one which a few minutes before had sent his ship sky-high. He knew precisely what was going to happen: the trap-door would open, and the German captain would come out to survey the damage he had wrought.

Crouched on the narrow deck and taking up a strategic point, the lieutenant whipped out his revolver, and thanked God for its waterproof cover. Then he waited.

Presently the trap-door opened, and a man's head appeared. Instantly a bullet was buried in it, and within ten seconds the lieutenant had dragged the captain's body half out of the conning-tower, doubled it over the iron deck, and knelt on it so that it could not be drawn down.

Incredible as it may seem, he was master of the situation. Five minutes before he had been kicking the water; now he was victor.

But the victory was not quite as cheap as that. Would another man appear? If the lieutenant shot him, would others follow? He had begun with six shots in his revolver. Would he need them all?

Slowly the hours dragged by. Cramped, cold, hungry, the strain of keeping an eye on the trap-door was telling. And yet, who shall say what the strain was on the men below—the victors who found defeat in the very moment of triumph? What were *they* thinking? Had they the faintest idea that *one* man alone was keeping them at bay?

Then a ship appeared—a British destroyer ploughing her way to the scene of disaster. She came up with the submarine which could not sink (for the trap-door could not be closed), and as soon as she was alongside, the British lieutenant calmly handed over his prize!

138

The greatest surprise of Mary's life was receiving half a crown on her fourth birthday. She carried the coin about the house, and was seen sitting on the stairs admiring it.

'What are you going to do with your half-crown?' her mother asked.

'Take it to Sunday School,' said Mary promptly.

'To show your teacher?'

Mary shook her head. 'No,' said she. 'I'm going to give it to God—He'll be as surprised as I am to get something besides pennies!'

139

All of us know Holman Hunt's famous picture, 'The Light of the World', showing Christ knocking at a door.

And, of course, we have noticed that the door is shut, and that there is no latch. Perhaps we can never remind ourselves too often of the story, so often told, that when a brother artist pointed out to Holman Hunt that he had forgotten to give the door a latch, he replied: 'Ah, my friend, that is the whole message of the picture. There *is* a latch—but it's on the *inside* of the door.'

140

During the Franco-Prussian War a company of Prussians was marching through a French village when they were fired on by an unseen enemy, six of the company being killed. So enraged was their captain that he vowed an immediate reprisal, but apparently the village was deserted; at any rate, not a living soul could be found there. Still angry, the captain marched on to a small town where he rounded up the first six Frenchmen he came across, locked them in the mayor's house, and promised to have them shot at dawn.

That evening the six prisoners were visited by a pastor who did what he could to comfort the unfortunate men. One of the six had a wife and five small children, and with tears he begged the pastor to appeal on his behalf. Couldn't the pastor do *anything*? Couldn't he go to the authorities and plead for him?

Having given the condemned men his blessing, the pastor was bold enough to call on the Prussian captain, who received him coldly and scorned his passionate appeal.

'Sir,' said the pastor quietly, 'This man is young, and has a wife and children. I am old and have neither. It can make no difference to you which six men you shoot. I beg of you to set *him* free and take *me* instead.'

Staggered by this request, the captain considered the suggestion a moment, and then said grimly that the pastor might have his way if he were fool enough.

So the change in personnel was made. The night dragged on, and the time of the execution drew near. But meanwhile, news of the old man's sacrifice had come to the ears of the Prussian general; and so greatly was he impressed by what the pastor had done that he ordered his release—and the release of the other five prisoners also.

141

In 1945 somebody wrote to the *Paisley Express:*

Roy is back again. He's been fighting overseas a long time. He's been here and there, and it is over five years since he went away—five momentous years, and a lot has happened, and I've done many things, just as you have in all these days, and I've been to many places, and I've forgotten a lot.

Well, Roy is home again, and he called to see me last night, and said, 'Say, do you remember the afternoon I went away?'

I said vaguely, 'Well, yes.'

'Do you remember what you did?'

'Did? Didn't I see you off at the station, old chap? I seem to have a hazy notion . . .'

Roy smiled as he said: 'You promised to take my mother home to tea, *and you did.*'

Roy says so. Well, bless you, just fancy Roy remembering a little thing like that!

142

The audience was melting away, many in the crowd still talking of the rounds of applause given to the brilliant pianist, or commenting on his marvellous technique. One member waited at the side door, and when the pianist hurried out he stopped him, saying smilingly, 'I just wanted to tell you that you've improved quite a lot!'

'Indeed?' The pianist was not sure how to take the compliment —if it *was* a compliment.

'There's no comparison,' continued the stranger, 'between your playing today and the way you played last time I heard you. When I think of that last time, and of the way you thumped, and the awful discords you gave us, the improvement is truly astonishing.'

The pianist strode angrily across the pavement to the waiting taxi. He had no desire to be made a fool of at that moment. But the stranger held his arm. 'Forgive me,' he said, still smiling. 'You see, I'm just back from Australia after twenty-five years. You won't remember me, but I remember you—I was your next-door neighbour when you were about four; and really, you know, you *have* improved.'

It was the pianist's turn to smile.

143

Great men give little thought to the honours heaped upon them. One day Tennyson was listening to a group of friends talking about the House of Lords when he began to speak but stopped abruptly.

'You were going to say something?' someone asked.

'Yes,' Tennyson answered. 'I was going to say what I would do if I were a lord, *and then I remembered I was one.*'

144

Once upon a time a poor farmer taking a sack of corn to the mill knew not what to do when it slipped from his horse and fell into the road. The sack was too heavy for him to lift, and his only hope was that presently someone would come riding by and lend a hand.

It was not long before a rider appeared, but the farmer's heart sank when he recognized him, for he was none other than the nobleman who lived in a castle near by. The farmer would have dared to ask another farmer to help, or any poor fellow who might have come along the road, but it was not for him to beg a favour of so great a man.

However, no sooner did the nobleman come up than he dismounted, saying, 'I see you've had bad luck, friend. How fortunate it is that I'm here just at the right time.' With that, he took one end of the sack, the farmer the other, and between them they lifted it on the horse.

'My lord,' said the farmer, 'how can I repay you?'

'Easily enough,' the nobleman replied. 'Whenever you see anyone else in a difficulty, do the same for him.'

145

A motorist pulled up in a village in the north of England. It was a warm, sunny day as he took a stroll around, and he saw nothing unusual in a man sitting on a chair near the open door of a white cottage in a garden crowded with colour. 'Nice garden,' remarked the motorist.

'Very,' replied the man in the chair. 'Gives me a lot of pleasure, this garden. I like looking at it.'

The motorist said he wasn't surprised: and added, 'I expect you spend your spare time gardening?'

'Oh, no,' was the reply. 'It's the wife. She does the gardening. I just tell her she's made a good job of it.'

'You believe in taking things easy?'

'Just that. I sit around and give orders. She obeys when she's a mind to. It's my legs—gone on strike, as you might say. Won't work. Don't blame 'em. North Africa.'

The man in the garden was grinning lovably as he spoke; but the motorist, suddenly realizing something of the tragedy behind it all, looked grave. 'So it happened in the War?' he said. 'Can't anything be done?'

The hero chuckled. 'They've done everything except take my legs off,' he declared. 'I've been in and out of hospital for years —seen more of the Old Country since the War than I ever did before. The doctors have given me up as a bad job, but I don't worry. Bit of luck, really.'

'Luck?' repeated the astonished motorist.

The grey eyes in the thin face twinkled. 'Sure, that's what I said—*luck*! During the War I hardly dared to come home on leave—the wife was a terror for making me dig the garden. But now, well, *she* does the digging, and I just sit here feeling sorry for all the poor married men who aren't as lucky as I am!'

146

One of the most striking things about Christianity is the fact that it has spread so far from beginnings so small.

When we think that at the first Whitsuntide there were no more than a score or two of persecuted believers, it is astonishing that the work Jesus began, and left apparently so incomplete, should ever have gone on.

This thought seems to have impressed even the earlier Christians, for there has come down to us a quaint legend to account for it. We are told that when Our Lord had finished His ministry on earth and had returned to heaven, the angel Gabriel met Him, saying: 'Lord, Thou hast done wonderful work among men, but hast Thou made any plans for carrying it on?'

Then answered Jesus: 'I have given the message to Peter and John, and to a few fishermen; and also to Martha and Mary and other women. They will tell their friends, and they in turn will pass it on till the whole world shall know.'

But Gabriel was not impressed by this reply. 'Lord,' he said, 'these fishermen will be busy with their nets, and the women have housework to do. May they not forget to pass the message on? Surely Thou hast other plans?'

Then the Lord smiled radiantly. 'No,' said He. 'I have left the message with these, *and I am counting on them.*'

147

In 1901 a man who was down on his luck knocked at a door in Winnipeg, and begged a slice of bread. The good people refused to give him merely a slice of bread, insisting on his stepping into the kitchen, where they were all at breakfast. So the tramp enjoyed bacon and eggs and a hot drink; and after thanking them, he went on his way and was never seen by the kindly folk again.

As it happened, the beggar ended his search for work in New Jersey, where he prospered. Seventeen years later he died worth £1,600, every penny of which he left to the Winnipeg family that had given him a good breakfast.

148

Years ago there was a porter at Victoria Station, London, who had one delight in life. His idea of having a good time was not to get blind drunk; not to go dog-racing; not even to cheer himself hoarse at a football match. He liked to sit an hour in St James's Park, *and watch the ducks.*

A stoutish, red-faced little man, he had a wife and three children. His wife declared he was the best husband ever. His three children—two girls and a boy—grew up to be useful citizens. His small house was always spick and span. He was nobody much, but he lived happily, kept his temper when travellers were asking which platform a train went from, and was greatly respected by all who knew him.

'Eh,' said he once, 'you don't know *how* near I've come many a time to committing manslaughter . . . summertime, hot weather, crowds and crowds, and everybody pushing and shoving and jolting, and everybody shouting: "Which platform for Worthing?" '

Then he would grin mischievously, and add: 'It was them ducks kept me out of jail. Fact! Every so often I used to go and sit by the lake, and say nothing to anybody, and just look at them ducks . . . and I always went home feeling I could face another week of it at Victoria.'

149

Livingstone and Stanley were journeying together from Lake Tanganyika when a rumour spread that they were Arab slavers.

Nothing could have been more dangerous, for, hated as they were, slavers carried their lives in their hands in that wild region.

At one point the natives approached threateningly, ready at the least provocation to destroy the two travellers. Long exposure to the sun had tanned Livingstone and Stanley so much that it was easy to mistake them for Arabs; and when a drunken youth incited the savages, the rabble attacked the two explorers and determined to murder them.

'Kill the Arabs!' was their frenzied cry. Spears were raised; the mob was thirsty for blood.

But Livingstone, unafraid, did not step back. He did not flinch. In as ugly a predicament as a man could find himself, he remained erect. Calmly, and with a smile, he rolled up his sleeve and showed them his arm. The hand was brown—the arm white. 'I am no Arab,' he said.

It was all very simple, but it saved his life.

150

Late one afternoon during World War II a small boy who lives near my home looked up at me appealingly as I passed the gate. Smiling wistfully, he murmured, 'I don't suppose you've time?'

'Time for what?' I asked.

'Everybody's too busy,' he replied, as if he had a grievance against humanity for being in haste. 'But it wouldn't take long. It's only round the corner and across the road.'

'Well?'

'Mummy's poorly today,' he explained, 'and Daddy's in a tank, and there's nobody to take me to see the cows, and I always like to go because they miss me.'

'Come,' said I. 'I'll take you.'

So we went to see the cows. The small boy gazed at them and said, 'Good-night, cows.' Then we walked homeward in the twilight.

H. L. GEE.

151

Not long ago a lady who lives in a Midland town was introduced to one of her husband's business acquaintances. 'I'd like you to meet a friend of mine from Manchester,' said her husband.

'Oh, *Manchester*!' murmured the lady. 'I know Manchester. At least,' she added after a pause, 'I once spent two days there.'

'And what did you think of it?' asked the man from Manchester.

'Well,' said the lady, 'I hardly dare tell you.'

'Surely it wasn't as bad as that?' asked the citizen of no mean city.

The lady smiled. 'Oh, I don't mean in *that* way,' she hastened to assure him. 'Manchester is an amazing city—that immense area near Piccadilly, for instance; and the Town Hall—friends took me over it, and I can well believe it's one of the biggest in England . . . I know my feet ached with walking so far. And then, of course, that huge round Library, and the John Ryland's Library, and the Cathedral, and Chetham's Hospital . . . oh, there was so much to see.'

'But what impressed you most?' asked the man from Manchester.

Again the lady smiled. She hesitated. 'Oh,' she said, 'I'm afraid you'll laugh at me. But, you see, it was early in June, and the friends who were showing me round happened to take me into a rather poor quarter of the city. We came to a very dull street of little houses, and on nearly every window-sill were jam jars filled with buttercups. They were like golden torches in a dismal place. Ever since then—only *please* don't laugh—I've never thought of Manchester without thinking of buttercups!'

152

One sunless day in April 1771 a very little fellow at Chatham was sitting disconsolately on his luggage, which had been dumped by the stage coach.

He had expected his uncle, Captain Maurice Suckling, to meet him, but no one came to speak to him, and no one cared anything about him.

The boy had not much luggage to sit on, and the world seemed very big. The *Raisonable*, his uncle's ship, lay near at hand, but the boy did not know how to get aboard—everyone seemed much too busy to take any notice of *him*. Hopeless and forlorn, he remained on the quay hour after hour, looking on at the bustle and stir, watching the ships with their black and white timbers, their network of rigging, and their companies of sailors. He hoped someone would come along and claim him, but no one did, and his heart sank. If ever there was a day in his life when he knew what fear was, it was this day, his first day at Chatham.

At last a sailor, taking pity on him, saw him aboard the *Raisonable*. Years after, when the boy had grown to be a man, and had become England's greatest admiral, he used to say that his first day at Chatham was the most wretched he had ever known.

He was Horatio Nelson.

153

When somebody asked Marshal Foch how he managed to win World War I, he is reported to have said: 'By smoking my pipe, not getting excited, and reserving all my strength for the task in hand.'

154

Monsieur Brassier was ruffled. Yes, yes, he had had trouble, heaps of it, and all caused by a thoughtless customer who had come into his shop and upset everything! He had lost francs out of it, many francs!

'He comes into my shop, monsieur,' he explained to one of his regular customers, 'a man with a beard and very bright eyes. My assistants were hurrying to go to appointments to prepare ladies and gentlemen for the ball—you know what a grand affair it was last night. He comes into my shop, this man, and sits in this chair, monsieur, this *very* chair, and I throw the towel round his neck, and I take up the brush to lather him when he says, "One moment, pardon me, monsieur."

'I wonder what can be the matter. He takes a pencil from his waistcoat, and searches in his pocket for paper. He cannot find it. He looks round anxiously. Then his eye falls on a paper on the table there, and he snatches it up and begins writing. "Just one moment," he says to me who have a dozen customers waiting.

'Never, monsieur, did you see such scribble, never. No man could read it. The moment become a minute, five minutes. I say, "Excuse me, monsieur, but I have many customers . . ."

'He says, "Yes, yes, very good, one moment," and goes on and on. I cough. I shake him by the arm. I say, "Monsieur, it is imperative that I ask you to leave this chair," but he goes on till the page is full. Then he jumps up suddenly, and runs out of the shop without his shave, without his hat, *without paying me a sou*! Diable, monsieur, I find afterwards I am ruined, for the list of appointments for my assistants can nowhere be found . . . for he has run off with it!'

Says the customer: 'Friend Brassier, I saw this man dashing out of your shop. Know you who he was? He was *Victor Hugo*; and you, monsieur, have surely helped him to compose something that all France will be proud of!'

The barber is silent a moment. 'Victor Hugo!' he repeats. 'Writing in *my* shop? In this very chair? *Juste ciel!* I am a proud man, monsieur!'

155

In London's cruel ordeal during the continuous raids with which Hitler hoped to bring England to her knees, Sir Winston Churchill visited a bombed area while the ruins were still ablaze. Speaking to an old lady whose house had been shaken but not severely damaged, he said: 'And how do *you* feel after a night of horror?'

'Oh, not so bad,' was the gallant reply. 'After all, there's one thing about these raids—they *do* take your mind off the war!'

156

Declared an Irishman once: 'I'd give fifty pounds to know where I'm going to die.'

'Why do you want to know *that*?' asked his friend. 'You'd be no better for knowing.'

'Faith,' said the Irishman, 'but I would. If I knew where it was I'd never go near the place!'

157

In 1936 the world lost a voice which had moved unnumbered people to tears, a voice full of sweetness and pathos, the voice of Dame Clara Butt. For years she sang to immense and always appreciative audiences, and once she sang *alone* in the depths of despair.

Then a girl in her early 'teens, she had a friend, Alice Jenkins, whom she loved dearly. Music linked them together, for Alice was a brilliant musician, and Clara was already singing at concerts. The two went everywhere together.

Then Alice became ill—mysteriously ill. Day after day Clara called to inquire about her friend, but she could never see her. Each day the news was bad. One day it was more alarming than ever. The next day she was told that Alice was dying.

Sensitive and passionate, Clara would not leave the house. She stayed in one of the rooms on the ground floor—sitting, standing, sitting again; pacing softly to and fro. She was praying with all her soul—praying for the girl upstairs by whose bed her mother and a nurse were waiting for the end.

Suddenly Clara did a mad thing. She had picked up one of the many pieces of music lying on the piano. It was the piece she had sung and Alice had played over and over again. Both loved it. There and then Clara sang it—sang it loudly, her young powerful rich contralto filling all the house:

'Beat on, true heart, for ever;
Shine, bright, strong, golden chain!'

And to the mother and nurse in the bedroom there came a strange feeling, almost frightening, as Alice opened her eyes, listened, smiled—and from that minute began to get well.

158

Long ago two knights came riding towards a statue—a huge figure of Victory holding a shield.

Arriving almost at the same moment the knights, who had come from different directions, stood looking at the figure in wonder, one exclaiming, 'Marvellous. And I declare the shield is pure silver.'

'Surely you are mistaken,' said the other knight. 'Anyone can see the figure holds a golden shield.'

'Silver,' said the first knight.

'Gold,' said the second.

'Nonsense,' said the first.

'You insult me,' said the second.

At this point they drew their swords; and, as was the custom of the gallant and headstrong in those days, they were about to fight when a maiden ran between them crying: 'Good friends, put up your swords. The shield you have been looking at is silver on the one side, gold on the other.'

159

How often have you finished a letter with the words, *Yours sincerely*? But have you ever paused to wonder what this common and formal ending means?

It has been suggested—though it is *merely* a suggestion and nothing more—that *Yours sincerely* has something to do, however remotely, with the potters of ancient Rome.

There were, of course, good Roman potters and bad. The good potters made good drinking and cooking vessels; the bad ones made bad vessels *which looked good.*

For what happened was this: Unscrupulous potters did not hesitate to make a cracked pot look sound by filling the crack with wax. You could turn such a pot round and round in the market place and never discover the flaw, so cunningly was it hidden; but when you took the pot home and poured hot water into it, the wax melted, and you found, too late, that you had been had.

Well, the bad potters patched their pots, and often got away with it; but the good potters broke any pots that had cracks or flaws. They scorned the use of wax for hiding a crack. So, a pot *without* wax was genuine, sound, reliable; and thus—so, at least, it has been suggested—there came into being the phrase *sine cera*, which was the Latin way of saying, without wax. Whether or not our phrase *Yours sincerely* really is indirectly derived from this ancient Roman phrase is uncertain, but it is challenging to think, when next you write *Yours sincerely*, that you are assuring somebody you are altogether genuine and honest; in other words that you are precisely what you seem.

160

Things were not too gay when Geoffrey went home one lunch-time. His wife was anything but cheery; and twice she 'ticked him off' in no uncertain manner and with a pretty sharp tongue.

There were quite a few things Geoffrey did not do. He did not answer back. He did not sulk. He did not hit his wife on the head. He did not leave home for ever. He did not call her names.

No, Geoffrey just kept on, much as usual. After lunch he went back to work; but when he got home at teatime his wife was wearing another frock. She looked smart. Tea was all ready.

'I was just tired out this morning,' she explained. 'And it was *so* sweet of you, Geoffrey, not to say anything when I was horrid.'

161

'Eh,' exclaimed Mrs Emily Bee of Granada Street, Limehouse, 'don't I wish *he* could see it?'

It was the eve of George the Fifth's Silver Jubilee—May 1935—and Mrs Bee, a widow with a very small pension, was tired out. What a time she'd had, to be sure, but how she'd enjoyed it! Loyal to the backbone, she'd done all she could to make one corner of Limehouse gay.

First she'd hung red, white and blue festoons outside her small and dingy house. Then she'd taken down her front curtains, washed them, and dyed *them* red, white and blue. Then she'd arranged a row of chairs outside her beflagged front door, every chair painted red, white and blue. It had been her example that had fired all Granada Street with enthusiasm, and brought out no end of bunting. 'Eh,' repeated Mrs Bee to her neighbours, 'don't I wish the King could see it?'

But it was no good wishing, so Mrs Emily Bee went to lie down for half an hour—not that it was any use . . . there was too much noise outside. Sad indeed that a loyal body couldn't get a wink of sleep nohow! But wasn't Granada Street noisier than usual? Cycle bells were ringing furiously. There was cheering—wild cheering. Thousands of feet were running along the street. Maybe there was a fire?

Up jumped Mrs Bee, losing two hairpins as she hurried downstairs, her soiled apron still covering an old frock she had been going to change if only . . .

Bless us all, children singing! Policemen—no end of 'em—just outside her house. And crowds of people—all London, or nearly—jostling in Granada Street, Limehouse! Heaven preserve us—somebody's knocking at the front door, and her hair all over the place, as you might say, and her apron not too clean, either; and there, by the kerb, a magnificent car all spit and polish, and somebody stepping out. Mrs Bee's heart missed a beat—it was Princess Elizabeth and her Grandma', if you please; and behind them a fine gentleman raising his hat . . . raising his hat to Mrs Emily Bee! Lord, how the lamp-posts swayed. She did not hear what he said to her—she just knew that he was George the Fifth, King of England, Emperor of India, Defender of the Faith . . . it all ran round in Mrs Bee's head.

The car moves off. The crowd cheers louder than before; and Mrs Bee, dazed but smiling, sits down heavily on one of her red, white and blue chairs, and murmurs to a neighbour, 'Eh, you don't know how glad I am I'd done my best when the King called!'

162

'I was glad to see you at church last Sunday evening, Miss Sprague,' said the Minister.

'Thank you,' replied she. 'As a matter of fact, I *always* make a point of attending when *you* are preaching.'

The Minister was flattered, and said so.

'Oh, don't mistake me,' Miss Sprague hastened to add. 'It's only that when the Reverend Rogers preaches I can't get a seat anywhere, but when *you* are preaching there's always lots of room.'

163

After a perilous journey in the Antarctic, Sir Ernest Shackleton wrote: 'When I look back I have no doubt that Providence guided us not only across the snowfields but across the storm-white sea. I know that during that long and raking march of thirty-six hours over the unnamed mountains and glaciers of South Georgia it seemed to me often that we were four, not three. I said nothing to my companions; but afterwards Worsley said to me, *Boss, I'd a curious feeling on that march that there was another person with us.*

164

A charming young lady was driving a car when she noticed a number of men climbing a pole to repair the telephone wires. 'Idiots!' she exclaimed. 'Do they think I've never driven a car before?'

165

The hymn, *The Lord's my Shepherd, I'll not want*, by William Whittingham (and revised by Francis Rous and the Westminster Assembly Divines) is, as everyone knows, a rendering of the 23rd Psalm. It has long been part and parcel of Scottish life, and is now usually sung to the tune *Crimond.*

Of this hymn the Rev. D. P. Alford once wrote: 'When I was chaplain of the Scilly Isles one of my parishioners, a Scotsman who was dying, found the greatest consolation in the metrical version of this psalm. His wife said to me: *It is no wonder that psalm comforts him, for he has said it every night before going to bed ever since I have known him.* They were a very elderly pair, and had been married many years.'

166

In 1685 Sir John Cochrane, one of Argyll's supporters, was in prison in Edinburgh, a rebel condemned to death. Once the warrant for his execution reached the capital, his life must end.

Grizel, his daughter, had done all she could to secure his reprieve. The Earl of Dundonald was working on the prisoner's behalf, and feverish attempts to set him free were being made by a host of influential sympathizers. But the day of the execution was drawing near, and at any hour the warrant might be given to the warden of the castle. If only his friends could gain a few days' grace, their efforts might succeed, for Sir John had many friends at court. The days slipped by, however, and at last only a few hours, at most, could be hoped for before the warrant came.

It was then that Grizel had a scheme she dare not share with anyone except one trusted friend. Leaving home secretly she hurried to the Border, and in a cottage four miles from Berwick she laid careful plans with the help of her old nurse. Then she rode on to Belford where the post took the mail from Durham, but Grizel no longer looked like a girl. You would have taken her for a Cavalier, for she was dressed as a dashing young man, two pistols in her belt.

At the inn she contrived to empty the shot out of the post's pistols, and then went on ahead till she saw him coming along the road. For a time she jogged along at his side, finding him glad to have a companion. They talked pleasantly enough till they reached a desolate region. Then came the supreme moment of Grizel's life, the moment when her heart beat so loudly that she thought the man at her side must hear it; the moment when she knew she must not fail. Out came her pistols. She was a highwayman in an instant.

But the post was not easily intimidated. At first he laughed aloud—this girlish fellow, he thought, was joking. Then, realizing his mistake, he turned savagely, whipped out his pistols, and when the command, 'Stand and deliver,' was repeated, fired point-blank. Neither pistol went off, but a pistol was held at his head (though he did not perceive how the frail hand trembled). Suddenly swinging off his horse, the post made a dash at brave Grizel, but she proved too quick for him. Snatching his saddle-bag, she set spurs to her horse and galloped off.

Afterwards, tearing open the bag, she found the royal warrant, burnt it, and reached home safely.

It was fifteen days before another death warrant could reach Edinburgh, and in the meantime Grizel's father received a royal pardon.

167

All of us, of course, know the story told in St Luke's Gospel of how, when Jesus was born in Bethlehem, there were shepherds watching in the fields by night, and how the angel of the Lord came upon them and brought them glad tidings of great joy. We read that after the angels had sung *Glory to God in the highest*, the shepherds went even unto Bethlehem, and found Mary and Joseph, and the Babe lying in a manger.

Legend tells us that among the shepherds was a lad named Ephraim, and that when the shepherds set out to find Jesus he took a lantern and went along with them. Had the shepherds been less excited they would have noticed Ephraim, and would most probably have ordered him back; but in their eagerness they hurried into the little town and crowded into the stable, Ephraim with them. When they fell down to worship the new-born King, the boy dropped on his knees also. But when the shepherds left the stable to spread abroad the glad tidings, Ephraim remained behind.

For, says the legend, his quick young eyes had noticed something the others had missed—Mary wrapping her cloak about the

Holy Child because, shortly before dawn, the air was chill. So, without a word, Ephraim ventured humbly and reverently to draw near, holding up his lantern so that the small flame might warm the air, if ever so little, about the Babe. For two hours he stood there, his arm aching and throbbing all the time, but his heart full of love and adoration; and at last, when the sun was up and the morning light came in at the stable door, he crept away on tiptoe.

Then it was that the miracle occurred, for as soon as Ephraim was in the open air, the sunshine all about him, he tried to blow out the flame of his lantern, *but could not*. All that day it burned with a soft, clear light; and it went on burning as softly and as clearly all that night. Day and night the lamp burned steadily—as steadily, indeed, as Ephraim's love burned in his heart. Ephraim grew to be a man—loved by all for his gentleness and sweetness—and still, day and night, his lantern shone its pure light upon all things; and so it continued to burn until Ephraim was old and lay dying.

The legend says that death was kindly to Ephraim; and that towards nightfall the lamplight grew brighter and clearer until it shone like the sun itself, and a voice said; 'Behold now, Ephraim, your lamp had never gone out because your love has never wavered. Lo, I am the Light of the World. Come, enter into the joy of thy Lord.'

168

Schubert never lived to know true greatness, though a vague prophecy of it stirred him one day when, almost too poor to buy paper on which to write his compositions, he heard a military band playing his own immortal march. It was a hint of fame to come.

A tale is told of how he and a few friends were talking and drinking in a Viennese tavern one afternoon when an odd thing happened. They were in the last place for the composition of music, since they were half-deafened by the rattle of mugs and the babel of loud voices. Amid all this sat Schubert glancing over the pages of a book of poems which one of his friends had given him.

'I have a pretty melody in my head,' said Schubert, looking up suddenly. 'I could put it down if only I had paper with lines on it.'

A friend grabbed a bill of fare from a near-by table, ruled some lines, and handed it to Schubert. The rattling of the mugs went on. The laughing and talking continued. But there, amid squalor and noise, was born the imperishable music of Schubert's *Serenade*, as full of passion and sweetness as anything the world has ever heard.

169

For twenty years before 1915 the name of Charles Frohman, theatrical manager, was known on both sides of the Atlantic. We believe he was the first American manager to have controlling interests in English theatres. Certainly there was never a busier man. Frohman was *always* working. No one could imagine him resting. Time was money to him, seconds saved pounds in his pockets, and he had never a moment to spare. He was here, there and everywhere—organizing, directing, producing, altering, improving; you never saw such a man. He never seemed to need time to breathe. And how impatient he was if compelled to waste ten precious seconds!

In his later years he had offices at the Globe Theatre, a private sanctum reached by a lift.

One morning Frohman ran into the Globe, stepped into his lift, went half-way up, *and stuck between floors*!

There was consternation among the staff: Frohman—the busiest man in London—was wasting time; the priceless minutes were flying by. Engineers were sent for. Mechanics worked feverishly. Supreme efforts were made—and at last the lift was drawn up.

'Look out!' yelled somebody, expecting the roof to go off as the angry manager dashed out of his prison. 'Now there'll be trouble—Frohman's had nothing to do!'

But Charles Frohman was smiling when he came out. 'Say,' he observed, 'that's the first real rest I've had for years.'

170

Johnny had been indoors a few days with a slight chill, but one afternoon his mother said: 'I've some shopping to do. If I leave you at home, will you promise not to go out of doors?'

'Yes, Mother,' replied Johnny.

So, while his mother went into town, Johnny looked out of the window and wished that he, too, might go out. He saw the birds in the back garden. He saw the flowers. He sighed once, then again, and after that a third time. 'If I went into the garden for half a minute, nobody would know,' said he to himself.

Opening the back door, he stepped into the sunshine. Then he heard voices. Climbing on a box, he looked over the high wall, and was surprised to see many people in the garden next door, all of them in fine clothes, the gentlemen having carnations in their buttonholes, the ladies wearing flowered hats. A tall young man stood arm in arm with a lady in white. Their backs were to the wall, and a photographer, with his head under a black cloth, was shuffling about behind a camera. It was all so very interesting that Johnny remained peeping over the wall till the photographer said, smiling: 'There, that's all for today, I think!'

When the ladies and gentlemen went indoors, Johnny thought that he ought to return to the living-room; so he ran back to the house, closed the door, picked up a book, and was busy reading when his mother arrived. 'It's *so* nice to know I can trust my little boy,' said his mother.

Johnny beamed in saintly fashion.

And that would be the end of the story were it not that a few days later Mrs Smith popped in to see Johnny's mother while Johnny was at school. 'I just looked in to let you see the wedding photographs,' she explained. 'Here's one showing them coming out of church—doesn't Susan look simply radiant? And here's a picture of them cutting the cake! And we had this one taken in the back garden. . . .'

'H'm, *very* interesting,' murmured Johnny's mother. 'And I seem to know the little boy who is peeping over the wall!'

171

They were good neighbours. The old folk next door were interested in the business man and his wife and two children. Many little kindnesses and courtesies were exchanged, as well as smiles over the garden wall.

One springtime, however, the faintest shadow came between them. Somehow they did not see each other as often. What had been a warm friendship cooled imperceptibly. Each was polite, but the good feeling seemed to have gone, and the humour which had been so delightful was missing. In the quiet of their home the old people would say, 'What in the world can they be doing so early in the morning?'

When the children had gone to bed, the business man and his wife would say, 'It's so strange—and so thoughtless of them.' Each wished to complain to the other, but neither wanted to make trouble.

At last the old lady could bear it no longer; so one day she made it her business to waylay the man next door. Looking over the wall, she said she hoped he would forgive her, but really her husband was getting no sleep on account of it. Was there any need to be hammering at the bedroom wall so early in the morning—it woke them at five, and sometimes even sooner.

'That's very odd,' said the man next door. 'As a matter of fact, for weeks now I've been going to ask *you* why you were up so early, and what you could possibly be doing in the bedroom to disturb us like that.'

'But we don't do anything,' said the old lady in astonishment.

'Neither do we,' said the business man.

Then they looked at each other and laughed, and all the good feeling and neighbourliness came back.

It was the builder who found the cause of the trouble. 'I've known 'em do it before,' he said. 'It's them starlings. They've pecked away at the mortar in the chimney till there's hardly any left.'

172

From a remote corner of Yorkshire comes this old tale of Farmer Brearley who had been to market and was about to drive home again.

'Let's see, now,' said he thoughtfully, looking over the parcels in the trap. 'I've got my sack of meal, and my new fork, and my sheep-salve. I reckon that's the lot.'

So he climbed up and drove off at a canter, but once or twice he looked round and scratched his head. 'I reckon that's all,' he said uneasily. 'I reckon so.'

At last he drew rein at his own door, where his daughter stared in astonishment. 'Eh, Father,' she exclaimed, 'whatever have you done with Mother?'

173

Mary was dusting the stairs when somebody opened the back door, and called out, 'Are you there, luv?'

'Coming,' said Mary, in a flat voice.

She left her dusting and went into the kitchen, where she found her neighbour, Mrs Salmon, a motherly soul, and twice Mary's age. 'Eh, there you are, luv,' said Mrs Salmon, beaming. 'I've minced the cold meat and there's more than me and my Old Man can eat, so I've brought the rest round here. I thought mebbe it'd save you a bit, you know—and three bairns can put it out of sight in no time. Anything the matter, luv? You look a bit down, as you might say.'

For a moment Mary did not answer. She was very near to tears. 'Oh, it's nothing,' she said. 'I'm just fed up, that's all . . . fed up with housework. If I dust today, it'll need dusting tomorrow. I seem to spend my life washing up and washing up, and as fast as I clean anything it needs cleaning again. I'm fed up.'

Mrs Salmon nodded. 'Eh, luv,' she murmured, 'we all feel that way now and again, don't we? 'Course we do.' She paused. She was looking out of the kitchen window; and she stood looking so long that Mary glanced up questioningly.

'Silly of me,' said Mrs Salmon. 'But I was just looking at that there cherry tree at the bottom of your garden; and I was just thinking God must get fed up with it—making it all white and wonderful, same as it is now, and having to do it all over again *next* year. Or does He love us that much that He don't mind doing it over and over and over—same as you're going to keep on making this here little house clean and nice and like a bit of heaven for them *you* love?' She beamed again. 'Come on, luv,' she urged. 'I could do with a cup of tea. You come round with me—you'll feel on top of the world in no time.'

174

Twenty-two miners at Tylorstown, in Glamorgan, found themselves trapped in the dark when something went wrong with the cage machinery at the pithead. They were suspended in a shaft 2,000 feet deep, and there remained for an hour, wondering all the time what was the matter.

But the miners did not fret. *They sang.*

175

During the Korean War a company of Americans had a recreational centre in a hut behind the firing line. Over the door they proudly printed the words, *Second to None.*

When a British hut close by was completed somebody wrote over the door, *None.*

176

Perhaps there are some who have not heard the old story of the American millionaire who came upon a gardener at Oxford, and said: 'I sure fancy a lawn like this way back in Chicago. How do I get agoin'?'

The old English gardener looked at him with smiling eyes. 'You'll need some of our native soil,' he said.

'Oh, that's okay,' the hustler declared. 'We'll soon have a few hundred tons of that shipped over.'

'And some grass seed,' said the gardener.

'Okay,' the American agreed.

'And you must take care the ground is drained and levelled to begin with,' the gardener explained. 'And you need a good top dressing. I'd sow the seed in autumn; and the grass requires rolling and cutting in the spring, and then rolling and cutting again all the summer through.'

'I get you. And how long do we have it rolled and cut?'

'Well,' said the English gardener, thinking it out slowly, 'if you want to get it into really first class condition, I'd say *two hundred years would do it.*'

177

World War II is recent enough for most of us to recall the agony of parting known to so many in those grim and dangerous days. As a rule, the sailor, soldier or airman who was being seen off at the railway station, waved to a gallant sweetheart or wife; and even if he *knew* she would be crying a moment after he left, it was grand to remember a smiling face.

Perhaps the little wife who was seeing her husband off one day in 1942 was playing *her* part like the rest of them; but although *she* could pretend to be cheery, their small son was unable to disguise his feelings.

How tightly he held his mother's hand as the trio stood on the station platform! They had arrived much too soon, of course, and it was a wretched ordeal waiting for the moment of parting. Husband and wife bore up bravely; but the little chap sobbed all the time, and would not be comforted. His father tried to joke with him, and his mother gave him a penny to put in a slot machine—it was no use, the child was brokenhearted.

Suddenly the sobbing stopped and the tears were brushed aside! The small boy was looking up, eyes shining as if a fairy had appeared from nowhere. 'Good afternoon, sir,' said a deep voice. 'I'm the driver of locomotive five-eight-five-three. Care to look inside the cab?'

It wasn't true! He was dreaming! Little boys don't stand on the footplate! 'Come on,' coaxed the engine driver.

So the small boy walked along the platform and climbed into the cab of locomotive 5853. He touched a lever. He turned a wheel. He was lifted up to examine pressure gauges. Finally, the fireman opened the door of the furnace so that the small boy —now happy beyond all telling—might help to throw a shovel of coal into the fire to make his Daddy's train travel at sixty miles an hour.

A minute later locomotive 5853 was steaming out of the station —an Army officer waving to a smiling wife *and* a smiling son . . . thanks to a very knowing engine driver.

178

One day a miller and his son drove a donkey to market, intending to sell it. They had not gone far, however, when they were met by a number of girls who said among themselves, 'Fancy these silly fellows walking when they might ride!'

The father, overhearing this remark, told his son to mount. After a while they met some old men, one of whom exclaimed, 'Do you see that young scapegrace riding merrily while his father trudges along? Isn't it an example of the thoughtlessness of the younger generation?'

As soon as the son heard these words he jumped off the donkey and helped his father to mount, and in this manner they went along the road until they met some peasant women who shouted angrily: 'You cruel fellow, making yourself so comfortable on the donkey, and leaving your poor son to walk!'

The good-natured miller at once told his son to mount behind him, but as they were drawing near the town a shepherd called out, 'Pray, friend, does that donkey belong to you?'

'Yes,' said the miller.

'One would not have thought so by the unmerciful way you treat him. Why, you two are far better able to carry the poor animal than he to carry you!'

Hearing this, the father and son at once got down, tied the donkey's legs together, and having slung the animal on a pole, began carrying him across a narrow bridge in the town. The sight of a donkey being carried in this manner was so novel that the people left their shops and houses to enjoy the fun; and they laughed so loudly that the donkey, taking fright, kicked violently and fell into the river, where he was drowned.

179

From East Yorkshire comes this story of the school teacher who was trying to stamp out dialect in a lonely village. One of her scholars having written the word *putten* in his composition, the teacher said severely, 'Look at this sentence and tell me what is wrong.'

For a moment the lad stared hard at the sentence. Then, with a sudden inspiration, he replied, 'Why, Miss, Ah've gone an' putten *putten* wheer Ah owt ti hev' putten *put*.'

180

One day, it is said, Frederick the Great of Prussia rang his bell, but no one answered. He rang again, and still no one came; so he opened the door, and found his page fast asleep in a chair.

The King was about to shake the youth and upbraid him for his ill service when he noticed a letter half out of the boy's pocket. Glancing at it, he saw that it had been written by the lad's mother, and that in it she thanked him over and over again for sending her so much of his wages month by month. 'God will surely bless you, my dear boy,' she concluded.

This touched the King; so, after he had slipped a handful of ducats into the lad's pocket, he rang again—more vigorously than ever, and the moment the page appeared the King said accusingly: 'You've been asleep!'

'Yes, sire,' the boy confessed.

'Feel in your pocket,' ordered Frederick the Great; and when the astonished lad stammered his thanks, the King added, 'Always remain worthy of a good mother. So long as you do I will see that neither of you ever wants for anything.'

Thus fortune came to the page while he slept, for Frederick the Great kept his promise.

181

Aesop tells us that when a farmer saddled his horse to go to a neighbouring market he saw a nail was wanting in one of the horse's shoes. But he said, 'It's only *one* nail. I needn't trouble about *that.*' So he rode off.

About half-way on the journey the horse cast the shoe, so the farmer said, 'If there were a forge near, I'd have that shoe put on again. Anyhow, my horse has still three good shoes; I dare say he will do very well.'

But the ground was full of sharp flints, and soon the horse began to go lame. Suddenly two robbers sprang out of a wood, and though the farmer dug his spurs into the horse's sides, the poor animal was unable to run, so the robbers took from the farmer all his money and his horse as well.

182

As I was being carried on board during a brief moment's consciousness I heard the doctor say: 'He'll never reach Gibraltar.' From that moment I determined I would live.

LORD FISHER, many years before he died.

183

During a war between England and France an English drummer-boy was captured by the enemy. When asked who he was he replied that he was a drummer-boy, but as he had no drum this answer was not enough to remove the suspicion that he had been sent out as a spy. Accordingly, a drum was brought, and he was ordered to play two marches, which he did with much skill.

A French officer, however, even then not quite satisfied, ordered the lad to beat a retreat.

'A retreat, sir?' asked the English drummer-boy proudly. 'I do not know what that is.'

This spirited reply pleased the French officer so much that he dismissed the boy there and then.

184

As she had never used a telephone before, it was something of an ordeal for the old lady to go to the call-box, read the instructions, fumble with the receiver, and finally get in touch with the operator.

'It's Leslie, my grandson, you know, dearie,' she murmured confidentially. 'I just wanted a wee chat with the dear laddie, if you don't mind.'

'Number?' asked the operator.

'Oh, I couldn't say, dearie. It's Leslie, you know; he's on holiday, and I thought it would be such a surprise. . . .'

'Exchange?'

'Oh, I don't want to exchange anything. I'm just staying here in this box, but I thought perhaps you could get him for me. He's staying with friends in Aberdeen, dearie. . . .'

Strange to relate, the old lady *did* get through, the operator being wonderfully patient and wonderfully resourceful. So granny had a wee chat with her grandson. Then she rang off.

But that wasn't quite the end of the matter. The operator was rung up again. 'Can I help you?' she inquired mechanically.

'Oh, hello, dearie,' said a familiar voice. 'It's just me again. Leslie was *so* surprised; and you, you've been *so* kind, you know . . . I've put twopence in the box for yourself.'

185

At twenty-one Jacques Laffitte, son of a poor carpenter of Bayonne, set out to seek his fortune. He was nobody. He was without references from influential people. He had no brilliant academic career behind him. But he was young and full of hope.

So Jacques arrived in Paris; and there, with his usual thoroughness, he sought employment. Days became weeks, and still he was unsuccessful. Nobody in Paris took the least notice of him. If only he had had a letter from some distinguished Frenchman. . . .

One morning Jacques applied at the office of the famous Swiss banker, M. Perregaux. M. Perregaux himself, as chance would have it, received the young man, asked a few questions, shook his head, and regretted there was no vacancy at the moment.

Sadly and more discouraged than ever, Jacques left the banking establishment, walking slowly across the courtyard. As he did so, he paused, stooped and picked something up; then he sauntered into the busy street, wondering whether or not to return to Bayonne.

But at that moment he was overtaken by a man who tapped him on the shoulder. 'Excuse me, sir,' said he, 'I am an attendant at the Bank. Monsieur Perregaux wishes to see you again.'

For the second time that morning Jacques faced the great man. 'Pardon me,' murmured M. Perregaux, 'but I happened to be watching you as you crossed the courtyard. You stooped and picked something up. Would you mind telling me what it was?'

'Only this,' replied Jacques, wonderingly, as he took a bright new pin from the lapel of his jacket.

'Ah,' exclaimed M. Perregaux, '*that* alters everything. We always have room here for anyone who is careful about *little things*. You may start at once.'

Thus Jacques Laffitte began his long and amazingly successful association with the Bank, ultimately assuming complete control of what later became Perregaux Laffitte et Cie.

186

The incident occurred during the brief war between Britain and the United States—1812 to 1814—when, more by good luck than good management, an American privateer bore down on a small Welsh collier in the Irish Sea. Having captured the vessel, the American captain went on board, and was shown into the tiny cabin. After a word or two he said, 'Say, what's this box with a slit? Queer idea, ain't it?'

'That?' the Welshman replied. 'Oh, that's just our missionary box. We hold a service in the cabin every Sunday, and each of us puts a penny in the box. That's all.'

The American commander stood fingering his lip. Then he said, 'You do *that*, eh? Wal, I reckon it's no use interferin' with folks like you. You seem to think of others a bit—so, I guess you can just say I came on board for a friendly chat. See?'

Then he climbed down into the boat, leaving the Welsh collier to make her way to port.

187

There is something fine about this story of Garibaldi, the great Italian patriot.

Born in 1807, he won fame as a soldier after being condemned to death and escaping—almost by the skin of his teeth—to South America. When he returned to his country he had visions of a new Italy, and was prepared to do great things at any cost. But he had first of all to gather followers upon whom he could rely, so he began a campaign in which thousands flocked to his banner.

It is recorded that he was in a village one day when he saw a group of young men at a street corner. Making himself known to them, he urged them to enlist. 'What do you offer us?' one of their number demanded. 'Suppose we join up, what do we get for it?'

It was a fair question, and a lesser man might have answered with fair words and dazzling promises. Not so Garibaldi. 'Friends,' said he steadily, 'I offer you hardship, hunger, rags, thirst, sleepless nights, foot-sores, long marches, countless privations, disappointments and the hope of victory in the noblest cause that any Italian ever yet fought for. Will you join?'

And the amazing thing is that they did.

188

I met him on Westminster Bridge. He stopped me, pointed to the Clock Tower, and asked, 'Is that Big Ben?' I said it was.

The little man, who wore a grey cap, a brown overcoat and black shoes, had come up from Lancashire that afternoon. 'It's my first visit to London,' he said, smiling.

Big Ben was about to chime the hour, and the little man waited expectantly. Then, as nine o'clock began to strike, he set his watch, looked up curiously, and remarked, with a show of emotion he would like to have hidden: 'I always put my watch right by Big Ben, you know. My missus in Blackburn will be putting our kitchen clock right this very minute.' He paused, and then said: 'Somehow, you know, it sort of makes you proud you're British, doesn't it?'

ARTHUR PAGE.

189

A stirring scene it must have been when Elijah stood alone, yet something of the kind happened in England in 627; and Goodmanham, on the Yorkshire Wolds, must ever be our English Mount Carmel.

For months Edwin, King of Northumbria, had halted between two opinions. In spite of all the teaching and preaching of that austere missionary, Paulinus, the King found it difficult to decide between paganism and Christianity.

We cannot wonder. Born and brought up in the faith of his fathers, it was a hard thing to go over from the old to the new, and though the old faith was weak, and he saw much that was good in the new, the King lacked confidence to make an irrevocable decision.

One day he and his court listened again to the words of Paulinus. Many of his councillors were already sure in their own minds that their gods were worthless, but still the King held back. What if the old gods were real after all? Suppose he betrayed them—and they took vengeance? What then?

It was left to Coifi, the High Priest, to strike a blow for Christianity. As the King wavered, Coifi sprang to his feet. 'O King,' said he courageously, 'I have long ceased to believe in gods which cannot hear or answer prayer. I believe this man has a message for us, and that he can show us the way to heaven. Sire, give me a spear and a horse, and let me do my will.'

The spear was given. The horse was brought. Mounting, Coifi rode furiously along the white road which goes uphill from Londesborough to Goodmanham, where stood a pagan temple, perhaps only a rough green hedge about a few great wooden idols, stark and grim on the bare Wolds. Followed by his priests, he dashed up to the foremost idol and flung his spear into its ugly mass. Then he reined in his horse and stood motionless.

He was waiting. If the gods were angry, would they not there and then strike him dead? Would not a flash of lightning wither him, or the very earth open and swallow him? But there was neither flash nor tremor. Then Coifi commanded his priests to set fire to the idol; and by the time the King and his retinue rode up to the scene, the temple was in flames—and there, unharmed, stood Coifi, his spear still in the foremost idol.

It was all dramatic, crude, primitive, but it was the one thing needful to turn the balance in the King's mind. He was satisfied, convinced.

Riding back through Londesborough, Edwin went on to York, and there Paulinus baptized him in a tiny chapel, part of which we see today in the crypt of the Minster.

190

Jennifer is four.

Sometimes when her mother has tucked her up in bed and given her a good-night kiss, Jennifer is asleep in 'two ticks'. But not always.

'Mummy,' she calls.

'Well?'

'I'm thirsty.'

Then, later: 'Mummy, have you put my dolly in her pram?'

One evening she had called and called—a drink; her doll; the door to be opened a little wider so that the landing light shone into her room. And at last: 'Mummy?'

'What is it *this* time?'

A long pause, and eventually: 'It's all right, Mummy. *I jus' wanted to know you were there.*'

After that Jennifer was asleep in 'two ticks'.

191

One Monday morning a London minister found a note which had been pushed under the front door. He read:

> I was very worried all last week. Yesterday I dropped into your church in time for the evening service, and I would like you to know that what you said has helped and cheered me very much indeed.

As it happened, the minister had himself been depressed for some days. Reading that letter helped and cheered *him* enormously.

192

Ben Higginbotham, who had worked in a Lancashire cotton factory, was a cheery soul. His motto was, 'Well, it might ha' bin warse'.

One day he had an accident, and soon afterwards he was compelled to have both legs amputated at the knees. For weeks he lay between life and death, but gradually he made a remarkable recovery. A friend visiting him in hospital, remarked, 'Na then, owd lad, Ah reckon you'll hev a job ti find bright side o' this here misfortune.'

'Nay, nay,' murmured Ben faintly, 'it might ha' bin warse. Tha sees, lad, *Ah allus suffered wi' cowld feet.*'

193

I talked in 1942 with a little man who was in his shirt sleeves. 'Yes,' he said, pausing in his digging to look at the heap of bricks behind him, 'the bomb went right through the roof. Direct hit! Luckily my wife and I were in the shelter. And there was another bit of luck about it, too—the house fell into the street. If it had tumbled *this* way, *my onion bed would have been ruined.*

H. L. GEE.

194

There is in Austria a monastery which, in former times, was very rich and continued to be rich so long as it gave freely to the poor; but when it ceased giving away, it became poor itself, and so remains to this day.

MARTIN LUTHER.

195

In East Africa is a gravestone. The inscription reads:

Lord Baden-Powell
Chief Scout of the World
Born February 22nd, 1857
Died January 8th 1941
⊙

The circle with a dot in the middle is—as every Boy Scout knows—the Scout sign for, *I have gone home.*

196

Samuel Peploe (1668-1752), a notable churchman who became Bishop of Chester, had a hot temper and a determined manner, but was much respected. He was Vicar of Preston (Lancashire) in the troublous times of the first Jacobite rebellion—the Fifteen. The town was a Jacobite stronghold. the people having great sympathy with the Old Pretender; but the Vicar, a loyal subject who did not care who knew it, would make no compromises, and went on with his duties unflinchingly, saying what he thought and risking the consequences.

At last the rebellion came to a head, and Jacobite troops poured into Preston. Peploe did not waver. When it was time to go to church he went as usual.

Suddenly the service was interrupted by a party of rebels who, entering without ceremony, stalked down the nave and greatly alarmed the folk who had gathered for worship. One insolent fellow, pistol in hand, put the weapon to the Vicar's head and said, 'Stop praying for the Hanoverian usurper or I shoot you dead.'

Peploe, perfectly self-possessed, replied, 'Soldier, you do your duty as I am doing mine.' Then he went on calmly with the service.

No shot was fired; and rumour says it was for this act of courage and loyalty that George the First made the Vicar a Bishop.

197

There was once a man who lived seventy years, and died very greatly loved. On his gravestone are these words: HE PREACHED GOODNESS BY BEING GOOD.

198

One day during World War II we came upon two little maids sitting on a doorstep. They were busy writing.

'What are you doing?' we asked.

They looked up shyly, and said: 'Making lists.'

'Lists? What of?'

'Well,' one explained, 'if you go to the shops and ask for lump sugar or a banana, you can't get them, can you?'

'No, of course not.'

'Well, we're making a list of the things you *can* get.'

THE PILGRIM.

199

The winter afternoon was dark and grey over old Strasbourg. Little flurries of snow came whirling down between the chimneys and a biting wind blew in the narrow streets. Above the roofs, rising high into the clouds, stood the great cathedral, its stones dim in the gathering gloom, its windows catching the lights within.

Fine people were hurrying up the broad steps—ladies with furs, gentlemen in splendid attire, many of them coming in their carriages. Little Hans watched them. Perished with cold, ragged, an unwanted bit of humanity, he snuggled between two buttresses—a retreat from the wind—and wished *he* dare go into the cathedral where all was warm and bright, and where (as he could dimly hear) the organ was pealing loudly.

Suddenly a little girl left her mother as she came up the steps, ran towards him (all loveliness as she smiled) and thrust a big rosy apple into his hands. 'That's for you, little boy,' she said.

Then she and her mother went in at the great west door, and Hans stared at the apple. He thought at first he would eat it there and then, but he wanted to keep it for a time, so he held it in his hands, and went timidly to the door of the cathedral. Most of the folk were in, and the service had begun. No one turned him away. He plucked up courage and crept inside, slinking into a pew at the back.

Only vaguely could he understand the service, but it was wonderful. He loved the singing, the colour, the warmth. Then something terrible happened. Before he realized it, dignified men coming down the aisles were taking up the collection, and Hans—poor Hans—had nothing to give. He would have run out had he not been too frightened to move. What was he to do? Others were giving money—he could hear it. He had nothing . . . nothing to give God except his apple, and he could not give *that*. He dare not. What would all the people say? What would the man in the fine clothes say—the one standing on the steps amid all the bright candles at the far end? And wouldn't God be angry, too?

It seemed to Hans as if all eyes were fixed on him when, in an agony of fear, he timidly placed the red apple on the plate. He held his breath, but no one spoke, and the man who took the apple did not frown. He allowed it to remain on the plate with the silver coins. Slowly he walked along the aisle and up the steps to the choir, where he handed the plate to the priest, who blessed the gifts and then reverently placed them on the altar.

And behold, as little Hans watched, the apple changed. It became shining gold—the most precious of all gifts, and well-pleasing in the sight of God.

His joy was boundless.

200

Dame Ethel Smyth once told an audience that every misfortune has a silver lining. 'I sprained my ankle in St James's Street the other day,' she said, 'and thus learned how to spell *ankle*.'

Perhaps she caught this habit of looking on the bright side from an Irish maid, to whom she complained when indoors with a chill that she had noises in her head. 'They sound like a kitten mewing,' Dame Ethel declared.

'That's nice,' said the maid. *'It's company for you!'*

201

There are many stories of the kindness John Wesley showed to children, and we think this one is typical of the Little Man on Horseback:

While visiting Midsomer Norton he was the guest of Mrs Bush, who kept a boarding-school, and one evening during supper two of the boys quarrelled, and began fighting. Mrs Bush brought them before John Wesley, who did not rebuke them. 'Now boys,' he said, 'you must be reconciled. Go and shake hands with each other.' They did so. 'And now come to me.'

He then took a piece of bread and butter and, having folded it, directed them each to take half. 'Now you have broken bread together,' said Wesley solemnly. Then, handing them a cup of tea, the grand old preacher bade each drink some of it, saying, 'You have now drunk of the same cup, and I will bless you.'

So, laying his hands upon their young heads, and tenderly invoking a blessing on them, Wesley sent them away cured of their angry feelings.

One of these boys, who became a magistrate of Berkshire, took much pleasure in relating this story of the gentleness of the great preacher.

202

It was the morning of one of the most memorable days in the history of the world—18 June 1815. Unknown to the generals on the field—Napoleon, Wellington, Blücher—the fate of Europe was to be decided and years of war were to end in a lasting peace.

Blücher was sure of victory, so sure that he carefully selected a very fine cigar in order to treat himself to a smoke when the victory was won. Having put the cigar in his pocket, he went riding out to crush Napoleon and remake the map of Europe.

After the bitter fighting and when victory had been secured, Blücher took out his cigar. Gruff old warrior that he was, he snipped off the end, and was about to smoke when, glancing aside, he noticed a soldier who had lost both arms. With great deliberation the general lit his cigar, and then placed it between the lips of the wounded man.

In after years Blücher used to say that he had never enjoyed any other cigar quite as much as the one he did not smoke.

203

A slum child, an evacuee from London in World War II, walked in a field of daisies. After a while she looked up at the foster parent whose hand she was holding, and whispered timidly: 'Do you think I might pick just *one*, and send it home to Mummy?'

204

One day St Francis of Assisi beckoned to a young monk and said, 'Let us walk into the town, and there preach to the people.'

So the old monk and the young one walked from the monastery

along a quiet country road. As they went they talked gravely, each sharing spiritual experiences with the other. In this manner they came to Assisi, where they strolled through the market place, up and down many a side street, and so back to the gateway of the monastery. Only when they were in the shadow of the gateway did the young monk remember their errand. 'But, Father,' he exclaimed in surprise, 'we have forgotten to preach to the people.'

Laying his hand on the young man's shoulder and smiling, St Francis replied, 'My son, we have been preaching all the time. As we walked we were observed. Scraps of our conversation have no doubt been overheard. Our faces and our demeanour have been seen. Thus have we preached, thus delivered our sermon.' Then he added, 'Remember, my son, it is no use walking to preach if we do not preach as we walk.'

205

Granny's wonderful chair has been brought up to date.

A few days ago we were in a home where Joan Marion, who was four last month, had wonderful things to show us. There was a doll's house, a shop, a teddy bear, and a cupboard filled with toys. She talked while showing us her treasures, making up astonishing tales about them.

Suddenly she stopped, looked at the clock, and said, 'Hush; it will go in a minute now.' She hurried to the armchair, sat down, smoothed her frock and straightened her hair. The clock struck five, and within a few seconds the telephone rang. The little lady in the chair lifted the receiver, and said politely, 'Hello. Is that Granny?'

It evidently was.

For ten minutes Joan Marion sat listening. Then she explained that for some weeks Granny had not been able to go out, but that every day at five she rang up and told Joan Marion a story.

Hexham Courant.

206

A high-school girl was sitting next to a famous astronomer at a dinner-party. 'What do *you* do?' she asked, after they had been chatting a few minutes.

'I study astronomy,' he replied.
'Goodness!' exclaimed the girl. 'I finished astronomy last year.'

207

Huang Tao, a greedy little boy, saw a jar of olives on the table. His mother was in another room, and this seemed to be his chance to eat as many olives as possible. Usually he was allowed only two or three at a time, but now he could have at least six or seven! Squeezing his hand into the jar he grabbed as many olives as he could hold, only to discover that he could not free his hand. The harder he pulled, the more he hurt himself. As he was very small—scarcely more than a baby—he lost his presence of mind and began to cry. When his mother rushed into the room she quickly realized the cause of Huang Tao's trouble. Said she: 'My dear child, if you try to take fewer olives you will have no trouble in releasing your hand.'

208

A lovely story was told by Neville Chamberlain when, as Prime Minister, he addressed artists at the Royal Academy Banquet in 1938.

He was reminded, he said, of the observation made by a monk looking at the picture of the *Last Supper*. He had sat nearly three score years in the presence of that picture, seeing his companions dropping off one by one. More than one generation had passed away, yet the figures in the picture remained unchanged until sometimes he wondered whether *they* were not the reality and *we* only the shadows.

209

He always had money to spare. A student at one of our universities, he ran a sports car, was often on the Continent, and never hesitated to buy rare books at high prices if they took his fancy.

It was a surprise to us when we found him lodging in a back street, where he had two rooms in a very small house overlooking back-yards and broken dustbins. Insisting on our staying for a cup of tea, he went down himself to fetch the tray.

'She finds it hard work coming upstairs,' he explained as he brought in the tray with its very ordinary white cups and saucers.

'You mean your landlady?'

'Yes,' he said. 'She and her old man are both over seventy, but very charming. They lost a son in the Great War. I happened to hear about them quite by accident; and I thought it would help them if I let them put me up. After all, it isn't the view I want, but somewhere to store my books; and, of course, the rent I pay makes all the difference in the world.'

THE PILGRIM.

210

One day during World War II Mrs Chapman was just about at her wits' end. She loved her son passionately, and was greatly distressed when, at the age of three, he nearly died of diphtheria. Happily, he came through; but only just. And even after the crisis the doctor shook his head. 'Douglas has had a bad time,' he said. 'It's been touch and go, and now he ought to get away. He needs *cold, dry* air. . . . Switzerland's the spot if there are to be no after effects.' But Switzerland was out of the question.

A mother who loves much is not easily cornered, however. In spite of the war, in spite of many difficulties, she found a way, not to Switzerland, but to a nearby ice rink. Surely there was plenty of cold, dry air in that spot! She muffled up her precious bairn. She provided him with leggings and gloves. And so a little chap whose life had been despaired of, was pushed on the ice on a pair of skates. Bit by bit he 'found his feet' and began to enjoy life on the rink. Health and strength returned.

That is only the beginning of the story. Douglas Chapman went on the ice in order to get well—that and nothing more. But notice how sometimes the unexpected happens: Douglas began to skate. Soon he was at home on skates. He became expert when only six, and was then 'spotted' by Mr Mitchell of the Empress Hall, London. In 1952 he made his successful début as a skating star in the pantomime on ice, *Puss in Boots*.

Today Douglas Chapman is the world's youngest skating star —a shining future is before him, and even now he is earning enough to repay something of what it has cost his mother to make him the clever and vigorous laddie he is.

So the worst turned best . . . the weakling became strong; and though the door to Switzerland was closed, another door opened on a brilliant career. A mother's despair became an undreamed-of triumph.

211

In March 1952 Dr Townley Lord, President of the World Baptist Alliance, and Editor of the *Baptist Times*, was among the speakers at a great Methodist Rally in the Birmingham Central Mission. With a rare twinkle in his eyes he said: 'It is very kind of the Methodists to invite a Baptist to share in this Anniversary. May I be permitted to mention that I was born a Methodist, and that I remained a Methodist until at last I saw the light, and joined the Baptists. . . .'

Later in the meeting Sister Gwen Appleton gave a report on the work of the Mission, and with infinite good humour and a rare smile, she began: 'I should like to thank Doctor Townley Lord for his inspiring address, and to add, if he will allow me, that I was brought up a Baptist until, in my teens, I saw the light and joined the Methodists. . . .'

212

An Australian soldier in Crete who had been cut off from his regiment was plodding along a country road, hungry and exhausted, and tired of having to hide every time he saw anybody. He had not eaten for days, and finally decided to risk detection and beg food from the next peasant he met. The next peasant happened to be a very old man, hobbling along almost bent double with the weight of a sack he was carrying. The soldier stopped him. As he could not speak Greek, he told his plight by sign-language. The old fellow watched the pathetic gestures in silence; then, straightening his back, he burst into a roar of laughter. 'Why, lad,' he said, 'you look as if you might be hungry! Have some tucker!' After opening his sack, which was full of food, he explained that he, too, was an escaping Australian, whose disguise was good enough to fool any Hun in World War II.

So the two joined forces and continued on their way to the coast. All went well until their food supply dwindled away. At last they became so weak they could hardly walk. One day, meeting a shepherd driving a flock of sheep, the two Australians made frantic signs to show they were dying of starvation. The shepherd chuckled. 'Well, boys,' he said, 'you can take a sheep apiece and eat it if you want to!' *He also was an escaping Australian!*

From that time the old man, the shepherd and the soldier drove the sheep till they came to the sea—and it is good to know that there they found a fishing-boat and escaped to safety.

The Children's Newspaper.

213

Writing of the discovery of radium by her mother and father, Eve Curie says:

Purified as a chloride, radium appeared to be a dull white powder much like common kitchen salt. But its properties were stupefying. Its radiation passed all expectation in intensity; it proved to be two million times stronger than that of uranium. The rays traversed the hardest and most opaque matter. Only a thick screen of lead proved able to stop their insidious penetration.

The last and most moving miracle was that radium could become the ally of human beings in the war against cancer. Radium was *useful*—magnificently useful, and its extraction no longer had merely experimental interest. A radium industry was about to be born.

Since the therapeutic effects of radium had become known, plans for exploitation of radioactive ores had been made in several countries, particularly in Belgium and in America. But engineers could produce the 'fabulous metal' only if they knew the secret of the delicate operations involved.

Pierre explained all this to his wife one Sunday morning after reading a letter from some technicians in the United States who wanted to exploit radium in America, and asked for information. 'We have two choices,' Pierre told her. 'We can describe the results of our research without reserve, including the processes of purification. . . .'

Marie made a mechanical gesture of approval, and murmured: 'Yes, naturally.'

'Or else,' Pierre went on, 'we can consider ourselves to be the proprietors, the "inventors" of radium, patent the technique of treating pitchblende, and assure ourselves of rights over the manufacture of radium throughout the world.'

Marie reflected a few seconds. Then she said: 'It is impossible. It would be contrary to the scientific spirit.'

Pierre's serious face lightened. To settle his conscience, he dwelt upon the matter, mentioning—with a little laugh—the only thing which it was cruel for him to give up: 'We could have a fine laboratory, too.'

Marie's gaze grew fixed. She steadily considered this idea of gain. Almost at once she rejected it. 'Physicists always publish their researches complete. If our discovery has a commercial future, that is an accident by which we must not profit. And radium is going to be of use in treating disease. . . . It is impossible to take advantage of *that*.'

She made no attempt to convince her husband; she guessed that he had spoken of the patent only out of scruple. The words she pronounced with complete assurance expressed the feelings of both, their infallible conception of the scientists' rôle.

Pierre added, as if settling a question of no importance: 'I shall write tonight, then, to the American engineers, and give them the information they ask for.'

A quarter of an hour after this little Sunday morning talk, Pierre and Marie headed for the woods on their beloved bicycles. They had chosen for ever between poverty and fortune. In the evening they came back exhausted, their arms filled with leaves and field flowers.

EVE CURIE: *Madame Curie.*

214

It was the sight of a pauper's funeral, at which four drunken fellows let a coffin fall in the street, that turned young Lord Shaftesbury's thoughts to the poor whose voice he afterwards became. Born in 1801, the greater part of his eighty-four years was spent in a glorious battle for the 'under-dogs'. Let us take one moment out of his long experience:

Here he is, this tall, handsome man with a graceful figure and regular features, with all the breeding of generations of Ashley Coopers—a peer of the realm, an aristocrat whom the Queen and the Prime Minister do not hesitate to consult on a score of problems, a dignified gentleman, now venerable, who regularly takes his seat in the House of Lords. But notice his environment. Is it the Upper House or Windsor Castle or his club or his country seat? It is none of these. It is a wretched hall in one of the vilest slums in London.

Lord Shaftesbury has received a 'round robin'—a petition from forty thieves, forty of the worst men in London, forty men as desperate, as dishonourable (one would think) as all London's underworld could muster. They have asked him to meet them in a spot where a man might be conveniently murdered.

Lord Shaftesbury, unafraid, attends the meeting.

In this hall with the forty thieves—and another three hundred and fifty unwashed, unshaven men of the Bill Sykes type—he is calm and dignified. Is it not a glorious moment for him as he stands among them, and does it not thrill us as we hear his quiet voice speaking words of courage and comfort? Are there many things finer than the picture of this noble English gentleman kneeling to pray with the dregs of London, and then promising to give them all a new chance—promising, and *keeping* his promise, so that most of them emigrated and 'made good'?

215

'Here, Andrew,' said little Flora, 'here's sixpence for Christmas.'

Andrew looked anxiously at his sister. 'Naw, naw,' he said. 'I canna gie you anything this year, Flora, so just you gie me threepence, and you can ca' the other threepence a Christmas box frac me.'

216

Long ago, says a story still told in Turkey, a sultan wished to find an honest man whom he could trust to gather his taxes.

'Do as I say,' said one of his counsellors, 'and you'll find the man you need.'

Applications were at once invited for the post, and several hundred men came to the palace. The counsellor arranged for them to walk along a dark corridor before arriving at the audience room, where, as soon as all were assembled, the counsellor said, in the presence of the sultan, 'Gentlemen, we should like to see you dance.'

It was odd that only one of the company began dancing, all the others standing still as statues, all looking extremely uncomfortable. 'Here's your honest man,' declared the counsellor, pointing to the man who was still dancing.

Then he went on to explain that he had arranged for open bags of money to be placed in the corridor. All but one of the applicants, it seemed, had filled their pockets while walking along the corridor.

217

Accompanied by his daughter, a child of seven, an English clergyman was on his way to the United States. It was Sunday, and at the captain's invitation the clergyman had conducted a service, and had preached on the love of God.

It had not been easy to do so, for the clergyman had lost his wife only a few weeks before, and his sense of loss and utter loneliness had tried his faith severely.

Father and daughter had been walking the deck for some time. Presently, standing side by side, they leaned over the rail, and gazed across what seemed endless miles of sea. The little girl, naturally serious and especially so after the shock of losing her mother, was silent; but presently she said: 'Daddy, does God love us as much as we loved Mummy?'

'He does,' replied her father. 'God's love is the biggest thing there is, my dear.'

'How big?' asked the child.

'How big? I will tell you. Look across the sea, my dear. Look up. Look down. God's love is so big that it stretches round us further than all this water. It is higher than the blue sky above us. It is deeper than the deepest depth of the ocean over which we are now sailing.'

The child pondered this, her face thoughtful, the tears not far away. Suddenly she held her father's arm with both small hands; and, turning upwards a face radiant with joy, she exclaimed: 'Oh, Daddy—how wonderful that we happen to be right in the *very middle* of it!'

218

Mark Hambourg, the eminent pianist, was spending Christmas with the British political agent in Peshawar when his native servant, Rawji, appeared in the morning with a salaam and said: 'It is Christmas Day, Master. Do I not get a Christmas present?'

'Why on earth should you get a present?' Mark Hambourg answered, indignant at his asking for one. 'No one has given *me* a present.'

'I give you one, Master,' said Rawji, producing from behind his back a posy of flowers.

Much affected, Hambourg rewarded his servant with a good tip. At the end of the week, when the servant brought his account, the expense items included: 'For Christmas present to Master . . . 2 rupees!'

Adapted from MARK HAMBOURG'S *The Eighth Octave.*

219

Coming out of church one Sunday morning, a West Riding man was greeted by his friend, Joe Dyson, who had been awaiting him twenty minutes. 'Tha's late,' said Joe.

'Aye.'

'Parson been a bit long-winded?'

'Aye.'

' 'Appen he hasn't finished *yet*?'

'Oh, aye, he finished a long while sin, *but he won't stop*!'

220

They nicknamed him Old Dobby. His name was Dobson—Mr Charles Dobson—and he kept a grocer's shop in a downtown neighbourhood of the city. And *was* he mean?

Old Dobby never knocked off an odd halfpenny. He never paid a lad to deliver goods for him—the customer had to take them herself, or leave them. His shop was open earlier and closed later than any other—which *proved* how miserly he was. And Old Dobby lived alone—too mean to employ a housekeeper. Younger folk said he's been too selfish to get married, but older folk recalled that he'd been married long ago. Or was that just another legend?

Still, you had to admit, however much you disliked it, that Dobby was useful. He sold everything. True, he never knocked a halfpenny off and always demanded cash payment, but he never put a penny on; and, really, it was a miracle that year after year, with never so much as a day's holiday, he ran the house and shop unaided. So it went on. The toddlers grew up, had children of their own, and even grand-children, and Dobby was still there, brisk and smiling as he leaned over his counter, and murmured, 'Will there be anything else?'

One morning the shop door remained closed. Eventually the police broke in, and found Old Dobby leaning over his counter. He'd died while checking up the day's takings. Poor Old Dobby —folk round about began to realize what an institution he had been all their lives . . . and then, oddly enough, the gossips began talking, and bit by bit the truth came out that those dozen poor children who had been sent for a week to the seaside every August, that annual Old Folks' Festival in the Lloyd Hall, and the Children's Christmas Party at the Clifton Restaurant, had all been staged and paid for—unbelievable though it seemed—by Old Dobby.

221

I had a bit of good fortune the other evening. I did not come into money or earn promotion. I just met Wilkins.

He was taking a stroll and I was taking a stroll, and we met, and we stood, and we talked, and the evening sunshine was bright and warm, and a bird went on singing above our heads, and the world was very peaceful and pleasant; and Wilkins told me about an interesting week-end, and we chatted very amicably with no thought as to how quickly the hands of the clock were going round, and we shared a bit of humour, and were sympathetic about a mutual friend who is ill, and then we parted.

And that was all.

But it was pleasant meeting Wilkins unexpectedly like that, and talking about things and people, and being friendly. It doesn't sound much, does it? But I enjoyed it.

STEPHEN A. WOOD

222

Sir James Barrie tells us somewhere how he met Robert Louis Stevenson one winter's day in 1879 in Edinburgh.

'As I was crossing Princes Street I ran against another

wayfarer,' he says. 'Looking up, I saw that he was a young man of exceeding tenuity of body, and that he was wearing a velvet jacket. He passed on, but he had bumped against me, and I stood in the middle of the street, regardless of the traffic, and glared contemptuously after him.

'He must have grown conscious of this, because he turned and looked at me. I continued to glare. He went on a bit, and turned again. I was still glaring; so he came back and said to me, quite clearly: "After all, God made me."

'I said: "He is getting careless."

'He lifted his cane, and then he said: "Do I know you?"

'He said it with such extraordinary charm that I replied wistfully: "No, but I wish you did." '

Is it not a lovely example of the way in which what might have been a quarrel ended in mutual admiration?

223

Let us go to Berlin at a time when a boy of thirteen is making a stir by his skill as a pianist. He is Felix Mendelssohn, and his tutor is Zelter.

'Felix,' says Zelter one wonderful day, 'we are to go together to Weimar, the home of the great philosopher, Goethe.'

We will follow them to the pleasant old German town with its tree-shaded roads, and come to the lovely house in a large garden. Here it is that Zelter turns in, taking Felix with him. 'We are going to see Goethe?' asks Mendelssohn, breathlessly.

'To see Goethe—and play to him.'

In they go, finding the poet and philosopher in the garden. They are invited into the drawing-room, where there is a piano. A few friends come in and sit round, and Felix Mendelssohn plays for them, nervously at first, afterwards with the rapture of forgetfulness. He plays as he would have played to the crowned heads of Europe, for this old, white-haired man will live when crowned heads are forgotten.

An hour passes. The last note dies away. The immortal Goethe crosses the room, rests his hand gently on the young shoulder, and asks, 'How can I reward you?' His voice trembles slightly.

A moment Felix Mendelssohn hesitates. Then, looking up boldly, he says, '*Sir, I should be glad if you would kiss me.*'

224

In 1924 Mr Cecil Firth explored the chapels connected with the Heb-Set Temple near the beautiful pyramid temple of Zoser, and by chance came upon two inscriptions of extraordinary interest. One had been written by a Greek tourist who had gone to see Sakkara. He was careful to write on one of the great stones that he was giving himself a holiday in Egypt after fighting many campaigns, in one of which he was the sole survivor of his regiment.

Close by was the second inscription, written 30 centuries later, the work of a member of the Australian Light Horse who had fought in Gallipoli and Palestine in World War I. He, too, had visited Sakkara while on leave, and had recorded the fact that he was the sole survivor of *his* squadron.

225

'This,' declared the auctioneer during a sale of household goods and furnishings in Wakefield, 'is a first-class radiogram, and is in perfect working order. Listen!'

As he spoke, he switched on. Instantly the sale-room was filled with a loud and distinct voice saying: 'What am I bid for this lot? Forty pounds? Thank you, ladies and gentlemen. I've forty pounds bid for this lot. Any advance on forty pounds? Going . . .'

The remainder of the broadcast appeal was drowned in wild laughter—as we may well imagine. The explanation was simply that *by chance* the auctioneer had tuned in to a school broadcast dealing with auctioneering.

226

It is related that Sir Henry Irving's handwriting was at times almost illegible, but he told J. B. Booth that apparently his shocking scrawl had its virtues. 'I once gave a scallywag formal notice of dismissal,' he declared. 'It seems that only the signature was readable, so the fellow used the note as a free pass to the Lyceum for many years.'

227

Have you heard the story of the lady who, when shopping, was tempted to buy a pound of tomatoes from a barrow-boy? When she had walked a few yards she stopped, examined her change, and concluded that the vendor has given her a shilling too much. So she went back and told him.

'You're right, ma'am,' declared the barrow-boy, pocketing the shilling. 'Here, just give us hold of that there bag a minute.'

To the lady's surprise he opened the bag, picked out a bad tomato, and put a good one in its place. 'You was honest with me, ma'am,' he replied, seeing her questioning glance, 'and I'll be honest with you.'

228

Serbians tell this tale of three poor brothers to whom an angel, disguised as a beggar, appeared as they walked by a river. 'What would you like best?' asked the beggar, speaking to the eldest.

'This river, if it ran wine,' was the answer. The river became wine at that moment, and men sprang up and began pouring the wine into barrels.

The second brother said he would like a farm. At once a field of crows became a plain, with cattle and farms and dairies.

But the third, when the question was put to *him*, declared he would like a good wife. So the angel persuaded the king to allow the young man to marry his daughter.

Now the king soon regretted what he had done, being ashamed of having a peasant for a son-in-law, so he drove his daughter and her husband from the palace, and they became so poor that they had to live in a cottage. But they loved each other, and were happy.

A year later the angel returned. Appearing again as a beggar, he asked the first brother for a cup of wine, but the man turned him away—the river running water as he did so.

'A cup of milk,' was the beggar's plea to the second brother, who refused even so modest a request—and, as he did so, all his cattle became crows.

Coming to the cottage, the beggar asked for food, the youngest of the three brothers inviting him into his poor home, and showing him every kindness while his wife baked a small loaf. And, lo, as she cut the loaf the beggar vanished, and the cottage also. Husband and wife were sitting at a banquet in a palace all their own!

229

'I have one preacher I love better than any other on earth,' declared Martin Luther. 'It is my tame robin who preaches to me daily. After he has taken his crumbs, he hops to a tree close by, lifts up his voice to God, and sings his carols of praise and gratitude. Then he tucks his head under his wing and goes to sleep, leaving tomorrow to look after itself.'

230

There is a story of a teacher who had received her month's salary, and was putting it into her handbag when a small boy asked confidingly, 'Is that money?'

'Yes,' said the teacher.

'Is it your wages?' was the next question.

The teacher said it was. There was a pause during which the child looked very thoughtful. At last he whispered, 'Where do you work, miss?'

231

Albert Schweitzer, born in 1875 at Kaiserberg, was a weakly child, though he soon became strong when his father moved to a pastorate at Gunsbach, near the Vosges mountains. He was one of a family of five, and was much better off than most children in the village, sharing a happy and cultured environment. To his schoolfellows he appeared extraordinarily queer. Instead of shooting birds he would frighten them away in order to protect them; and his teachers were aggravated by his habit of giggling, and his knack of setting the whole class laughing.

One story of his childhood, however, shows his kindness to others—the kindness which sprang from his soul. He had been fighting one of the village boys, and was getting the better of him when the lad cried out: 'Yes, if I got broth twice a week, as you do, I'd be as strong as you are.'

This incident showed the parson's son that he was not regarded as one of the village boys, but as a member of a favoured class. He determined there and then that in clothes, at least, he would appear as one of the village boys. He refused to wear a new coat which had been made for him, his excuse being that it was too good. He went hatless, and wore fingerless gloves. For this stubbornness his father boxed his ears, but young Albert had made up his mind to be as humble as his companions; and it was this humility which later caused him to sacrifice fame and fortune in Europe, and—after taking a medical degree—to devote his life to improving the conditions of the native people of Equatorial Africa.

232

The very young clergyman went into the pulpit with his head in the air. Somehow he got through the preliminaries, but five minutes after announcing his text he lost the thread of his discourse, and was compelled to bring his sermon to an abrupt and most unsatisfactory conclusion. Consequently he came out of the pulpit humbled by his failure, and very conscious that he had made a bad impression.

'Eh, well,' said a kindly deacon in the vestry afterwards, 'it's a pity. You see, if only you'd gone *up* the steps same as you came down, you'd have come *down* same as you went up.'

233

A husbandman, says Aesop, wishing to protect his corn from the cranes, set a net in his field. One morning he took several birds, and among them there happened to be a stork. 'Spare my life,' cried the stork. 'I am no thieving crane. I am a poor, harmless, innocent stork, the most pious and dutiful of all birds. I always honour and help my parents.'

'That may be,' interrupted the husbandman, 'but seeing that I've caught you in the company of those who were destroying my corn, you must suffer with them.'

With these words he killed the stork.

234

In what was perhaps the blackest year of World War I, a girl of twenty-four found herself a widow.

She lived in a very poor quarter of a Midland city, and she had dreamed of a little home in the country once the war was over—

a cottage, a garden, children, sunshine; but when her husband was killed her hopes faded.

It seemed as if the blow were harder than she could bear; and in the first terrible weeks she did an odd thing almost every day. She did it because she could not help it. Doing it tortured her very soul; but somehow even that torture brought a kind of compensation. Every day she opened a cupboard and looked again at the neat brown two-piece which had been her going-away costume. It reminded her of her wedding day . . . and then the tears, the hot tears, would run down her cheeks, and she would sob for an hour or more.

One morning the back door opened, and Tony, a very little boy who lived next door, walked in gravely and unceremoniously. He pointed to his tiny pair of trousers, and said—rather proudly —' 'Oles—lots 'oles.'

When his mother called for him, she admitted that she had mended the trousers till they wouldn't mend any more.

That evening the widow did a brave thing. Opening the cupboard, she stared at the going-away two-piece. Then she took down the skirt, *and out of it cut a pair of trousers for Tony.*

But that is not really the wonder of the story. The wonder is that although the widow always felt a sharp pang whenever she saw Tony running about in what she was pleased to call *her trousers*, from that moment life for her seemed just the least bit more tolerable.

235

The Armada had sailed at last. Philip of Spain was to wipe England off the face of the earth, and danger was at our very doors in that memorable year 1588. It was then that Elizabeth I, in order to enhearten her people, appeared among the soldiers at Tilbury, and showed herself every inch a queen.

Mounted on a noble charger, with a general's truncheon in her hand, a corselet of polished steel laced over her magnificent apparel, and a page in attendance bearing her white-plumed helmet, she rode bareheaded from rank to rank with a courageous deportment and smiling countenance; and amid the affectionate plaudits and shouts of military ardour which burst from the animated and admiring soldiery, she addressed them in the following brief and spirited speech:

'My loving people, we have been persuaded by some th
careful of our safety to take heed how we commit ourse
armed multitudes for fear of treachery; but I do not desire to liv
to distrust my faithful and loving people. Let tyrants fear: I have always so behaved myself that, under God, I have placed my chiefest strength and safeguard in the loyal hearts and good will of my subjects. And therefore I am come among you at this time not as for my recreation or sport but being resolved in the midst and heat of the battle to live or die among you all; to lay down for my God and for my kingdom and for my people my honour and my blood even in the dust.

'I know I have but the body of a weak and feeble woman, but I have the heart of a king, and of a king of England, too.'

236

A touching story is told of the fading years of Emerson's life. When attending Longfellow's funeral, he looked down into the grave, and said: 'I have forgotten my friend's name, *but he was a beautiful soul.*'

237

One spring some time before the American Civil War, a boy in search of work came to Worthy Taylor's prosperous Ohio farm. The farmer knew nothing much about the boy except that his name was Jim, but he gave him a job. Jim spent the summer cutting stove-wood, bringing in the cows and making himself generally useful. He ate in the kitchen and slept in the haymow.

Before the summer was over, Jim had fallen in love with Taylor's daughter. When the farmer refused to let him marry her—telling him bluntly that he had no money, no name and very poor prospects—Jim put his belongings in his old carpet bag, and disappeared.

Thirty-five years passed, and Taylor one day pulled down his barn to make way for a new one. On one of the rafters above the haymow he discovered that Jim had carved his full name—*James A. Garfield.*

He was then President of the United States.

Reader's Digest, 1950.

A frail woman afire with an intense religious enthusiasm was possessed with the conviction that in some way she was to do a special work among the Chinese people. If to the East she might not go, at least she could go to the East End of London. So Catherine Hine learned her way about the labyrinth of streets where dwell the laundrymen, the stewards and sea-cooks, the restaurant keepers, and the drivers of more questionable trades.

She had a great gift of inspiring confidence and compelling honesty; and by its aid she gained a remarkable insight into the Chinese character. Moving continuously among these people, she grew accustomed to their alien appearance, their weak and narrow eyes and high, gaunt cheek-bones. They for their part responded eagerly, and soon she gained from them the name of 'Little Teacher'. Her slender knowledge of the Chinese language, self-acquired, was extended by hard study, often late into the night; and a tiny classroom was opened in which the 'Little Teacher' laboured to make known the lesser mysteries of English and the greater mysteries of God.

It was labour which took heavy toll of her strength, but it prospered beyond imagining, and it was a wise decision of Headquarters to further it by giving it recognition as a special missionary effort associated with the slum operations in the same district. A little hall was rented for her. It was decked with Chinese symbols, and to enter it was like passing into another world. But it was the flag of the Salvation Army with its bright significance, carefully explained to them, which most of all appealed to her disciples. For them it was like one of their own ideographs; to see it, ever afterwards, was to be reminded of the 'Little Teacher' and the spirit of their preceptor.

To one of her converts, on his departure for his native land, she gave an Army flag by way of keepsake. They laughed at him when he returned to his village in China's far interior; laughed at his flag and at his strange new creed. But he was patient as the 'Little Teacher' had been patient with him, and in time he too began to gather followers. Then came a wave of trouble. Civil war raged: murder and rapine stalked the land. Word was brought that a rebel army was marching on the village. Torture and death had been the lot of native Christians everywhere along the rebels' path, and fear laid hold upon the small community.

They sought their leader with crumbling faith. 'Now is the time,' they said, 'to show us if your teaching has been true. Either this God can save us or He is a lie. Tell us if we can trust Him now.'

Deep in his soul he doubted. Often had God come close to him in times of less urgent need, but now He seemed infinitely remote. Here was indeed a test. If prayer could move His arm, as 'Little Teacher' had said . . .

Little Teacher! How would *she* have acted? She would have talked to God in her own intimate fashion. He looked at her flag, hanging from the wall of his room, and he took it down and prayed. He made reply to his questioners that God would certainly protect them. Then, flag in hand, he went out to meet the raiders—alone.

The colours carried by the self-appointed envoy were recognized by the leader of the rebels. He also had lived in London and had known and reverenced the 'Little Teacher'. By curious question and excited answer the two men proved the bond between them, and the hand of death was stayed. The raiding column passed on its way, nor was the slightest hurt inflicted on any in that village.

HUGH REDWOOD: *God in the Slums.*

239

I am indebted to my friend, F. Austin Hyde, for the story of the Yorkshireman who, having reached the age of ninety-eight, was interviewed on his birthday by an energetic and good-natured reporter in his early fifties. 'Thank you for granting me this interview—this very *pleasant* interview,' boomed the genial reporter. 'And may I say that I sincerely hope, sir, I shall have the pleasure of congratulating you on your hundredth birthday?'

The Yorkshire veteran nodded his head slowly. 'Aye, why,' said he, 'you look to be in middlin' good health, young feller. I doan't see why you shouldn't.'

240

An Arab possessed a horse of such exceptional strength and beauty that every Bedouin who saw it or heard of it wished to buy it. One tribesman offered first two camels, then all the camels he possessed, but the owner of the fine horse refused to part with his prize. Thereupon the would-be purchaser decided to obtain it by guile.

Disguising himself as a beggar, and feigning illness, he lay by the roadside on a route the owner of the horse was to pass. Presently the rider came to the spot. Touched by the sorry plight of the supposed sick man, he at once dismounted and offered to carry him to a place where medical aid could be obtained. But the beggar did not stir. 'I have been without food for days,' he moaned. 'I cannot rise; I have no strength left.'

Gently lifting the beggar, the owner of the horse placed him in his own saddle, intending to mount himself and ride to an oasis, but no sooner was the sham invalid safely on the horse than he galloped off.

At last the owner called to the thief to halt, and when the rogue was at a safe distance he did so. 'You've taken my horse,' said the owner, 'but I implore you never to tell anyone how you obtained it.'

'Why not?' the other demanded.

'Because one day another man may lie by the roadside really ill, and if your deceit is known, men may hesitate to assist him.'

At this the thief was so struck with shame that he rode back and promptly gave up the animal to its rightful master.

My Magazine.

241

We called at the vicarage and found a blind man and a girl sitting in a sunny corner of the garden. In answer to our query, the blind man smiled, saying, 'Oh, no, *I'm* not the vicar, and this isn't *my* garden. But the vicar, who is very kind, allows me to sit here whenever William can find time to bring me along.'

'William is your son?'

Again the whimsical smile. 'Oh, no. He's a farm labourer who happens to live next door to me, and is very kind. He brings me along nearly every evening in the week, and Elsie takes me home.'

We did not dare to guess who Elsie was, so we inquired tactfully.

'Oh,' said the blind man, 'she's a bit of sunshine, and lives at the lodge. She's reading *Essays of Elia* to me now. This is the second time we have borrowed it.'

'From the county library?'

'Oh, no,' said the blind man. 'Miss Wilson, the schoolmistress, lends us books. She is very kind.'

OPTIMIST.

242

For weeks he had put pennies and small pieces of silver in his money-box. Now the thrilling moment had come. The red tin box was taken down from the shelf, and the little fellow eagerly unlocked it. Out came the hoard of money. When it was counted it amounted to fourteen shillings and fivepence! 'Why!' exclaimed the owner of the fortune, 'I never thought I should get *so much* out of my box!'

'You wouldn't,' said his father, 'if you hadn't put so much in.'

243

Aesop tells us that one day two boys, one the son of rich, the other the son of poor, parents, were standing on the seashore when pirates sprang out of the bushes and dragged them aboard their vessel with the intention of selling them as slaves. A storm having arisen, however, the ship was driven out of its course and wrecked, and with the exception of the two boys all perished. The lads reached an island inhabited by savages, and were at once taken prisoner.

Now at home the rich boy, knowing that he had plenty of money, had learned nothing; but the poor boy had been very useful to his father in making baskets. So, having cut some willow-twigs, he began to make a little basket; and while he was thus engaged, the savages gathered round to watch. When he had finished the basket, the boy presented it to the person who appeared to be their chief, whereupon all the rest, men and women, desired also to have baskets made for them, and at once built a hut so that the lad might proceed with his work in comfort. They also promised to supply him with food.

Seeing that the other boy was idle, they desired that he, too, should make baskets, but when they found he was unable to be useful they beat him, and would have killed him had not the little basket-maker begged them to spare his companion's life. They then ordered the rich boy to strip off his beautiful velvet jacket, and from that time on to wait on the poor boy, and carry willow twigs for him.

244

It was George Whitefield who gave Savannah its famous orphanage, and it was his greatest friend in America, Benjamin Franklin, who paid to the founder's eloquence the greatest of all tributes. As Franklin wanted the orphanage to be built in Philadelphia, Whitefield's decision to establish it at Savannah was a disappointment—so great a disappointment that the American Jack-of-all-trades made up his mind to contribute not one penny towards its maintenance. His resolution, however, was broken the next time he heard Whitefield preach. What happened is told here in Franklin's own words:

'I silently resolved he should get nothing from me. It happened that I had in my pocket a handful of copper, three or four silver dollars, and five pistoles in gold. As he proceeded I began to soften, and decided to give the copper. Another stroke of his oratory made me ashamed, and I determined to give the silver; and he finished so admirably that I emptied my pocket wholly into the collector's dish, *gold and all*.'

245

The Rev. Bernard Snell once told the story of a little girl who was seen carrying a baby. 'Isn't the baby heavy?' somebody asked.

'Oh, no,' was the reply. 'He's my brother.'

246

One summer's day when George Cave, later Viscount Cave of Richmond, was walking in St James's Street, London, arm in arm with the girl who was soon to be his wife, he said to her: 'My dear, I'll buy you a diamond necklace when I take silk.'

Estella Matthews, his witty and romantic sweetheart, glanced up laughingly into his face. 'No,' said she. 'A pearl necklace when you take silk, and diamonds when you are Lord Chancellor!'

A tall man who happened to pass them at that moment wondered who in the world these two dreamers could be, for he had overheard a fragment of their conversation. Young George Cave raised his hat, and then whispered to Estella: 'That's Arthur Balfour.'

As it happened, Arthur Balfour lived to see the lover in his Cabinet; and when Lord Cave lay dying he was able to say to his beloved Estella: 'I have had everything that I ever wished for; and you have had your ambition for me, for I have been Lord Chancellor.'

247

A Newmarket man joined up during World War I, and after a period of training was ordered to France. When he said 'Good-bye' to his wife, his dog jumped into the railway carriage, and did all it could to accompany him. But it was left behind.

One morning, a month later, the soldier's wife missed the dog. She looked everywhere for it, but it could not be found. No one had seen it. The police were asked to help, but day after day passed and the dog was still missing. The soldier's wife was grieved, not only because she had lost a faithful friend, but because she knew that if ever her husband came home he would be sorry indeed. At last she wrote and told him what had happened, and six weeks later she received a letter from the Front. To her amazement she read that the dog had by some marvellous means made his way to his master's side.

How did the dog reach a port? How did it cross the Channel? How did it know what direction to take in France? Amid those miles of trenches, with scores of thousands of men around, by what sense did the dog find its way to the hand it knew?

248

Glenalmond School is in Perthshire, and in its chapel is the name of an old boy who made the supreme sacrifice.

The story of the loss of the *Birkenhead* in 1852 is well known. A troopship, she went down suddenly off Cape Agulhas where she had struck a rock. In an instant death took toll of hundreds on board.

The soldiers, among whom was Alexander Cumine Russell, were lined up on the deck, most of them to die standing at attention; the women and children were rushed to the boats, one of which Russell was ordered to command. Successfully lowered, the boat pushed off with its burden of wretched, terrified humanity, Russell, like many others, seeing the ship go down and watching the waves overwhelm the courageous troops who remained on board till they were scattered by the inrushing waters. Many a hand was flung up from the whirlpool, and many ghastly things were witnessed in those awful moments. It was all terrible, but Russell must have been thankful that he had at least a chance of life.

Then came a scream from a woman in his boat. A man was seen struggling in the water only a yard or two away; and the woman, beside herself with grief and terror, cried, 'Save him! Oh, sir, save him—he is my husband!'

Russell saw her frantic children. He saw the agony in her face. He felt the eyes of the man beseeching him. Then, without a word, he plunged into the water, helped the other man into his place, *the only one in the crowded boat*, and turned to swim till he could swim no longer.

'God bless you,' said a score of broken voices.

It was thus the old boy of Glenalmond School went to meet his glorious death.

249

After the morning service a lady hurried up to the Minister. 'Oh,' she exclaimed, 'thank you *so* much for your beautiful sermon. All the time you were telling everyone about their shortcomings I kept wishing my husband were here—it would have done him a world of good.'

'I wasn't thinking of your husband, madam,' said the Minister. 'I was thinking of *you*.'

250

Long ago, says a legend, a small boy lived in a cottage on a green hill. He was happy, but not perfectly happy for there was one thing he wanted more than anything else in the world.

Every day towards evening he would sit on the doorstep, his chin resting in his hands as he stared across the wide valley at the house with golden windows. How brilliantly those windows shone—dazzlingly and wonderfully, and so alluring that he never tired of gazing at them, wishing all the time that he were lucky enough to live in such a wonderful house as the one far across the valley.

Day after day and indeed year after year the house with the golden windows fascinated this little fellow; and at last, when he was old enough to go to school, he made up his mind to see the house of his dreams.

One summer afternoon he set off on his exciting quest. But the journey proved to be longer and harder than he had expected, and the sun was already below the horizon when he trudged uphill and reached his journey's end. And how terribly disappointing that end was, for instead of being a fine house, as he had always imagined, the house with the golden windows was no more than a cottage; and the windows, the dazzling golden windows, were only ordinary windows after all.

Weary and hungry, the young and very disillusioned explorer found hospitality on the hill. An old man and woman lived in the cottage, and when they learned how far the little chap had walked and what he had set out to find, they shook their heads and smiled sadly. 'Well, well,' said the old woman, 'it's growing late. You must eat some supper, and then we'll put you up for the night—it's much too late to think of going back now.'

So the small boy stayed the night; and as he was very tired, he was asleep in next to no time. Early in the morning he awoke, sat up, peeped out of the window and made a discovery which astonished him, for there, far across the valley, was another house with golden windows, each window flashing as dazzlingly and as marvellously as anything he had ever seen before. He was looking at the windows of his own home—and how glad, how very glad he was later in the day to be back in the house with golden windows.

251

Josefo, the goldsmith, was working even when Florence was on holiday. His craftsmen took the matter philosophically, but little Andrea was rebellious, for he wanted very much to see the procession and join in the festival. Tools had to be sharpened, however, and work had to be done. Besides, Josefo was already angry with him for drawing on the wall. And unfortunately there was a still more serious offence to be dealt with—a crime of which Josefo was still ignorant.

One of the workmen had discovered that Andrea had been up to his pranks again. The little rascal had torn off a piece of parchment (parchment was dear in those days) *and drawn on it*! 'Now,' said the craftsman, 'there *will* be trouble!'

In came Josefo at that moment. When he heard about the parchment he gave Andrea a look which almost withered him, and caused the seven-year-old to creep into a corner. But when Josefo saw what was *on* the parchment he did not shout. He did not throw anything at Andrea. He did not kick him down the stairs. He said quietly, 'Andrea, come here.'

Trembling, Andrea obeyed.

'Who drew this?'

'I did.'

'You may have the rest of the day off to see the festival,' said Josefo. 'I will use this design for the cardinal's bowl we are to make, and tomorrow I will show it to Gian Barile, the artist.'

Josefo kept his word—and thus began the career of Andrea del Sarto, the amazing Florentine painter.

252

Once upon a time there was an old Arab who had three sons. Calling them together, he said, 'Sons, my end is near. I bless you all. To my eldest I give half my camels, to my second one-third, and to my youngest I give one-ninth.' Soon afterwards he died.

Now the old man had seventeen camels, and the three brothers were greatly perplexed to know how to share them as their father had bidden. They pondered long over the problem, and it seemed that they must either kill some of the camels and cut them into pieces, or disobey their father. At last they went to their father's old friend and asked his advice. As soon as he heard their story he said, 'I will help you. I honoured your father. I am old. I have but one camel, but take it—it is yours.'

Gratefully the three sons took the old man's camel, finding that it was now easy to divide the camels as their father had wished. The eldest took half—that was nine camels; the second took one-third, which was six camels; and the youngest took one-ninth, which was two camels.

Only when each had received his fair share of camels did they discover that there was a camel to spare; so—out of gratitude to their father's friend—they returned his camel.

253

Those of us who are bad writers and have the habit of scribbling may well find a moral in this story from Spain.

According to the *Citizen*, published in April 1911, there were pretty goings on in southern Spain, and a woman there was indignant indeed. She declared she would not pay, but pay she had to, for the Court ruled quite rightly that if people cannot read your writing it is at any rate as much your fault as theirs.

What happened was that the woman despatched an order for a thousand oranges. She used the Spanish word *naranjas*, but she scribbled it so badly that it looked like *naranjos*. A day or two later there came to her door a score of heavily laden wagons, and in the wagons a thousand young orange trees, a fine sight, to be sure—all healthy, and all ready for planting. The word *naranjos* is Spanish for orange trees, and here they were.

The woman said it was ridiculous and that people were stupid. The fruit-grower said her a's were like **o's**. The judge said she must pay.

254

A Leeds man boarded a Headingley tramcar in City Square, but discovered too late that he had no money with him. The conductress must have noticed his anxious manner, for she asked: 'Now then, love, what's up?'

'I want to get to Headingley,' he said, 'but, I've no money.'

'That's all right love,' she murmured.

Her soothing tone reassured him, and he asked: 'What shall I do, then?'

'Do?' said she. *'Get off!'*

NORTHERNER II in the *Yorkshire Post*.

255

I was duly rebuked this morning. As I went home to lunch my neighbour's wee bairn, Andrea, hugged me, and said, 'I'se glad you've come!'

Well, that was charming; so I said, 'And what's the meaning of all this, eh?' For, though I apologize for the thought, I fancied she might be hoping I had something in my pocket for her.

With grave eyes she looked at me and said, 'Oh, nofing—I'se just glad, that's all!'

To be loved for no ulterior reason, ah, *that* is to be loved indeed!

H. L. GEE.

256

Some years before World War II a motor-cyclist had the misfortune to knock down a hen. He pulled up at once, and apologized to a woman who was standing at a gate near-by.

'It's all very well to say you're sorry,' snapped the woman, 'but sympathy doesn't help much. I've lost one of my best hens, and you owe me ten shillings.'

The motor-cyclist felt that this was too much. He offered six shillings; but the woman refused to take less than ten. In the circumstances the motor-cyclist felt bound to pay the sum demanded, and he had actually put his hand in his pocket when the hen, which was still lying in the road, gave a flutter, stood up, and ran through the hedge.

'Good afternoon,' said the motor-cyclist; and off he went, his money in his pocket.

We feel sure Aesop would have added, by way of a moral: *It is sometimes wise to be satisfied.*

257

While journeying from Berlin to Warsaw, Chopin and a friend had to wait at a village until the horses were changed. To while away the time, Chopin sat down at an old piano which he found in a room of the inn, playing so wonderfully that his companion walked in, and was followed by other passengers. The postmaster and his wife joined the little crowd. Their daughters came softly into the room. All listened entranced, and when the horses were in the shafts and the coach was ready to start, the small audience begged the musician to play just one more piece.

At last Chopin rose. He smiled at the company—a very small audience for one used to playing before vast assemblies in the capitals of Europe. It was then that something was said which gladdened his heart even more than the loudest applause could ever have done, for a venerable Pole murmured: 'Sir, if Mozart had heard you he would have seized your hands and shouted, *Bravo!*'

258

One day Augustine, the first Archbishop of Canterbury, was invited to preach at some distance from the place where he was staying at that time. Being ignorant of the route he should take, he engaged a guide to direct him, but the man mistook the way. Instead of following the usual road, he led Augustine along a by-path, eventually bringing him to his destination in time for the service.

When Augustine returned home, he learned that this mistake had saved his life. Some of his enemies, knowing the route he *should* have taken, had hidden by the highway, intending to kill him. Thus an error had frustrated their plans, and had enabled Augustine to continue his great missionary labours.

259

Very old is the story of two quarrelsome fellows who were walking by the sea when they found an oyster.

'I saw it first,' said one.

'I picked it up,' said the other.

So they fell to wrangling over the oyster in a ridiculous fashion, and might have come to blows had not a lawyer joined them. When they asked him to decide who owned the oyster, he agreed to settle the matter provided they would accept his decision.

'Let me see the oyster,' he said. 'A very fine one it is, to be sure, and quite fresh, I declare. Now, my friends, it seems perfectly plain that your claims are equal, and therefore half goes to one, and half to the other.' So saying, he swallowed the oyster, giving one shell to each of the stupid men.

'But you've taken it yourself!' they exclaimed angrily.

'*That* was my fee,' said the lawyer, smiling.

260

In his delightful book, *Adventure in Poplar*, the Rev. William H. Lax tells us that in the Mission Sunday School there was much sorrow because a small girl had died. The other children were asked to bring a penny to provide a wreath. One of the youngest scholars elected to give her penny to Mr Lax himself, saying as she pushed the sticky coin into the minister's hand, 'Please, sir, muvver 'as sent a penny for Jinny's wreath, an' she ses as if it was *your* funeral she'd 'ave sent a shillin'!'

261

Every year Lion Sunday comes round for London, and in October a special sermon is always preached in Leadenhall Street, a thanksgiving for a man's singular escape from death.

One of the quaintest stories London has to tell is this tale of Sir John Gayer, a devout man and a bold traveller whose most remarkable adventure gives the City a yearly sermon of unique interest.

Why is the Lion Sermon preached?

It is linked with Sir John, who was Lord Mayor in 1646, in that year leaving a sum of money to St Katherine Cree's for the preaching of a sermon in memory of his miraculous deliverance. If we are to believe the quaint tale told of him, he was travelling in Asia, somewhere near Turkey we think, when he chanced to wander from his companions.

While walking alone he met a lion in the way. A brave man was Sir John, but he had not expected to meet a lion, and was not ready for the encounter, nor had he a weapon with which to defend himself. Happily he did not try to run away. He did not anger the beast by attempting to frighten it. Being, as we said, a devout man, he dropped on his knees, closed his eyes (thus the story has been handed down to us) and prayed that God would save him.

When he opened his eyes (as we are informed) the lion had vanished.

It has long been said that Satan trembles when he sees the weakest saint upon his knees, and it seems to be true of lions.

262

Rothschild—a name to conjure with! We have visions of unlimited wealth, of men with millions at their fingertips, of financiers who controlled the very destinies of nations. There was old Mayer Rothschild, who made a fortune in Frankfurt in the eighteenth century; there were his five amazing sons who settled as bankers in Frankfurt, Vienna, Manchester, Naples, and Paris; and there was that fine Lionel, who died in 1879 after a life spent in winning emancipation for the Jews.

But we are concerned only with little Constance Rothschild, who knew and loved the village of Aston Clinton. The Rothschild who had his great house there was a generous philanthropist, and he it was who gave the village its day school. But the school was only big enough for boys and girls of about eight upwards.

One day Constance was asked what she would like for her birthday. She, the daughter of a Rothschild, might have asked for a queen's necklace or the finest horses in the world. 'What would you like for your birthday?' they asked.

She replied, '*An Infant School, please!*'

She got it—or rather, the village did.

263

In a little house at Kirriemuir, not so very far from Dundee, sat a mother with a white, drawn face. She had lovely eyes and—when not so anxious—a sweet smile, and her goodness shone in her gentle features; but on this day she was sad indeed, and so worried that for once she had no thought of glancing at the six hair-seated chairs, the first the family had ever been able to boast of, and of which she was very proud. For the postie had brought a letter with bad news. David, her boy at school, was ill, and the mother must hurry if she was to see him alive.

Quickly she ran round the house. She made her preparations in a calm way that alarmed her other children, among them James Matthew, who was six. When all was ready, she went out —the children with her. She hurried to the station, a little wooden affair, for Kirriemuir in 1866 was by no means a place of great importance. She bought a ticket. She stood waiting for the train. Then her husband came from the telegraph office. 'He's gone,' he whispered huskily, and they all turned and walked home again.

Day after day the mother lay in a darkened room, a look on her face which frightened little James. One day his father said, 'James, *you* must comfort her.'

So the little fellow went timidly into the dark room and looked at the bed. His mother whispered, 'Is that you?'

James thought she meant David, his brother. So he said, 'No, it's not him. *It's only me*.'

The droll, sad little words touched a spring in his mother's heart. She drew him towards her, and they cried together. It was the beginning of a marvellous love between James Matthew Barrie and his mother.

264

Two men walking in Leeds looked up to see a car with neither driver nor occupants moving slowly by the pavement.

One of the two was impulsive. With him to think was to act. The other was prone to reflect first and act afterwards. The impulsive man, realizing that if the car gathered speed there might easily be a serious accident, wrenched open the door, sprang into the driver's seat, and applied the brake.

We may forgive him if he afterwards glanced at his companion and expected commendation. But his friend had no praise to offer. While the impulsive man had been acting gallantly in the public interest, *he* had been contemplating. He argued, that, although cars have been known to run away from time to time, they do not as a rule travel up a slight incline. From this he deduced that if there was no one in the car there must be someone pushing it. His deduction proved to be correct, for as the brake was put on with a jerk a red face looked over the roof, and someone wanted to know why someone was interfering with an honest man.

265

There were three of us in the railway compartment—a young lady who nodded as I got in, a man reading a book in a corner, and my humble self.

'Thank goodness *you've* come,' said the young lady in a low tone as the train started. 'I was just aching for somebody to talk to.'

She glanced at the elderly man in the corner, his eyes on an open book. 'I've spoken to him *three* times,' she said, 'and he's never even condescended to look up. Just sits there reading; hasn't a word to say; isn't even civil enough to reply.'

So we chatted awhile until the man in the corner closed his book, stretched his arms, reached down his suitcase, peered inside and took out a large paper bag from which he drew sandwiches, fruit, biscuits and cake. 'Help yourselves,' he said, smiling at the two of us. 'There's more here than I can eat. Just nod to me . . . *I'm stone deaf*!'

A contributor to the *Newcastle Journal.*

266

Thomas Carlyle tells us that two miners went down a Cornish mine in order to prepare a charge for blasting the rock. The method in those days was to cut a hole in the surface, fill it with gunpowder, and prepare a sort of train. The charge was duly laid and the match placed in position when one of the men, thinking the match a little too long, used a lump of rock to cut it in two. In so doing he ignited it.

Both men saw the danger. The fuse was alight, and they had made no preparations for retreat. Instant death stared them in the face, a horrible death which must have sickened them even to think of it. They raced to the shaft where a basket hung by a rope, the two miners reaching it at the same moment. Then, in what must have been an eternity, they realized there was only room for one.

For a fraction of a second they stood facing the most terrible alternative imaginable. To climb into the basket meant a chance of life; to stay behind meant death.

The hesitation lasted no more than a moment. With splendid courage one man said to the other, 'Go aloft, Jack; I'll be in heaven in a minute!'

Jack went aloft.

There was a terrific roar, a shaking of the very earth. In the deathly silence which followed, another workman went down the shaft to see if anything was left of the hero who had chosen to stay. By what seemed a miracle, the rocks had been thrown in such a way as to make a wall about him, shielding him from the direct force of the explosion. The hero was dazed, but unhurt.

267

Three fishermen on the pier were looking out to sea. Presently a piece of driftwood floated towards the shore. Said one humorously, 'Yon's a board.'

There was no reply to this gratuitous information until the second fisherman, a noted wag, remarked, 'Aye, mebbe it's Board o' Trade.'

Again there was a long silence. Eventually the third fisherman began to shake his head slowly. 'Nay,' he observed solemnly, 'It can't be. *It's movin'*.'

268

Her name was Penelope, but she was Poor Penny from the first. '*Poor* Penny,' they would say, tickled to death as they said it, '*poor* Penny—leave it to poor Penny.'

For Penny was the eldest of the family, and before she was fifteen she was mother and housemaid and nurse and head cook and bottle-washer!

Yes, it was Penny who stayed at home and looked after the others when their mother died. It was she who ran the home and saw to things; and she who, later, nursed her father through a long and fatal illness. That somebody once wanted to marry Penny was the family joke . . . fancy *anybody* wanting to marry *poor* Penny!

Meanwhile Geoffrey grew up and got on; Maud married exceedingly well; Arthur became a noted journalist, and Marion eloped with a colonel and lived in Paris. At long last, and only after her father had died, poor Penny married a draper who had waited years and years for her.

Well, the patient draper never set the Thames on fire, but he was careful and humorous and kindly and able eventually to move into the suburbs and do a bit of gardening with Penny's help. As for Geoffrey, he lost most of his money, after which his wife went off with another man; Maud, who had simply *everything*, was bored to tears; Arthur worried himself to his grave at forty, and Marion, proud and painted, was glad in the end to live in the little flat poor Penny provided for her.

Today, white haired but fresh-complexioned, bright of eye and almost always *smiling*, poor Penny is actually the richest of all the family—rich in the love of her devoted husband, rich because all her life she has loved much.

269

A down-and-out was wandering in the streets of Paris one day. Shabbily dressed, out of work, hopeless, he had not money enough for a meal. To his surprise someone tapped him on the shoulder, and the down-and-out turned to look into the face of Alexander Dumas, the greatest French writer of his time. They had been friends thirty years before, these two, but life had led them along different paths, the one to misfortune and poverty, the other to success and wealth.

'Friend,' asked Dumas, 'where are you dining?'

The other shrugged his shoulders. 'Alas,' said he, 'nowhere.'

'You are wrong,' replied Dumas. 'You are dining with *me*.'

So the two went to the author's fine house with its many servants and magnificent table. When the meal was finished Dumas excused himself, saying he must go to his work. 'I shall expect you here tomorrow,' he said.

The next day his friend appeared, and the next, and the day after. On the fourth day the down-and-out felt unable to trespass further on his friend's kindness. At dinner he said, 'I cannot come any more. You are very kind, but it is not right that I should receive and give nothing in return. I *must* earn my daily bread.'

'Ah, yes, to be sure, to be sure,' Dumas replied, leaning back in his chair and looking at the ceiling. 'It is only right. I will tell you something you can do for me, if you will. I shall esteem it a great favour. I will ask you to go every day to the Pont Neuf, and make a careful reading of the temperature. It is a matter of much importance to me, for the temperature affects my box-office receipts at the theatre.'

Proud to serve, the old man made a daily practice of bringing his useless record, staying to dinner every evening until his life was done.

270

Once upon a time the sun and the wind had a quarrel, and the wind said, 'I'm stronger than you. I'll prove it. Let's see which of us can make that ploughman take off his coat.' So the wind blew hard, but all his blowing could not drag the coat away.

'Now,' said the sun gently, 'let *me* try.' He beamed, and soon the man exclaimed, 'How hot it is!' Then he unbuttoned his coat. Presently he threw it open; and at last, off came the coat.

271

January 1881 had been a month of heavy snow, biting frosts and high winds. On the nineteenth day a vessel ran ashore upon the dangerous rocks in Robin Hood's Bay, Yorkshire. There was no lifeboat there at that time, and a fishing coble must have perished instantly in a sea so violent. The nearest lifeboat was at Whitby, but it was unthinkable that she could sail in the teeth of a raging gale across six miles of madly tempestuous sea. Besides, there was Black Nab in the way, and after that the wave-battered walls of North Cheek. Little wonder, then, that many of the good folk of the bay town looked into the seething cauldron at their doors, and believed that the hapless ship was beyond all human aid.

Not so the crew of the Whitby lifeboat. No sooner were they acquainted with the terrible predicament of the wreck than they determined to drag the lifeboat over the moors! It seemed a mad resolve, for the upland region had been almost impassable for weeks. Snow lay deeply drifted; windswept patches of ice made the one road extremely hazardous. That conditions were wholly unfavourable everyone knew, yet the boat was taken from her house, the strongest teams of farm horses were requisitioned and hurried into harness, and crowds of men and women willingly gave their assistance. So the 'impossible' was attempted.

Never was there wilder folly, never more noble purpose, more resolute determination. Each obstacle was overcome by almost superhuman strength and perseverance. Narrow streets and awkward corners were miraculously negotiated. Snowdrifts were overridden by sheer force. Treacherous hills were conquered bit by bit, until—the inhospitable moorland region having been crossed—the lifeboat was safely directed down the steep cliff-road to the water's edge at Robin Hood's Bay, and a marvellous rescue successfully effected.

272

There is living even today in the backwoods of Formosa a wild race of head-hunters. In the eighteenth century the Chinese were forcing them back to the mountains, and the natives—who believed that heaven was to be gained only by men with blood-stained hands—lost no opportunity of raiding the Chinese outposts, cutting off heads, and carrying them home.

A terrible vendetta thus continued.

At last a simple, earnest Chinaman, Gaw Hong, was appointed magistrate of the district. Unlike his predecessors, he was kind, honest and friendly, and the head-hunting natives quickly learned to respect him, and at last to love him. Bit by bit he won a wonderful power over them, and to his great joy there came a day when he was able to persuade the people of his own district to forsake their head-hunting practice. From that moment the vendetta between the natives and the Chinese began to die out.

But a great feast approached, and the natives came to Gaw Hong pleading to be allowed to make human sacrifice for this special occasion. Only so could they hope to appease their gods. Gaw Hong, greatly troubled, asked for time to think over the matter, and when he saw that the chiefs were determined, he was still more troubled. He knew that if they took the head of any of the Chinese, the old enmity would break out again, and the vendetta would go on as before. At last, calling the head-hunters together, he said very quietly, 'I have found a way out of your difficulty. You may take *one* head, and one only, but you must kill the first man who comes through the wood on the day I appoint.'

It was agreed.

At dawn on the appointed day one of the head-hunters waited in secret. Amid the shadows he lurked, and presently a man came on slowly. An arrow sped, the man fell, and a moment later the head was carried with joy to the waiting chiefs. Then the bag was opened—*and there was the head of Gaw Hong.*

We are told that the shocked head-hunters agreed never to kill for sacrifice again; and we believe they have kept their word for over 150 years.

273

During the American War of Independence a company of soldiers in the Army of Defence were one day tugging at long ropes as they tried to hoist a heavy beam. Time and time again the beam slipped a few inches in spite of the commands of a little corporal who kept shouting, 'Heave away, there! Heave away!'

For some minutes a gentleman in civilian clothes watched this odd pantomime. He saw the beam rise. He saw it fall. At last he ventured to say to the little corporal: "Do you not think that if *you* lent a hand, the beam could be swung into position?'

The pompous little corporal turned crimson. 'I?' he demanded. 'But, sir, I am a corporal!'

Without more ado, the gentleman took off his frock coat, laid hold of one of the ropes, and when next the command, 'Heave away!' was given, he pulled with all his might. Slowly the beam rose once more, touched the cross bar, swung round, and settled where it was required.

'At last!' exclaimed the gentleman as he picked up his coat. Then, smiling, he added: 'By the way, Mr Corporal, if ever you have another job on hand like this, be good enough to send for your Commander-in-Chief. I shall be glad to help.'

He walked off, leaving the pompous little corporal thunderstruck at the discovery that his squad had been helped by George Washington.

274

From China comes the story of a man who was riding a donkey when he met a man on horseback. 'Ah,' said he to himself, '*he* can afford a horse while all I have is a donkey.'

Presently he met a poor fellow, wet with perspiration, pushing a heavily laden barrow. 'Ah,' said he to himself, '*I* can afford a donkey, but this creature has to push a barrow!'

275

At last, exasperated by the way my small son, David, dawdled at teatime, I said, 'I wish to goodness you'd eat that piece of cake instead of crumbling it on your plate.'

He ate the cake.

A quarter of an hour later I heard the click of the letter-box in the front door. David was lying on the rug by the fire, idly turning the pages of a picture book. 'Run along and bring the newspaper,' said I.

He was reluctant to obey.

'Do as I say,' I ordered.

As he got up slowly from the rug I saw tears coursing down his cheeks. 'I'm a bit stiff,' he murmured.

I put my hand on the smooth brow. It was hot. David had a chill—the beginning, as it proved, of a three-weeks' illness.

All that time I kept blaming myself, wishing I had been less severe, wondering why in the world I hadn't noticed it sooner.

You never feel so small as when you know you have been unjust.

H. L. GEE: *Of Countless Price.*

276

One day early in the eighteenth century an ill-dressed, hollow-cheeked fellow stood leaning over the parapet of one of London's bridges. He looked so utterly wretched that anyone might have been forgiven for thinking he was about to find a quick way out of his troubles. Indeed, a passer-by, catching sight of the man's face, was so sure he had come upon somebody who was contemplating suicide that he patted the fellow on the shoulder, spoke a few kind words, and slipped a guinea into his hand.

But this Good Samaritan had not given a guinea to a down-and-out. He had given it to one of the richest men alive. We have all heard of Guy Fawkes who somehow became mixed up with gunpowder, treason and plot; but London's other Guy—Thomas Guy—was a miser, living like a rat in a hole, pinching, scraping, saving, not because he was mean, but because he had the warmest heart of any man in England, and delighted to do good by stealth. He it was who built Guy's Hospital, and endowed it with a million pounds!

It was to this fabulously rich philanthropist that the passer-by had given a guinea; but the odd thing is that in all Thomas Guy's long and curious life nothing warmed his heart or gave him such intense joy as that gift he did not need.

277

Once upon a time there was a monkey who thought too highly of himself. He boasted that he ought to be made Lord of the Sky because he could jump further than any other living creature.

Walking in the forest one day God met the proud monkey. 'I hear you are quite good at jumping,' said God.

'Quite good!' repeated the offended monkey. 'Quite good, indeed! I'm the best jumper in the world. I can jump a hundred miles—a thousand miles.'

'Really?' asked God. 'Then listen. Sit in my hand, and if you can jump out of it, I will make you Lord of the Sky.'

'Pooh!' exclaimed the monkey. 'That's easy—easy to a fellow like me. Watch!'

Then the monkey crouched on all fours, took a deep breath, and made the biggest jump of his life. He sprang over hills and valleys, over seas and rivers, and came down at the very edge of the world. Had he gone another ten yards, he would have fallen into eternal space. And there, at the end of the world, stood four huge brown pillars, on one of which the monkey put a chalk-mark. Then he gave another great leap, and landed safely in the palm of God's hand.

'There you are,' declared the proud monkey. 'I reached the very edge of the world—and if you don't believe it, go and look for yourself. You'll see the mark I made on one of the four pillars I found. Now, what about making me Lord of the Sky?'

But God, looking down gently on the monkey, replied: 'Those four pillars, little monkey, were my fingers. Not even *you* can jump out of my loving hand. Away with you, and let me hear no more of your foolish boasting!'

278

The pitch was not exactly what would be required for a Test Match, for actually it was merely a length of concrete with a piece of matting on top. The teams were an eleven from Bowral High

School, Australia, and their implacable rivals, Mittagong School eleven, a pretty tough lot who were used to having a walk-over in almost every match. There was, however, one occasion when Bowral put up a stiff fight, for a boy there, a chap who was not particularly famous for his cricketing abilities, made things hum. A total of 156 was achieved, and of that number 115 runs were secured by this one boy.

His school chums, naturally delighted, hailed him as a conquering hero. They praised him, slapped him on the back, and called him a fine fellow. He would not have been flesh and blood had he not been pleased.

But there was a cold douche the morning after victory. Addressing the assembled school, the Headmaster said ponderously: 'I understand a certain boy yesterday scored over a hundred in a match. That is all very well, *but it is no excuse for having left the bat behind.* See that it is recovered.'

So Don Bradman went for the bat.

279

Looking through a book catalogue the other day, a pessimist was about to order a volume by Dr R. Allestree, entitled: *The Causes of the Decay of Christian Piety*; or, *an Impartial Survey of the Ruins of the Christian Religion*, when he happened to notice the date of publication. It was not this deplorable year, but 1694!

280

A story told by the poet George W. Russell gives a charming example of Irish courtesy and wit.

An Englishwoman cycling in the west of Ireland took shelter in the only cottage in sight; and the cottager, his wife being at market, did the honours with cake and milk.

When the rain cleared off the visitor put half a crown on the table, but the labourer handed it back with the remark: 'Arrah, would the sun pay for shining in at the dure?'

281

One day in 1937 a motorist pulled up outside the north door of Liverpool Cathedral—the great pile of masonry rising in splendour above the city. As he did so a policeman crossed the road and came towards the car. The motorist sighed. Was there no place in England where one might park a car for half an hour?

The policeman put a smiling face in at the window.

'Good morning, sir,' he said. 'I've just come across to put your mind at rest. Your car will be all right here, sir; and, what is more, though I guess this is something of a shock, you can leave it as long as you like.'

He beamed, and then strode majestically on.

282

After the fall of France, a significant fable was spread in hopeful whispers throughout the stricken country. In its heroic humour was proof of a deep and abiding faith in ultimate liberation by the stubborn people across the Channel.

The story related that in July 1940, when England faced the enemy alone, Hitler invited Churchill to Paris for a secret conference. Churchill arrived by 'plane, and was escorted to the Château of Fontainebleau, where Hitler and Mussolini awaited him at a tea-table beside the famous carp pool.

The Führer lost no time. 'Here's what I've got to say to you, Churchill! England is finished. Sign this document admitting that England has lost the war, and all Europe will have peace tomorrow!'

'I regret that I cannot sign it,' replied Churchill quietly. 'I don't agree that we have lost the war.'

'Ridiculous!' exclaimed Hitler, pounding the table. 'Look at the evidence!'

Churchill sipped his tea. 'In England,' he said, 'we often settle a difference of opinion by making a wager. Would you like to make one with me? The loser will agree that he has lost the war.'

'What's the bet?' asked the Führer suspiciously.

'You see those big carp in the pool? Well, let's wager that the first to catch one without using any of the usual fishing equipment will be declared winner of the war.'

'It's a bet!' snapped Hitler, who at once whipped out a revolver and emptied it at the nearest carp. But the water deflected the bullets, and the carp swam on undisturbed.

'It's up to you, Musso!' growled Hitler. 'They tell me you're a great swimmer—in you go!'

The Duce shed his clothes and jumped into the pool; but, try as he would, the carp slipped through his grasp. At last, exhausted, he clambered out empty-handed.

'It's your turn, Churchill,' Hitler rasped. 'Let's see what *you* can do!'

Churchill calmly dipped his teaspoon into the pool, and tossed the water over his shoulder. Then again. And again.

Hitler watched open-mouthed. 'What on earth are you doing?' he demanded impatiently.

'It will take a long time,' replied Churchill, keeping right on dipping, '*but we are going to win the war*!'

COLONEL RÉMY: *The Silent Company.*

283

In spite of all the canny tales which are supposed to emanate from Scotland there has never been a dearth of Scottish philanthropists, and one of the greatest and most warm-hearted of all was William Quarrier, founder of the famous Orphan Homes. His motto was *Have Faith in God*—and no man ever lived up to his motto more adventurously.

In the days before the site at Bridge of Weir was bought, part of the House, accommodating boys only, was at the old Mansion House of Cessnock in Govan. This needed considerable renovation before the children could move in, but at that moment William Quarrier had not one penny with which to pay the expenses. He tells us:

'When we moved into Cessnock House we needed £200 for improvements, and during the first few months friends contributed £100 for the purpose. The alterations were almost finished and the tradesmen's accounts were already waiting to be paid, when I received a note from a friend who said, *Please call at your earliest convenience.*

'I called at once, and he greeted me with the words: "How do you stand at Cessnock?"

'I said we wanted £100 of the £200 required for alterations. He immediately wrote a cheque for £100, and handed it to me. "That will keep you easy," he said. "As it happens, a relative has died and left me his fortune, and this is the first bit of it. I desire to give it to Christ for the work in your hands". '

284

From Maidstone comes this story of two women who met in Week Street one morning. 'Oh, hello!' said the first, 'you look a bit flushed, my dear. Anything wrong?'

'No, not really,' replied the second. 'I've just been ticked off good and proper.'

'Ticked off? Who by?'

'My sister.' The woman shrugged her shoulders as she went on, 'I often call to see if there's anything I can get for her while I'm shopping. I was round at her house the day before yesterday, but she was out—she'd gone to see a neighbour. Her hubby was in, though, and promised he'd tell her I'd called, but he must have forgotten. Anyhow, when I looked in ten minutes ago, she just about bit my head off . . . said I'd time to waste, that I never went near, that I didn't care *how* bothered she was or *how* much she had to do. . . . Eh, deary me, she *was* mad!'

'And what did *you* say?'

'Me? Oh, I never said anything. I just came away, that's all. Poor Jean, she's worried about her boy overseas, and that invalid hubby of hers is *such* a care; and the weather's been trying, you know, and she's tired out. It would do her good to storm at me—relieve her pent-up feelings, you know.'

The first woman *had* to smile at the bright little body standing there on the pavement. 'Well,' she said, 'after *such* a reception I guess you'll never visit your sister again!'

'What nonsense!' was the reply. 'Why, I'm taking her a few strawberries *now*!'

285

A country fellow, seeing a large pumpkin growing on its small mean vine, exclaimed, 'How stupid for pumpkins to grow on such little vines! Now, if *I* had made the world I should have hung splendid pumpkins aloft in giant oaks. They would have looked fine up there—much finer than puny acorns.'

Being tired as a result of thinking such a great thought, the fellow lay down beneath a tall oak, but he had no sooner closed his eyes than a sudden sharp blow on his chin made him sit up. An acorn had fallen.

'Bless my soul!' he exclaimed, 'what a mercy pumpkins do *not* grow on oaks!'

286

A year or two ago there was in Scotland a little schoolgirl named Mary who was a very merry soul, fond of singing, and lively in spirit.

One winter's day she was taken ill. The doctor treated her for pleurisy at first, later for pneumonia; but somehow things did not go quite as they should have done. Mary was removed to hospital, and there specialists, doctors and nurses cared for her. The trouble was that they couldn't get her temperature to remain normal for twenty-four hours. Day after day and week after week she lay in the big ward—serious and curiously still. She never complained, but she was steadily becoming weaker. Mother, father, friends, doctors, nurses, all tried to quicken her interest, to stimulate her, to challenge her to fight for life, but all in vain. Mary lay without saying a word, and without even a hint of a smile.

One bright spring morning a nurse who had gone round the ward washing the patients, opened a window. When she returned later she stood still, astonished. There, at the foot of Mary's bed, perching happily on the iron rail, was a robin . . . and Mary, resting on one elbow was watching it!

How that robin sang! Presently he flew off, but an hour later he was back again. Spreading a cloth over the foot of the bed, Sister scattered crumbs, and soon the robin was back a third time. After that he seemed to *adopt* Mary—popping in time and time again every day, singing as he perched, winking at her with one bright black eye.

From that day Mary began to get well; and within a few weeks she was putting on weight, and getting back to her usual lively and merry self.

'Ah,' said Matron as Mary left the hospital, 'that little bird did what *we* couldn't do.'

'Yes,' said Mary, 'he *helped*, bless him . . . *but it was God, really, wasn't it?*'

287

One day when Booker Washington, the famous Negro educator, was in haste to catch a train, he hurried to a horse-stand and asked the driver of a cab to take him to the station. 'No,' replied the driver. 'I've never driven a black man, and I never will.'

'All right, friend,' retorted Booker Washington cheerily. 'Just hop in der back seat, and I'll do der drivin'!'

The astonished cabby did as he was bidden, and Booker Washington caught his train.

288

James Truslow Adams tells a story of an explorer in the Amazon region of South America who tried to make his little company endure forced marches. In one way or another he coaxed or intimidated with so much success that for two days the native bearers made surprising progress, but on the third morning he found them sitting around doing nothing.

When the explorer inquired why they were not preparing to break camp, the head man explained that they could not go any further until their souls had caught up with their bodies.

289

When General Mark Clark was asked what was the best advice that had ever been given to him, he replied: 'The suggestion that I should marry the girl who is now my wife.'

'And who advised you to marry her?' he was asked.

'She did,' replied the General.

290

In the most famous storybook of the Middle Ages we read of a certain king who wished to honour one of his generals, hero of a resounding victory. To the general's great delight the king decreed that he should be greeted with cheers when he entered the city, that he should ride in a triumphal car drawn by four white horses, and that his captives should follow with their hands bound.

It was a proud moment for the general when he began his entry, but before he had gone many yards he learned that the king who had decreed three honours had also appointed three annoyances to keep him humble.

A slave rode with him in his chariot to show that the greatest and the least are one; another slave struck him every time the people cheered, that his pride might be checked; and though the populace was allowed to hail him as victor, it was also permitted to jeer at him and shout insulting remarks to remind him that, great as he was, he was not without failures.

291

One of the happiest men I ever knew was Arthur Blands, a miner.

Football was the big thing in his life. He played it—centre forward—till he was approaching forty; and he followed the game with tremendous interest all his days. I used to marvel at his knowledge not only of the technique of the game but of the lives of the football 'stars'.

Every Saturday afternoon, in later life, Arthur Blands went to watch a football match, and I think he enjoyed watching the game as much as playing it.

I said *every* Saturday, but that is not quite true. One season he missed seven matches. It was when his mate, George Whitely, was ill; and instead of going to see the match, Arthur sat by George's bed and talked football.

And here's the odd thing: In his last days Arthur used to say to me, a rare twinkle in his eye: 'Yes, I've *played* in some grand matches, and I've *seen* some grand matches, but the ones I enjoyed most of all were the ones I missed.'

H. L. GEE: *Of Countless Price.*

292

I saw the King (George VI) knight three of his generals in the field, and decorate others. This was at Eindhoven in the autumn of 1944. He was quietly amused when the generals 'fumbled the drill'—one turned his back as he moved off; another was caught between a handshake and a salute, a third came to attention too far away.

But the King hung the ribboned Orders about them with studied care. No ribbon was left to curl or fold. He put each on slowly and thoroughly, patting it until it hung flat.

This was the first occasion on which the King had worn a battledress, and he told his generals he had 'taken it straight off the line', and had had it altered by his tailor.

He went to church that day. It was a simple service in a plain little Dutch building. The hymns were accompanied on a small harmonium—well loved, familiar hymns, sung with solemn vigour: *Soldiers of Christ, arise and put your armour on; Praise my soul the King of Heaven;* and *O Jesus I have promised to serve Thee to the end.*

We heard the sudden snarl of a 'plane and the quick answering boom of anti-aircraft guns, but the King, in prayer, with his face buried in his hands, did not move.

JOE ILLINGWORTH: *Yorkshire Post.*

293

Newcastle-upon-Tyne did a lovely thing in 1938.

For nearly forty years Mrs Jones, who was then seventy, had helped to clean the City Engineer's offices, doing her work well. At last she felt that she could wash and scrub no longer, so she retired.

But Newcastle would not let her slip quietly away. She was invited to tea at the Town Hall, and there she found herself the guest of honour. She was asked to accept a bedroom clock and a purse of money from the City Engineer's Department; and she was also presented with an armchair by the other cleaners.

294

A crow, ready to die of thirst, found a pitcher, but was disappointed to discover that the water in it was so low that with all his straining and stretching he was unable to reach it. He tried to break the pitcher, or to overturn it, but he was not strong enough.

At last he thought of a plan. Seeing some pebbles lying near, he dropped a great number of them, one by one, into the pitcher. Bit by bit the water rose until it nearly reached the brim, so the patient bird was at last able to quench his thirst.

295

Before General Montgomery left the Eighth Army in 1944, he addressed a representative gathering in a small opera house in Italy, when the reason for their long chain of successes was plain to see. Here was a friend in whom every man had the utmost confidence; here was a great leader who had complete confidence in every man.

The feeling was expressed simply as General Montgomery left the theatre. 'Good old Monty,' shouted a private.

'Cheerio, boys,' replied the general.

296

Andrew Marvell, poet and satirist, lived at a time when a worthless, sensual king was on the throne of England. He was Charles the Second, and the evil ways of his court and the follies of his incapable government were frequently ridiculed by a man whose silence would have been worth a considerable sum. The King, therefore, sent Lord Danby to search out the troublesome fellow, who was M.P. for Hull, and had little more money than the small fee the citizens were pleased to pay him.

My Lord Danby had somewhat to do to find where Andrew Marvell, poet and friend of Milton, lived; but he eventually discovered him up two flights of stairs. Unannounced, he pushed open the door and found Andrew writing at a table. 'I come with a message from the King,' said Lord Danby impressively. 'He wishes to know how he can serve you.'

'He cannot,' replied Andrew.

'He offers you a post of honour at court,' Danby continued.

'I cannot accept the honour,' replied Andrew without a moment's hesitation. 'For either I must appear ungrateful to His Majesty or be false to my country.'

Then Lord Danby said, 'Will you accept a thousand pounds from His Majesty, using it till such time as you may ask him for a further favour?'

At this Andrew stood up very straight, looked Lord Danby in the face, and called for his servant. 'Boy,' he said, 'what had I for dinner yesterday?'

The boy replied, 'A shoulder of mutton, sir.'

'And today?'

'The remainder, hashed.'

Then said Andrew, 'My Lord, tomorrow I shall have the sweet bone boiled.'

So Danby, perceiving how frugally the patriot lived, and how impossible it was to bribe him, returned to the King.

297

Mr Williams was very worried. One evening he called to see the Vicar. There, in the Vicar's study, he explained the difficulty in which he found himself.

'You see,' he said, 'I've been with the firm over twenty years, and I've had nothing to complain of until this last twelve months or so. I got on fine with the old man, but when he retired and his son took over, everything was different. I rather think the younger man resents my presence. He's always finding fault; always making things difficult for me. My position's become intolerable; but I simply *daren't* leave until I've another job to go to. . . . I've an invalid wife to think of as you know. . . .'

'Ever tried praying about it?' asked the Vicar.

Mr Williams was taken aback. 'No,' he admitted. 'It seems to me the sort of thing you've got to handle yourself.'

The Vicar nodded. 'Let me tell you about my operation,' he said, very well aware that his visitor was not at that moment particularly interested in that topic. 'It was years ago. The doctor said there was nothing else for it; and, as it happened, I'd always *dreaded* having to go into the operating theatre. Most people are afraid, but I'd a *horror* of it. I was ready to receive any kind of treatment; ready to take any number of drugs, but an operation . . .' Even as the Vicar spoke he shuddered. 'And so,' he went on quietly, 'I prayed about it. I asked God to spare me such an ordeal. You may think I was foolish, but that's what I did. And my prayer was wonderfully answered.'

For a moment there was silence in the room. Mr Williams shuffled uneasily in his chair. 'And you're going to tell me,' he said at last, 'that as a result of your prayers you got better without having to undergo the operation?'

The Vicar smiled as he shook his head. 'Oh, no,' he murmured gently. 'Not *that*. I was operated on all right . . . but as a result of prayer, *God gave me the courage to endure*.'

298

Sir Ralph Abercromby, born in Scotland in 1734, shares with Sir John Moore the honour of helping to restore discipline and military glory to the British Army. It was in Aboukir Bay that he met his end. A great soldier and a charming man, he always insisted on taking risks with his men. At the last he rode at the head of a company which beat the French and drove them back, but while he was doing so he was struck by a bullet. His men carried him out of the fighting, and took him on board the flagship. 'What is it you've placed under my head?' Sir Ralph asked as they laid him down.

'Only a soldier's blanket,' they said.

'Take it back to him at once!' was the imperious command.

It was his last order.

299

From Pickering in Yorkshire comes the story of the farm labourer who never could resist the temptation of claiming acquaintance with notable people. If, during his visit to one of the public houses, somebody mentioned any of the gentry, Jack would be sure to say, 'Oh, aye, Ah know *'im*!'

On one occasion someone happened to mention Lord Middleton. 'Lord Middleton?' exclaimed Jack, running true to form. 'Oh, aye, Ah know *'im*!'

'Mebbe thoo does,' replied one of his pals. 'But t' question is, does Lord Middleton know *thee*?'

300

In the days when Rider Haggard's books were 'best sellers' everyone knew Captain Frederick Courteney Selous, the Allan Quatermain of *King Solomon's Mines*. He went to his death, not in King Solomon's mines, but while leading his company into action in World War I. For years he had been known as the prince of explorers and big-game hunters, a pioneer in Central Africa, a trader and naturalist with an iron nerve and more escapes and adventures to tell of than probably any other man of his day. His lectures to the children at the Foundling Hospital are still talked of, for crowds flocked to hear him—the close-lipped man with silver hair, blue eyes, a pointed beard, and an icy reserve except when he opened his heart to little folk. He was always a walking puzzle, violently opposed to every doctrine, always different. In his lectures, the lion or tiger was always the hero of the piece, he the villain apologizing for shooting it.

It was popularly said that he was the bravest man alive, and perhaps popular opinion has rarely been nearer the truth.

Yet there was a day when Selous, strolling quietly across the Strand with heavy traffic surging by, grabbed his companion's arm, and said nervously, 'You know, *this just terrifies me.*'

301

One day, says Aesop, a lion was sleeping in his den when a mouse scampered over his nose. The lion, thus aroused from sleep, clapped his paw on the little intruder, and was about to put him to death, when the mouse begged him to spare its life. The lion, amused at the fright of the little creature, at once let it go.

Now, a short time after this, the lion, while ranging the woods in search of his prey, was caught in a snare. He tried with all his strength to escape, but finding he could not do so, he set up a roar which made the whole forest echo again. The mouse, hearing the voice and recognizing it as that of its former friend, ran to the spot, and assured the lion he would soon be free. So, with its sharp teeth the mouse gnawed at the fastenings of the snare, and thus set the lion at liberty.

302

Dumas' story of *The Count of Monte Cristo* is well known and finely done, but it remains fiction, whereas the story of Hugo Grotius is fact.

Who knows anything of Hugo today? We *should* know much of him, for three hundred years before the League of Nations was born he was telling men that war was foolish, urging them—in a famous book which the nations are still too dense to understand—to find other ways of settling disputes.

It is not with Hugo's teaching that we are concerned, however, but with a single incident in his life. As a young man he talked fearlessly about religion at a time when men had to believe what they were told, and it was little wonder that the famous Dutchman got himself into such trouble that he was sentenced to imprisonment for life.

So charming was he, however, that soon after he had entered the shadow of Louvenstein Castle he made friends with his warders, gained permission for his wife to stay in prison with him, and presently had his room piled high with books, the gifts of his many friends.

Every now and then some of the books were packed into a trunk and carried out. 'More books from Grotius!' the warders would declare, laughingly. 'More books!' At first they examined the trunk every time it came in or out, but after a time the soldiers at the gates grew tired of handling books, and said, with a great pretence of importance, 'Pass, books from Grotius!' It was a rare joke!

Month after month the books came and went. Then one day Hugo's wife packed a heap of books in the trunk, the guard who was watching her remarking that he couldn't for the life of him tell how Grotius could read such dry stuff. At last the trunk was filled, so the guard went off to fetch a couple of soldiers to carry the trunk out. *That was Hugo's opportunity*. The books were taken out quickly and hidden in a corner. Into the trunk jumped Grotius, and down went the lid. His wife made some excuse—Grotius had gone to another room, for he had free access to several parts of the prison—and without more ado the soldiers went off with their burden.

'Hello,' said the guard at the castle gate. 'More books? Pass, books from Grotius!'

It was a rare joke!

303

A motor-cyclist swerved suddenly, mounted the grass verge, crashed through a fence and came to a halt against a brick wall. His machine was smashed, and he himself—as he realized when he 'came to'—was badly knocked about. Opening his eyes, he saw a small girl holding her younger brother by the hand. 'Please,' begged the small girl, 'would you mind doing it again? Alfie laughed like anything!'

304

A traveller who arrived at King's Cross between three and four in the morning took a taxi to Russell Square. 'Queer job, yours,' he remarked. 'Do you *ever* go to bed?'

'Oh, yes, sir. I'll be snoring my head orf about dinnertime.'

'And how do you like your job?' asked the traveller.

'Oh, not so bad, sir, really. Get used to it after a bit. Not arf bad, it isn't. It's easier driving round London in the early hours than it is about noon; and then, of course, sir, there's the sunrises wot most folks miss. Not arf beautiful some of 'em, sir. Sort of make a chap feel as if he's in church, if you understand.'

305

Is it too late to tell a little tale of the immortal days of Dunkirk?

One summer evening a vicar in the south-east of England walked into his church and was surprised to find a small boy kneeling before the altar. Presently the boy stood up, turned, and hurried towards the door. In the porch, the vicar smiled as he asked the boy what he had been doing.

'Oh,' was the reply, 'I've been coming every evening this week, sir. You see, I was afraid my Daddy might be left on Dunkirk beaches, so I came to ask God to bring him safely home. *He has done!* And so,' concluded the boy, 'I came along this time just to say thank you.'

306

Her dream came true.

The dreamer was a poor girl, Eugenie Feneglie, who was born in Toulon in 1868. She was clever and very charming, and she had a wonderful voice. Left an orphan, she tried to earn her living by singing in cafés, pleasing the patrons so much that she dreamed of making a success in Paris.

So to Paris she went. Her quest for fame and fortune seemed hopeless at first, but she found both more quickly than she had ever expected. A theatre manager gave her a part in which she excelled, captivating all Paris. Wealth flowed to her hands. All who knew her delighted in her company, for she was gracious and good as well as talented. Every door in Paris was open to her.

Yes, her dream had come true. Known as Eve Lavalliere, she was rich and famous. But suddenly she vanished. Paris looked everywhere for her. She was not to be found. One day, however, someone came upon a woman in a village among the Vosges. She was poor, and she was helping poor people—nursing the sick and scrubbing floors for old women who could not get down on their knees. She was Eve Lavalliere.

'Come back!' Paris begged.

But Eve said, 'No. Paris can give me everything except one thing—happiness.'

So Eve remained the friend of the poor till she died in 1929.

307

I overtook him late one afternoon. 'Going home?' I asked.

He said he was; so I went along with him, and presently we turned off into a rather dull street. 'By the way,' I remarked, 'is this a short cut? It doesn't seem very inviting.'

He grinned. 'I don't come this way because I want to see it,' he explained. 'I come so that I may be seen.'

A few minutes later we looked up at the window of a dingy house. Someone waved to us, and we both waved back.

'I always make a point of coming this way if I can,' my friend explained. 'The man we waved to is a cripple—he's been in bed twelve years. Few folk ever call to see him, and life must be terribly dull. He knows I usually leave business a little after five, and he always looks out for me.' My friend paused; then he added, 'I'm not much to look at, but if it gives anyone any pleasure to see me, they're welcome!'

A contributor to the *Cornish Guardian.*

308

Everywhere in the park were the unmistakable signs of the litter lout. 'What in the world's the cause of this outrageous state of affairs?' demanded a local councillor, addressing one of the park keepers.

'Well, sir,' was the reply, 'last night we was told to distribute handbills requesting the public to keep our open spaces tidy . . . and this 'ere's the morning after.'

309

The Club Aluminium Company of Chicago was almost a 'Depression' casualty of the early thirties. The firm owed nearly six hundred thousand dollars and the number of its employees had dwindled from a thousand to twenty-four. Both creditors and stockholders were writing off their seemingly inevitable losses. But less than a decade later every cent of debt had been paid off, the volume of trade had risen to an annual four million dollars, and stockholders were again realizing a return on their investment. Club Aluminium is now going strong.

Some people called this survival and come-back a miracle of management, but the man who did it gives credit to the Sermon on the Mount. It was this 'manual of human relations' that gave Herbert Taylor the business concepts which took Club Aluminium from the verge of bankruptcy, and put it well on the sunny side of solvency.

Before taking over Club's management Taylor had no connection with it except as a customer. He held an executive position with another company that bought large quantities of Club Aluminium products. He had what most people called an assured future, with a five-figure salary at a time when every dollar looked as big as a wagon wheel. So, when the presidency of the defunct company was offered him and he accepted, many people wondered why he had made such a choice.

The underlying philosophy of the Sermon on the Mount was not only responsible for Taylor's later success with the company but was partly the reason for his taking it over in the first place. Some of the employees of the near-bankrupt company had originally accepted positions with it on Taylor's recommendations. Since most business concerns were then turning off men and hiring practically none, the Club Aluminium employees had nowhere to go. When the presidency was offered, Taylor felt he could not let the employees down.

As soon as he took over, Taylor called his department heads, and together they worked out the Four-Way Test, based entirely on the pattern of human relations and honest dealings set out in the Sermon on the Mount. It became a rule of faith and practice for all employees. It grew to be so deeply rooted in their consciousness that it was continually in their minds as they weighed every step of their business operations.

Here are the four test questions:

1. Is it the truth?
2. Is it fair to all concerned?
3. Will it build goodwill for the company and better friendship for our personnel?
4. Will it be profitable for all concerned?

The 'all concerned' clause included everybody—management,

employees, suppliers, customers and even competitors.

Employees were regularly paid a share of the profits in addition to wages, and this Golden Rule practice inspired them to work harder to make sure that there would be profits to share. They were encouraged to offer suggestions for improving the company's business, and to feel free to offer criticism of their company's employee relations. If an employee had to be discharged, he was told frankly why it was necessary. If he had qualifications that did not fit into the company's set-up but might be useful elsewhere, the management went out of their way to help him to obtain the right job.

In buying material or supplies, Taylor never asked other firms to sell at a loss even if they were in a trap. In one case a printer who got out a large order of promotional literature for Club Aluminium discovered after he was paid that he had underestimated his cost, and had lost a sizeable sum. Taylor accidentally learned of this, and promptly sent the printer a cheque to make good the deficit.

Under his Four-Way Test, Taylor tried to sell his aluminium ware at a price that was fair to distributors and consumers, and he did all he could to avoid hurting his competitors. He was certain that if he could put out high-quality pots and pans, and create a demand for them at a price which would not undercut a rival, the goods would sell on their merits. He impressed that idea on every dealer who handled his products.

One of the hardest places to apply the Four-Way Test was in advertising. The same screening questions were applied to every advertising layout placed on Taylor's desk. 'Is it the truth?' 'Is it fair to all concerned?' He rejected many a beautifully illustrated and persuasive advertisement because he thought it would give the wrong impression, even though it stuck to the literal truth.

One day Taylor picked up and read for the first time an expensive promotional pamphlet that his officials were already sending out. At first glance it seemed to be unimpeachable. It truthfully pointed out the advantages of waterless cooking for which Club Aluminium products were recommended; but buried deep in the text were a few sentences telling of the shortcomings of the boiling method. Taylor immediately ordered circulation of the pamphlet to be stopped, and went to some expense to recall every one of the booklets which had already gone out.

'We don't need to knock our competitors who sell equipment for cooking by the boiling method,' he explained. 'We sell our goods on their merits.'

One day during the darkest part of the Depression, and at a time when the company was still struggling, it was offered what looked like a windfall—a purchase order for half a million dollars' worth of Club Aluminium products. It was hard to put this bit of luck to the Four-Way Test, but they did. It hit a snag on Point 2: 'Is it fair to all concerned?' The company wishing to buy the half million dollars' worth of aluminium ware planned to use it in a premium-promotion scheme. Taylor reasoned that if the aluminium products were virtually given away to stimulate the selling of somebody else's goods, it would be harmful to Club dealers who were trying to sell the same aluminium ware at a going price. So—much as it hurt to do so—Club Aluminium turned the offer down.

Has this policy of rigid honesty paid?

Club Aluminium's phenomenal growth is the answer to that question. When Taylor took over he showed his faith in his principles by investing his entire savings of six thousand dollars in the enterprise at a time when no bank would risk a cent on it.

There is no doubt about it: Most of us prefer to do business with those who practise Christian principles.

ROSS L. HOLMAN: *Good Business*, 1953.

310

Two Yorkshiremen trudged from Leeds to London. Utterly worn out and thoroughly dejected they limped into Barnet, only to learn that they had still another ten miles to go.

'It's noa use, Bill,' groaned one, sitting by the roadside and caressing his aching feet. 'Ah'm dead beat, lad. Ah'll nivver tramp another yard, Ah tell thi.'

'Dang it,' replied Bill, 'tha mun stick it somehow. Wheer's thi courage, lad? We'll go on, thee an' me—efter all, *it's nobbut five mile apiece*!'

311

A young man died at twenty-five during World War I. But then, thousands of men died at twenty-five in those dreadful years. They died, and were forgotten by the world, remembered perhaps only in one or two sorrowing homes. They had lived their little lives and had gone the way to dusty death, and even if they had been good soldiers the war machinery had moved on relentlessly; the living were more use than the dead, so the dead were soon out of mind.

This young man was Gilbert Talbot, son of that great scholar and humble soul, Bishop Talbot, whose home at Rochester was the centre of many loyalties. The son, like the father, was deeply and superbly spiritual. He was also practical. Though a dreamer, he was never idle, and his heart went out to all who suffered.

When the war came, Gilbert Talbot found a job for himself, and did it with heart and soul. He carried the message of Jesus into the lives of men who prayed one day and died the next. There was something about him which made his goodness attractive, something which made men love him and trust him and believe in the word he had for them.

Then he was killed, and his work should have ceased. Strangely enough, it really only began then, for Tubby Clayton founded Toc H to his memory; and now the rare spirit of that young soldier is a power in the lives of thousands in every continent who live the life of the lamp.

312

One of the few fine things done in those wretched days when Englishmen had no better sport than that of fighting Frenchmen, is linked with the name of Edward the Third's Queen, Philippa.

Calais was at last in English hands, and Edward the Third, angered by the time it had taken him to capture it, was eager to punish the city. Then came six men with ropes round their necks. They were six of the chief citizens, among them Eustace St Pierre. They begged the King to hang them but to spare the city.

'Go,' cried the King to an officer, 'lead these men to execution.'

At that moment a sound of trumpets was heard—Queen Philippa had arrived with new forces from England, and Sir Walter Mauny lost no time in telling her what was happening. As soon as Philippa heard of the six men of Calais, she hastened to the King, saying, 'My Lord, the question I am to ask touches not the lives of a few mechanics, but respects the honour of the

English nation, the glory of Edward, my husband, my king. You think you have sacrificed six of your enemies to death. No, my Lord, they have sentenced themselves, and the stage on which they suffer will be to them a stage of honour, but to Edward a stage of shame.'

These words flashed conviction on Edward. 'I have done wrong, very wrong!' he exclaimed. 'Let the execution be instantly stayed, and the captives brought before us.'

St Pierre and his friends were soon brought in, whereupon the Queen thus addressed them: 'Natives of France and inhabitants of Calais, you have been sufficiently tried. We loose your chains, and thank you for that lesson in humility which you teach when you show us that excellence is not of blood, of title, or of station.'

'Ah, my country!' exclaimed St Pierre, 'it is now that I tremble for you. Edward only attacks our cities, but Philippa conquers hearts.'

313

It was a typical winter night in Russia. A bitter wind swept across the market place of the little town, driving the snow in heavy drifts against the door of the log-built store. High overhead, set in the empty blackness of the sky, the stars, like tired eyes blinded by the whiteness of the snow, blinked away the hours.

Suddenly, borne on the wind across the white plains, sounded the baying of a wolf. To the westward another answered, then another, and soon from all quarters came the howling of wolves maddened by hunger.

Horses, harnessed to a sleigh in front of the store, pricked up their ears and, raising their heads, anxiously sniffed the wind. At that moment the door of the store opened and two men, wrapped in skins and wearing close-fitting caps and leggings, came to the threshold and stood listening.

'The wolves seem well packed tonight, Alex. The sooner we start on the homeward trail the better.'

Alex, a heavily-bearded man, climbed slowly into his seat and carefully wrapped himself round with rugs.

'You're right, Ivan,' he laughed, gathering up the reins. 'We'll have a sharp enough run if the horses get the scent of the wolves.'

Ivan turned from the horses and took his place. Then, with a crack of the whip and the jingle of bells, the sleigh slipped past the store into the white vastness of the plains. Over the frozen ground it flew, on and on until the clear-cut line of the forest drew nearer and nearer.

They were well into the depths of it when Ivan, turning to his friend, exclaimed: 'The wolves have scented us, Alex. They're on our track.'

For some minutes the sleigh raced silently through the keen air. Then Alex spoke, and his voice was hard.

'The horses can't last long at this pace; see, they are flagging even now!' Two or three minutes of tenseness, and he spoke again: 'It's no use; we can't pull ahead of them. Cut one of the horses loose!'

One slash of Ivan's knife and a horse sprang from the traces—the horde of wolves closing on it a moment later.

Ahead the village lights twinkled, but Alex, turning again, saw that it was impossible to out-distance their pursuers. The wolves were gaining fast. Again Ivan unsheathed his knife. 'You have a wife and children waiting for you, Alex. I've no one. I can keep the wolves off long enough for you to reach the village. God speed you, friend!' And with a spring he leapt out.

The sleigh, relieved of his weight, bounded ahead once more; and when at last it stopped in the circle of the village lights, Alex was unconscious.

In the church of the little Russian village is a tablet set in the wall. On it are these simple words: *Sacred to the Memory of Ivan Rosinif. 'Greater love hath no man than this, that a man lay down his life for his friends.'*

My Magazine.

314

Monsignor Contini was once hearing a confession. At the end, the penitent who was kneeling before him said: 'Oh, Father, I was forgetting to tell you that I have stolen a pair of silver buckles.'

'Well, my son,' said Contini, 'you must promise to give them back immediately, or I cannot give you absolution.'

'Oh, Father,' replied the penitent, 'won't *you* have them?'

'Certainly not. I absolutely refuse.'

'But, Father, if when I give them back to their owner, he refuses to accept them?'

'In that case you will be able to keep them.' Then Monsignor Contini gave absolution to his penitent, who went away happily; but when, some time later, Contini left the confessional, he found that his shoes were minus their silver buckles!

THE MARCHESA STELLA VITELLESCHI: *Out of My Coffin.*

315

Few men have left a fairer name than Abraham Lincoln whose splendid life ran out in 1865. Though born in a log cabin, he won his way by sheer merit to White House. His first successes were as a lawyer, and one of the most stirring moments in his life was his vindication of young Armstrong.

The court was crowded for the trial. William Armstrong, son of the woman who years before had darned Lincoln's socks, was accused of manslaughter. He and other young fellows had been drunk, and some of their number appeared as witnesses to prove that in a free fight it was Armstrong who struck the blow which had killed Metzar.

Counsel, having proved that the dead man had been Armstrong's personal enemy, brought witnesses who left not a shadow of doubt that the young man was guilty. 'What time in the evening was it?' asked Counsel of one of the witnesses.

'Between ten and eleven,' was the reply.

'Was it not dark?'

'Yes, but the moon was shining brightly. It was light enough for me to see the whole affair.'

Counsel considered the evidence against Armstrong too strong to admit of reasonable doubt, and the plea allowed the prisoner was short and formal.

Then all eyes were turned on Lincoln—the youthful lawyer with the square jaw and burning eyes. Reviewing the testimonies of the witnesses, he revealed discrepancies and indicated a plot against the accused; and then, raising his voice and throwing his long arm above his head, he cried, '*And your witness testifies that the moon was shining brightly when the deed was done between ten and eleven, but Your Honour's almanac will show that the moon did not rise till an hour later.* Consequently I submit that the whole story is a fabrication!'

After retiring for thirty-five minutes the jury returned the verdict, '*Not Guilty.*'

316

A little maid ran indoors saying: 'Mummy, there's an elephant in the garden!'

Her mother (who seems to have had little understanding of small children) scolded her for telling a lie, adding that the child knew very well there was only an old tree in the garden. 'Go upstairs,' said she severely, 'and tell God you are sorry.'

Up went the culprit; but she was soon down again. 'Well,' her mother asked, 'did you tell God you were sorry?'

'Oh, yes,' was the startling reply, 'but God said: "Don't mention it, Miss Green. I took it for an elephant myself at first." '

317

Promenade Concerts have been a feature of the musical world since 1895, but the idea was anticipated over a century and a half ago when George the Third gave his patronage to a series of concerts in Hanover Square. The King, who was greatly interested, pressed his ministers to attend. He is said to have urged Lord North to go, but his lordship declined. 'Well, your brother, the bishop, goes,' said the King.

'I know,' said Lord North. 'And if I were as deaf as the bishop I might go, too.'

318

Most of us go through life with unsatisfied longings to do thrilling things—driving railway engines, appearing on television, or swimming the Channel. Some of us, therefore, may envy the achievement of Field-Marshal Lord Alexander who, when Governor-General of Canada, opened a firemen's handicraft exhibition at a fire station in Ottawa. Part of the station equipment included one of those very exciting slippery poles down which firemen slide from their bedrooms to reach the engine below.

To the amazement of sixty distinguished and dignified visitors, *down the pole His Excellency came sliding*! 'I've *always* wanted to go down one of those things,' he explained to the startled onlookers.

319

Speaking at Baltimore on the spirit of British women, Lady Astor said of the 1914-18 war:

A friend of mine in Devon had two splendid boys killed in the first three years of war. In the last year American sailors were stationed at Plymouth, and my friend and her husband did everything they could to make them feel less lonely. She entertained as many as she could for Christmas, and hardly ever was her house without them.

About January 1918, just before one of the fiercest battles, she said, 'I don't believe I could go on if Jack was taken.'

Next morning a wire came saying Jack, her last son, had been killed.

That was a Monday. On Thursday my friend had planned a party for the gallant American sailors. When she arrived at Plymouth, and I saw her white, stricken face, I begged her not to have the boys—they would remind her of Jack.

She looked at me with eyes I can never forget, and said, 'But, Nancy, they're a long way from home—we *must* do all we can.'

So the party went on; and the boys, never guessing her sorrow, were charmed by the cheerful kindness of their hostess.

320

Two Chinese coolies were having a heated argument in the street, and a crowd of interested spectators quickly gathered. Among the onlookers was an English tourist who, after watching and listening for several minutes, remarked to his Chinese guide that he expected the two men would begin fighting any moment.

'I doubt it,' replied the Chinaman. 'You see, the man who strikes first is thereby admitting that he has run short of ideas.'

321

This dialogue took place in a Liverpool police court a few years ago. Is it not proof that there actually *is* honour among thieves?

An ex-burglar, found loitering as though intent on picking pockets, appealed against a sentence for loitering.

Ex-burglar (after admitting a previous conviction for housebreaking); I would never stoop so low as to pick pockets.

Judge: What do pickpockets think of housebreakers?

Ex-burglar: I can tell you what housebreakers think of pickpockets.

Judge: You seem to place housebreakers above pickpockets?

Ex-burglar: I think it is a more honourable profession.

Judge: You mean housebreaking?

Ex-burglar: If you pick a man's pockets you may be taking the bread out of his children's mouths. If you break into a big house and steal diamonds you are not taking bread out of the children's mouths.

Judge: But if you break into a small house and take every penny a man possesses?

Ex-burglar: I would never do that.

322

From France comes the old story of Launomar, a shepherd of Chartres who died in 593 after being head of a monastery at Corbion. While the monastery was being built, Launomar lived in a wattle hut, a few devout monks with him.

One evening robbers stole the only cow the monks possessed, but as they were driving it from the meadow to the woods they lost their way, and when night fell they found themselves, to their consternation, again outside Launomar's hut. The monks closed in upon them, and there was no escape. Brought into Launomar's presence, the robbers fell on their knees and asked forgiveness.

'My kind friends,' replied Launomar, 'I want to thank you for bringing back our strayed cow. You must be tired and hungry. Pray sit down with us at supper, and stay the night in our hut.'

323

It was the 6th March 1835 when two men stood looking at each other, each feeling he would have given all he had to be anywhere else in the world.

Thomas Carlyle had been working for five months on his book, *The French Revolution*. Having stirred himself out of his moodiness and gloom, he had toiled night and day at the first volume, and when it was finished he had sent it (the only copy he had) to his friend, John Stuart Mill. The work was a desperate attempt to make a name and a sum of money; it meant everything to the author.

They say Mill's housemaid burnt the manuscript, using it to make a fire. Anyhow, Mill lost it. So he called on Carlyle, stayed two hours longer than he had intended, and made his confession. Carlyle would have taken a blow in the face more readily.

But he did what only a strong man could have done. After a period of depression, he compelled himself to turn once more to the task. Beginning all over again, he at last triumphed gloriously, giving the world a salvaged masterpiece.

324

Over one of the shops in a Lancashire town hung a clock, and every morning a man on his way to the cotton mill stopped outside, set his watch, and then went on. One day the owner of the shop happened to be standing at his door. 'Morning, lad,' said he. 'I notice there's never a day when you don't set your watch by my clock.'

'Aye, that's so,' replied the man. 'You see, I'm t' chap that blows t' buzzer at t' mill, and I've got to make sure I have the right time.'

'Well, by gum,' exclaimed the shopman, 'if that doesn't beat t' band! An' here's me been puttin' my clock right every day by t' buzzer!'

325

Georg Christian Neumark, then a very young man, was on his way to matriculate at the University of Königsberg when the party he was with was attacked and robbed by highwaymen. Neumark lost all his possessions except his prayer book and a very little money, and though he afterwards sought employment at Magdeburg and in three other German cities, he had no success. In the depth of winter he arrived at Kiel and was there befriended by a pastor who eventually secured for him a post as tutor to a judge. This turn of fortune's wheel proved to be the beginning of a series of successes, and on the day that he was appointed tutor, Neumark wrote the famous hymn, *Leave God to order all thy ways*, which quickly became immensely popular in Germany, and is now sung the world over.

326

In 1938 Yorkshire lost a wild-flower man, killed with a fellow scientist when a plane crashed in Tanganyika.

He was B. D. Burtt, who stood over six feet, and was an old boy of Ackworth School. As botanist of the Tsetse Research Department of the Tanganyika Government, he gathered thousands of flowers, sending over 30,000 specimens to all parts of the world. His love of flowers and all natural objects grew up with him from his earliest years; and those who knew him at Ackworth recall a remarkable race in which he ran.

Every year the school watches the famous Badsworth Run, and one year B. D. Burtt, who had longer legs than any other boy, ran in that race. It is now a tradition of the school that he outstripped everyone, and that he would have set up a new record if some flowers had not attracted his attention as he went panting along. Unable to resist them, he turned aside to gather a few, and then sprinted for the winning post, *arriving first.*

327

It was a sad day when Tom had to leave home for his period of Army training. His widowed mother dreaded it—and who can blame her? She kept a village shop, and one morning the shop door remained closed long after nine o'clock. The little body accompanied her son to the bus stop, and there the two waited in the rain. Half an hour later there was an awkward period of waiting on a railway station platform. In a way it was a relief when the guard blew his whistle, and the lad got into the compartment. His mother smiled bravely, waved, and stood watching till the train was out of sight.

Then she turned, walked briskly along the platform, dabbed her eyes, and tried to look unconcerned. Outside the station was the Vicar's wife. 'Oh, hello,' said she. 'Fancy seeing you! Care for a lift back?'

So the little widow travelled by car . . . the Vicar's wife chattering all the way, and somehow reviving the spirits of the lonely wee woman, cheering her, giving her something to look forward to, enabling her to open the shop and smile over the counter.

One need hardly add that it was not merely by chance that the Vicar's wife happened to be outside the station at that particular moment.

328

Once upon a time a little girl walking in the New Forest came upon her old friend, Roger, the shepherd. The good man was having much trouble with his sheep, and the child stopped to ask the reason. 'Where's Cap, your sheep-dog?' she inquired.

'Cap, Missie? He's in a bad way. I don't know what to do. Some boys have thrown stones at him and injured his paw so terribly that I think I shall have to hang him. I can't let him go on suffering like this.'

'Oh, don't say *that*. Let me have the key to your cottage, and I'll see if I can do anything for him,' begged the child.

The key was given, and the little girl hurried through the wood till she came to the shepherd's cottage. There she found Cap. The vicar, who was visiting next door, helped her with her work. She lit a fire, and with hot water fomented the injured leg. Then, begging an old petticoat from a neighbour, she used it as a bandage. Before she returned home she had done much to comfort the dog.

Next day she called again to look at the injury; and she kept on taking care of Cap till he was well enough to help Roger to look after the sheep.

She was Florence Nightingale.

329

During the retreat from Mons in World War I, a British regiment, worn out by weeks of constant fighting, collapsed in the square of St Quentin, too exhausted to care if they were captured. Lieutenant-General Sir Tom Bridges knew the advancing German army was close behind, yet it seemed impossible to rally men practically unconscious from fatigue.

Facing the square was a deserted toy shop. In a few minutes Sir Tom appeared, a toy drum slung about his neck and a shrill penny whistle clamped in his teeth. Playing the *British Grenadiers* and *Tipperary*—with flourishes—he marched round the square. Weary heads began to lift inquiringly from the cobblestones; and as the soldiers slowly sat up, Sir Tom's trumpeter dealt out the shop's supply of mouth organs. In ten minutes the regiment, weariness forgotten, was tootling *Tipperary* for dear life as it marched behind Sir Tom's penny whistle to safety.

330

The present is always an anxious time, and we may, therefore, be tempted to put off any ambitious project in the hope that tomorrow will be more propitious. That is essentially cowardly. What we need is faith and courage enough to challenge the present in the manner of that grand old squire, Sir Robert Shirley of Staunton Harold in Leicestershire. Over the doorway of the church he built—believed to be the only one erected during the Commonwealth—is this inscription:

In the year 1653, when all things sacred were throughout the nation either demolished or profaned, Sir Robert Shirley, Baronet, founded this church, whose singular praise it is to have done the best things in the worst times, and hoped them in the most calamitous.

331

Two brave men stood on the floating landing-stage at Liverpool. They were father and son, and the ordeal they went through was more painful than any words can tell.

The ship's siren sounded. 'Oh, well,' said the elder, 'I guess it's good-bye. God bless you, son.'

'And you. . . . Thanks for everything, Dad.'

They shook hands formally and in silence. 'Looks a bit like rain,' added the elder.

The younger glanced upwards. 'Yes,' said he, 'it might be a shower.'

Then he took quick strides up the gangway, the elder man remaining just long enough to wave before he turned on his heel and walked off briskly, erect, dry-eyed.

It had been hard, terribly hard, to part; but he was glad and thankful, and perhaps just the least bit proud, that he had gone through with it without breaking down; that all along he had insisted on his son accepting the appointment abroad; and that the boy had gone off happily and completely ignorant of the cancer from which he, the father, was suffering. Yes, it was indeed, 'Good-bye . . . good-bye for ever.'

The parting had been difficult for the son also; and he too, up there on the ship's deck, was glad and thankful the ordeal was over—and perhaps the least bit proud that to the end he had deceived the one who had so gallantly tried to deceive *him*. For the younger man had been told by the family doctor that there was no hope of his ever seeing his father alive again.

332

Who does not know the story of Zutphen?

Made Governor of Flushing in 1585, Sir Philip Sidney sailed for Holland, where he took part in some fighting and led a successful skirmish. Then came the battle of Zutphen, fought on a foggy morning, Sidney leading his company of men against the Spaniards. Suddenly the fog lifted and Sidney found himself a target for the enemy whose bullets whistled over his head. His horse was killed under him. He mounted another, and led his men with glorious courage. He was wounded, but kept his horse for a time, ordering the attack, directing his men though he was fast becoming weaker and more feverish.

When at last he was lifted to the ground, a cup of water was brought for him. He raised it to his parched lips—his fever now high, his wounds throbbing—and was about to drink greedily when he caught sight of a common soldier following every movement of his hand with longing eyes. Holding out the cup to him he said, 'Take it. Thy need is greater than mine.'

That he was a gallant soldier, a finished poet, a perfect courtier is sometimes forgotten, but these words alone endow his name with imperishable glory. He won immortality in a moment.

333

'Build me a magnificent palace,' said Gondoforus, King of the Indies, speaking to St Thomas. 'Here is gold and silver; build in my absence.'

When the King returned he found that St Thomas had given all the money to the sick and poor. In his anger he ordered the saint to be tortured to death; but the night before the execution Gondoforus dreamed that he himself was in Paradise, where he saw a magnificent palace, the angels saying, 'Behold the palace of King Gondoforus!'

Then the King ran to the dungeon, and set St Thomas free.

334

From France comes this story of the handsome Marquis of Hautmont, a gallant at the Court long years ago. Very proud he was, and proudest of all of his shield on which was written, *Love laughs at locksmiths*.

One day the King noticed that the Marquis and his own daughter, the Princess, were often together. Having no wish that they should marry, he remarked mockingly: 'Those are bold words on your shield. Are they true?'

'They are always true,' the Marquis replied.

'We will see about that,' said the King. 'I will lock the Princess in a tower, and if within a month you can enter, you may marry her. If not, die.'

The Marquis pretended to be filled with fear, but secretly he had a wooden bird made for him by clever craftsmen. It was so big that he could hide in it and play music on his flute. All who heard were amazed, and presently the astonishing bird was shown at Court, the King being so delighted that he bought it as a present for the Princess. No sooner was the bird carried into her presence in the tower than the Marquis hopped out, and said, 'You see, it's always true that love laughs at locksmiths.'

335

In 1950 ten-year-old Larry Lowe, of McMinniville, Oregon, saw notices of a pet show to be held in the city, but alas, he had no pet of his own. Happily, however, he had an idea. So, on the day of the show, Larry appeared with an entry in the 'biggest pet' class—*his four-year-old brother*!

Larry explained that, having no pet of his own, he had entered his mother's pet, for that was what she often called his young brother. The judges nodded, conferred for some time, and at the final adjudication awarded Larry the first prize.

336

My Lord Burghley, England's great Prime Mininster, is dying, and as Queen Elizabeth I (who has little compassion as a rule) is deeply moved by the news that her friend and counsellor is near his end, it is her royal pleasure to go to Exeter House to see him.

Let us watch her. Puffed and slashed sleeves are the height of fashion this year, and Elizabeth wears a gorgeous dress with sleeves puffed and slashed in wondrous style. Marvellously attired, richly jewelled, ropes of pearls about her neck, she is, at a glance, the first lady in the land. Moreover, high head-dresses are the order of the day, and Elizabeth sees to it that hers is the highest. Studded with diamonds, it towers above her head, so high, so amazing, that surely none but a queen would dare to wear it thus—and a Queen of England, too.

Here she comes, this autocratic, imperious woman, a splendid retinue attending her, ladies and gentlemen in waiting, soldiers to guard her carriage, courtiers to catch only the motion of a finger, pomp and splendour as befits a queen. As her carriage draws up outside Exeter House, servants run to open the door, and Her Majesty, proud, queenly, is conducted up the steps and into the house where my lord, little more than an old man tired of power, is waiting for the end.

Will Her Majesty be pleased to come this way? Will she turn to the right? Will she condescend to follow? Behold, she sweeps with rustle of silk and quiver of light until the door of Lord Burghley's room is thrown open. She is announced. She is about to enter—when tragedy occurs.

You think perhaps a messenger rushes in, falls at her feet and informs her that the Spanish Armada has been sighted? It is nothing so trifling. Is it that a conspirator who has been lurking in the shadows springs out, brandishing a gleaming dagger to strike the Queen in the name of the Roman Catholics? It is something infinitely more serious. In point of fact, it is that either the doorway to Lord Burghley's room is too low or Elizabeth's head-dress too high—anyhow, *she cannot get in.*

Was there ever a difficulty like this in the world before?

What consternation ensues! What a hubbub there is! Shall carpenters be called and the door made higher? Shall servants make a litter and bring out my Lord Burghley? What *can* be done? The courtiers whisper and look askance; the ladies in waiting are all a-flutter. Is there no one in the land with wit enough to get us out of this dilemma?

See, here is a servant of My Lord. A bold man he is, brilliant enough to have a place in Parliament, one might think. Falling on one knee (as the solemn historian, to whom we are indebted for this account, is careful to tell us) he makes a suggestion which none had dared to proffer. In short, he is brave enough to say, 'Your Majesty, would it be possible to stoop?'

Who would have thought of it?

Silence falls. Eyes turn to the Queen. She speaks. 'Fellow,' says she, and the speech is characteristic of her, 'for the King of Spain we would not bow our head—*but we will do so for your master*!'

So she got in after all, thank heaven!

337

A famous pianist crossing the Atlantic insisted on having his piano installed in his cabin so that he could practise six hours a day. 'But,' argued a friend, 'surely you can afford not to practise during the few days you'll be at sea? A short break wouldn't affect your playing.'

'If I missed practising one day,' said the great pianist, 'I'd notice the difference. If I missed three days, my public would notice the difference.'

338

The discovery some years ago of Hebrew manuscripts 800 years older than the famous *Codex Sinaiticus* was not only of immense importance to Biblical scholars but also extremely dramatic. The precious manuscripts include a scroll of the Book of Isaiah not known previously either in the original or in translation, and these ancient texts have already thrown a brilliant light on the Scriptures and on the Hebrew language.

It was a summer day in 1947 when a company of Bedouins, carrying goods along the dusty road leading up from the Jordan

Valley to Bethlehem, halted beneath steep sliffs. While eating and drinking they were surprised when one of their number, who had climbed to the mouth of a cave, picked up a broken earthenware jar and so made a discovery that enriched the world. Part of the cave had fallen in, and the Bedouin found more jars beside the one he had seen from a distance. All the jars were cracked or broken, and by the time his companions had joined him he was dragging parcels out of them. The parcels were wrapped in a kind of waxed linen.

Did they contain gold or silver or precious stones? Had the Bedouins stumbled on a fortune? All were excited, but their excitement turned to anger and disappointment when, after tearing off the wrappings, they brought to light nothing except yellow parchments.

By what appeared to be an amazing chance the jars with their wonderful treasures had been found; and by an even more astonishing sequence of events these early copies of the Scriptures escaped destruction. The Bedouins who ransacked the cave were ready to throw away the parchments in disgust until one of their number suggested that what was worth hiding might be worth buying. Thus the Hebrew scrolls were taken to Father Sowmy, librarian at St Mary's Orthodox Convent in the Old City of Jerusalem. A glance at them set him wondering greatly, and one Wednesday afternoon in February 1948 he rang up the American School of Oriental Research in Jerusalem. The telephone was answered by Omar, the cook, who later mentioned to Dr Trevor, the Director, that somebody had some parchments, and would like him to look at them. Dr Trevor was not very interested, and when told that the parchments were 'ancient Hebrew' he became still more sceptical. However, Father Sowmy related the story of their discovery, and Dr Trevor promised to examine the parchments the following day.

Promptly at 2.30 p.m. Father Sowmy, carrying a leather suitcase, arrived at the American School of Oriental Research, and there, in the twinkling of an eye, Dr Trevor realized that in his hands were manuscripts beyond the price of rubies.

As it happened, conditions in Jerusalem were quickly becoming increasingly dangerous. Arab and Jew were at each other's throats. Sniping and firing in the streets were everyday occurrences. Bombs were exploding here and there. Security for the valuable scrolls—as yet untranslated and still awaiting scholarly examination—there was none. So, in secret and behind close doors, the parchments were studied after having been carefully and laboriously repaired. By Easter they had been photographed, and the photographs successfully carried out of the turbulent country and conveyed to America. The original scrolls were smuggled out of Palestine by Father Sowmy himself.

Even today the full significance of this discovery cannot be assessed; but there can be no doubt that in the long story of Bible study no chapter is more thrilling than that of the way in which a treasure hid in a cave was brought out of darkness into the light of day; and how, through skill and devotion, that treasure was preserved from destruction so that its light might illuminate the pages of Holy Writ.

339

A certain man had given such offence that Alexander the Great would not pardon him. Hearing of this Aristotle went to Alexander and said, 'My lord, I will that this day thou shalt be more victorious than ever.'

Alexander answered and said, 'I will.'

Then said Aristotle, 'Thou hast subdued all the kingdoms of the world, but now this day thou art overcome. For if thou be not ruler of thyself then art thou ruled, yet if thou dost rule thyself then art thou victorious, for he that overcometh himself is most strong.'

Alexander, hearing the saying of Aristotle, remitted the offence done and was pleased. Wherefore it is written: *Better is a patient man than a strong man, and he that hath dominion over himself than a getter of cities.*

From a chronicle of the Middle Ages.

340

During the Great War a British destroyer lay pitching and rolling in heavy seas, her engines out of action. At the mercy of a screaming gale, she was in danger of foundering when the captain ordered oil to be poured on the water. While one of the seamen told off for this duty was on deck, a huge wave washed him overboard. No one expected to see him alive again, but—as by a miracle—another wave washed him back.

As one of the officers hurried forward, the seaman picked himself up, sprang to attention, and remarked, 'Sorry, sir; *lost the bucket.*'

341

An incident revealing the spirit of the Dutch people occurred at The Hague one day in 1942 when an officious Nazi marched into a department store and called out, 'Heil, Hitler! Where is the silk stocking department?'

A woman assistant promptly replied, 'God save the Queen! Third floor.'

342

Among the New Hebrides in the south Pacific is the island of Aniwa, where, years ago, every native knew that rain came down from the sky and never came up from the ground.

Yet here was a white man saying that he would bring water out of the depths of the earth. He was a good fellow, this white man, and no one wished him harm; but it was sad that the sun had addled his brain, and that now, quite mad, he was digging a hole in the ground. Rain came *down*; and in any case you could not get water without giving gifts to the Sacred Men, the Rain-Makers.

But the white man went on with his work, though old Namakei, who loved him, posted relays of men to watch, so that if the madness drove him to take his own life they might prevent it.

Day after day the white man laboured, digging a hole in the ground, strengthening the sides so that they should not cave in. No one would go into the well with him, and everyone laughed. If the god of this white man could bring water out of rocks, it would be very wonderful, but it could not happen—everyone knew that.

Twelve feet down the white man was nearly buried by falling earth. Twenty feet down he went, and the natives crowded round to see if he would vanish altogether. Thirty feet down he was working unaided. The patience of the natives was almost worn out, but the perseverance of the white man impressed them. Was he mad after all?

Then, one day there was a shout, a shout of triumph. Everyone rushed to the well, and up came John Gibson Paton with a jug of sparkling water which he offered to old Namakei, the chief. At first the chief drew back. Then he touched the jug. Then he shook it. Then he poured some of its contents on the ground. Then he dared to taste the liquid. 'It *is* water!' he cried. 'It is water brought up from the ground instead of down from the skies!'

A miracle!

343

One day, shortly before World War II, a journalist arrived at a Yorkshire village a mile from the River Ouse. It was a sunny morning in July, and as he parked his car near the churchyard he nodded to two old men who were standing near the lychgate. 'Nice weather,' remarked the journalist.

'Aye,' agreed the two old men.

Carrying his notebook and pencil, the journalist walked across the churchyard, paused to admire the fine old church, and then began to examine the south door. He noted the carving of the Norman arch, and the curious wrought iron on the door itself; and while he was busy making a sketch of some of the details he turned to nod again to the two old men who had come to join him. 'We've been watching you, Mister,' said one.

'Is there something wrong?' asked the other.

The journalist was amused by their curiosity. 'No, there's nothing wrong,' he assured them. 'It's this door, you know. I've come a hundred miles to look at it.'

The two old men seemed impressed; and they were still more impressed as the journalist went on to point out this and that—the beak-heads, the zigzag ornament, the curious faces carved by a Norman sculptor, and the iron-work on the door, one piece resembling a Viking ship, and all of it, as he told them, believed to be eight hundred years old. 'There are very few doors in all England as old as this,' said the journalist with enthusiasm. 'And *this* is one of the very finest. I've often seen pictures of it in books, but today I've come to take a really good look.'

'Now, fancy *that*,' exclaimed one of the old men.

'Aye, fancy that,' repeated the other. 'And to think that me and my pal has lived all our lives in the village, and yet, as you might say, we've never really seen this here door till you come along. Aye, fancy *that*, now!'

344

It is curious that, turning to the end of Sir Walter Scott's life, we come upon a story of his schooldays. But this in itself is significant, for with all the famous novelist had achieved, he recalled shortly before his death what had undoubtedly been a mean trick—one which weighed on his conscience, even if only lightly. Any boy might have done it—for it would have been done unthinkingly; but Sir Walter seems to have been sorry he did it.

As a boy at school he had long desired to beat another fellow in his class, though all his efforts had proved unavailing, the other boy being quicker in every way. One day Scott, very observant even then, noticed that whenever the clever boy was asked a question he invariably fingered a certain button on his waistcoat. There and then the idea popped into Walter's head that without that button his adversary might be vanquished.

By some clever trick the future novelist contrived to cut off the inspiring button, and when the class was questioned soon afterwards, and the brilliant boy was asked a poser, his fingers strayed at once in search of the button. Because the button was missing the bright boy seemed quite at a loss for an answer, but young Walter had an answer ready—and moved up one!

At the end of his life that boy was in the novelist's thoughts. 'Poor fellow,' he said of him. 'I often resolved to make some reparation, but it ended only in good resolutions. He's dead now, I believe.'

345

Abraham Lincoln, on hearing a friend speak angrily of someone, advised him to sit down and put all his abuse into a letter. 'It will do you good,' he said.

When the letter was written it was read to Lincoln, who commended it heartily for its severity. The writer was pleased, and asked, 'How would you advise me to send it?'

'Send it?' said Lincoln. 'Oh, I wouldn't *send* it. I sometimes write a letter like that—it does *me* good; *but I never send it*.'

346

Mrs Moody of Gorton, Manchester, was ironing about seven one Monday evening when Mrs Redshaw, from next door, popped in. 'Ah,' exclaimed Mrs Redshaw as she stepped into the kitchen, 'I guessed as much.'

'What do you mean?' Mrs Moody was not very pleased to see her uninvited guest.

'Why, love, just what I say. I told Herbert at tea-time I was pretty sure you'd be ironing half the night, and, you see, I'm right.'

'Well, you'll be telling me you've second sight next!' snapped Mrs Moody, hardly able to disguise the sneer in her voice.

'Sometimes I think I have,' agreed Mrs Redshaw, quite unperturbed as she threw her shawl over a chair-back, and beamed at Mrs Moody. 'D'ye know, love, I've a sort of feeling my hubby'll surprise us this evening—second sight, may be. Yes, I just happened to be looking out of the back kitchen window, and I saw you taking them clothes off the line, and I reckoned you was late with them, and that you wouldn't want to leave the ironing till tomorrow . . . so I just popped in, love . . . and give us hold of that flat-iron sharp. . . .'

For a moment it looked as if Mrs Moody were going to *throw* the flat-iron at Mrs Redshaw. She scowled. She went very red. Then, suddenly, she turned from the table, covered her face with her hands as she sat by the fire, and sobbed.

Mrs Redshaw went on ironing. Never a word of sympathy. Never a bit of cheer. She continued ironing for five minutes; then, when the shirt was finished and the pyjamas 'well on the way,' as she put it, Mrs Redshaw started talking about the price of meat, and so to the Women's Meeting at the Chapel, and from that to a whisper she had heard about the grocer's daughter. . . .

It was while Mrs Redshaw was ironing the last article that somebody opened the back door—Mr Redshaw, of all people, with something wrapped in newspaper. 'Come on, love,' urged Mrs Redshaw, 'put three plates to warm while I finish this here off. Didn't I tell you my hubby'd surprise us both? Let's have the kettle on, love, and we'll make a cup of tea after us fish and chips. . . .'

The miracle was that Mrs Moody laughed over supper, declaring that her poor old feet were wonderfully rested, and that she wouldn't worry any more because her husband had to be off work another six weeks, and that she felt she had 'go' enough to iron a dozen shirts, and that Mr Redshaw just didn't know what a lucky man he was.

'What, having to live with *her*?' demanded Mr Redshaw. 'There's only *me* could do it! She giving orders about fish and chips for three!'

347

An old farmer who was about to die called his two sons to his bedside, and said, 'My boys, my farm and the fields are yours in equal shares. I leave you a little ready money, but the bulk of my wealth is hidden somewhere in the ground, not more than eighteen inches from the surface. I regret that I've forgotten precisely where it lies.'

When the old man was dead and buried, his two sons set to work to dig up every inch of the ground in order to find the buried treasure. They failed to find it; but, as they had gone to all the trouble of turning over the soil, they thought they might as well sow a crop, which they did, reaping a good harvest.

In the autumn, as soon as they had opportunity, they dug for the treasure again, though with no better result. As their fields were turned over more thoroughly than any others in the neighbourhood, they reaped better harvests than anyone else. Year after year their search continued, and only when they had grown much older and wiser did the sons realize what their father had meant—that prosperity comes as a result of industry.

348

One day Edison was visited by Henry Ford, who, finding some difficulty in opening the garden gate, did not hesitate to say he was surprised that a man with Edison's ingenuity should allow his gate to take so much pushing.

Edison smiled. 'I use that gate for pumping water into the cistern,' he explained. 'Every time someone opens it he raises another gallon or two.'

349

Farmer Jed was sitting on the steps of his porch, moodily regarding the ravages of a cloudburst, when a neighbour pulled up in a wagon. 'Say, Jed,' he yelled, 'your hogs was washed down the creek, and they're all dead.'

'How about Flaherty's hogs?' asked Farmer Jed.

'They're gone, too.'

'And Larson's?'

'All washed away.'

'Huh!' exclaimed the farmer, cheering up. 'Tain't as bad as I thought.'

350

A Leeds man who was on holiday in the Yorkshire dales called for a chat with his old friend, Farmer Pulleyn. The two men walked up a lane, and paused to look over a gate.

'This *is* one of your fields, isn't it?' asked the man from Leeds.

'Aye,' said Farmer Pulleyn.

The visitor hesitated. He was no great judge of horseflesh, but he felt sure the grey mare in the field was a sorry beast. He was surprised to see her there, particularly as Farmer Pulleyn happens to be an expert as far as horses are concerned, and has carried off many a prize at agricultural shows. 'I suppose,' said the man from Leeds diplomatically, 'you'd some special reason for buying the grey mare?'

'Why?' murmured the farmer. 'Is there owt wrang wi' her?' Farmer Pulleyn was grinning, evidently enjoying himself as he leaned on the gate. 'I bought her for forty-five pounds,' he said. 'The chap I bought her off asked forty, but I got my own way in the end.'

The man from Leeds was more puzzled than ever. 'As a rule,' he began, 'a Yorkshireman pays *less* than he's asked, not more. What's the idea?'

'Well,' said Farmer Pulleyn slowly, 'it's *this* way. That there owd mare belonged to Timothy Platts who used to be the carrier in these parts. He gave a tidy sum for her over twenty years ago, and he thought the world of her. But he got too owd himself to keep on, and he went blind a while back. Now he's living with his married daughter. But she's no paddock, so he had to sell the owd mare. He'd let her get out of condition—him not being able to do much for her, you see. Fact is, she wasn't worth a tenner; only I happened to know that he always *thought* of her as she'd been when he looked after her same as if she were an only child. It would have broken Timmy's heart if he'd been able to see her; so I *made* him take more than he asked for her. And, of course, I've always a bit of grass that wants keeping down.'

351

According to *Punch* there was once a man with such unbounded faith in himself that his visiting card bore the words: *Railways built, photographs developed.*

352

I like to visit Mrs Smith.

I call now and then on Sunday afternoon, usually about four, and we have a cup of tea together. It sounds very commonplace, I know; but there it is.

We sit by the fire, this very old lady and I, and we drink our tea, and talk; and presently Mrs Smith slips into a reminiscent mood, recalling the bright days of long ago while I listen and nod and smile and enjoy it all immensely. Somehow, whenever I sit with Mrs Smith I forget the world of today, this torn and harassed and dangerous and unsettled and cruel world, and I seem to borrow from her the placidity of days gone by, to gather a new sweetness and freshness and quietness of spirit.

Sitting with an old lady and drinking tea may sound dull . . . but it can help one to face today with new resolution.

H. L. GEE.

353

Charles Haddon Spurgeon, London's greatest preacher last century, delighted to do good and to take folk by happy surprise. Busy as he was, he found time to visit many who were ill or poor or in need.

Often in his later years he used to tell the story of the closed door, and he would chuckle as he did so. It seems that after he had been preaching in the famous Tabernacle, somebody told him about a poor woman who could do with a little encouragement and some practical help. Nothing appealed more to Spurgeon's warm heart than sharing in a friendly conspiracy behind somebody's back. He listened carefully, made a note of the particulars, and promised that something should be done.

He was as good as his word. Only a few days later he hurried along a street of wretched houses, came to a door, and knocked.

But the door did not open. He knocked again; still the door remained closed, though Spurgeon knew very well that there was almost certainly somebody at home. A third time he knocked. Then he went off; but later in the day he approached the house again, walked briskly to the door, gave one resounding knock, and opened it.

'Well, what do you want?' gasped a nervous and surprised little woman.

'*Want*?' repeated Spurgeon. 'I don't want anything except to make you happy, my dear. I've come with a small gift—and I've reason to think it will be enough to pay what you owe in rent; and I hope there'll be something left over for yourself.'

At this news the woman sank into a chair, and wept. 'Oh,' said she between sobs, 'you've come as an answer to prayer; and to think that when I caught sight of you from the window this afternoon I daren't open the door because I thought you'd come for the rent.'

354

Sir John Rainsford once besought Queen Elizabeth on behalf of four prisoners. Said he: 'I beseech Your Majesty that, among the rest, four prisoners may have their liberty.'

'And who are these?' asked the Queen.

'Madam,' he replied, 'they are Matthew, Mark, Luke and John, who have long been imprisoned in the Latin tongue, and I now desire that they may go abroad among the people in English.'

355

Some years ago John Masefield talked about the making of stories, and one of the things he said was that the best story is the simplest, as we all know from the Bible, for there the immortal tales are told in the fewest and plainest words. To illustrate his point he related what a little girl said when asked what she had learned at Sunday School about the prophet Elisha. Her version was:

Little boys called him names. He told them that if they went on calling him names he would send a bear which would eat them. They did, and he did, and it did.

356

When we were in Lancashire long ago we were taken to see an old clockmaker. He showed us many ingenious pieces of mechanism, and afterwards accompanied us down the garden path. We left him leaning over his gate. He was in his shirt-sleeves, and had a pipe in his mouth.

Twenty years afterwards we happened to be in Lancashire again, and thought we would look at the village (only a few miles from Blackpool) we had visited once before. As we drew near we found everything changed. The green fields had gone, and in their place was a garden city. The quiet main street was busier than we had ever known it in the old days. Familiar landmarks were no more, and in their place were cinemas and banks and flats.

Then, amid all these changed circumstances, we found something which had hardly changed at all. The old clockmaker's house looked just as we had always pictured it; and there, *in his shirt-sleeves*, was the clockmaker himself, leaning over his garden gate and smoking his pipe as if it had never gone out in twenty years.

THE PILGRIM.

357

Somewhere about the year 1850 there lived in Pittsburgh, U.S.A., a Colonel Anderson who was concerned because so many of the local boys had no chance to read really worthwhile books. The Colonel believed that books could shape a boy's ambitions. He wished he could give every lad between the age of ten and twenty a dozen or more good books, but he had not the means. What he did was to invite any of the boys living near his home to use his library. Some refused. Some laughed. Some promised that they would, and never did; a few were grateful for the opportunity.

Among the most regular of all the borrowers was Andrew, a boy who was earning four dollars a week as a telegraph clerk. Every week he returned one book and borrowed another; and it was through Colonel Anderson that he grew up to love books so much and, in later years, to found the Andrew Carnegie Library Fund which has distributed over sixty million dollars.

358

An ambassador found Abraham Lincoln polishing his boots one morning during the Civil War. 'Mr President,' exclaimed the astonished ambassador, 'do you think the President of the United States ought to clean his own boots?'

There was a rare twinkle in Lincoln's eyes as he replied: 'Mr Ambassador, if the President does not clean his *own* boots, whose boots should he clean?'

359

There is a story of Robert Browning and a bore. They were at a dinner-party, and the bore had been claiming the poet's undivided attention for an unconscionable time. At last Robert could bear it no longer. With the acme of courtesy he availed himself of a pause in the bore's recitation to say, 'My dear fellow, how interesting! But I am forgetting my manners and monopolizing you.'

360

Come, let us to the Court today, for it is rumoured that an old hag is to be brought before the Lord Chief Justice on a charge of witchcraft. There should be somewhat to do, and perhaps a black cap, and the promise of a burning in the market place. Come!

Here is the Court, and here is Sir John Holt, one of the finest, and without doubt one of the fairest, judges in seventeenth-century England. This old woman before him is a witchlike creature, and many a judge would send her to the stake after merely looking at her. But we rather think Sir John will have more care—though we should not be surprised if she comes to a bad end, and that right speedily.

Will she plead not guilty? Faith, not she! She is doomed to the fire, then; doomed by her own folly. She does not deny she has magic powers and dealings with the Evil One, and here before Sir John she waves a bit of greasy old parchment which, she mumbles, will cure all manner of disease if you but sleep on it. There's proof for you! To business! She shall burn. . . .

But see, Sir John has taken the paper, and the solemn Court is startled by a burst of hearty laughter. It frightens the dusty clerks and stuffy lawyers, and rings oddly enough in this sad place. What's to do? 'Gentlemen of the Jury, *gentlemen*,' says His Lordship, wiping his poor eyes, 'when I was a lad at Oxford I lodged with this good woman, and being short of money I could think of no way to pay her. At the time she was suffering from ague, and to stop her pestering me I told her I'd give her something to cure the malady—and all others for that matter; and she, simple soul, believed an Oxford scholar must know everything, and was content to take a bit of old parchment I gave her with a dozen meaningless Greek words scrawled across it. "Sleep on it—it'll cure the ague," I told her; and by my faith, here is the very parchment, a scholar's joke turned to witchcraft!'

And now, amid the laughter of the Court, the last witch in England is set free.

361

This is not one of Aesop's fables, but a fable about Aesop, who one day was sitting by the road when a traveller asked, 'What sort of people live in Athens?'

'Tell me where you come from and the sort of people who live there,' Aesop replied.

Frowning, the man answered, 'Oh, I come from Argos. The people are a wretched crowd—liars, thieves, unjust, quarrelsome. I'm glad to shake the dust of the city off my feet.'

'I am sorry to tell you,' answered Aesop, 'that you'll find the people of Athens much the same.'

Presently another traveller came by and asked a similar question, and when Aesop inquired where he came from and what sort of people lived there, he replied, 'Oh, I come from Argos, where everybody is friendly. Honour, truth, virtue, kindness, all these are found among them. I love them all.'

Then Aesop smiled and said, 'Friend, I rejoice to be able to tell you that you'll find the people of Athens much the same.'

362

A famous painter was once asked what he mixed his colours with in order to produce such wonderful effects.

'With brains,' he replied.

363

The village postman had been enjoying a week's holiday with pay. Asked, a few days later, how he had spent the time, he replied: 'Why, the first day I pulls my onions, and the next I digs my taters. All the other days I kind of thinks the temporary postman seemed a bit lonely, so I goes with him on his rounds to keep him company.'

364

In Yorkshire they call it a 'two-up and a two-down'. The cottage is as small as that, and in it live a curate and his wife. The curate is a young man who feels he has a great work to do, and his wife (whose parents are very well off) has thrown in her lot with her husband, and is wishful to help him in whatever he undertakes.

One day a friend remarked to the curate's wife: 'Really, my dear, when I see you living in this little house I can't help feeling sorry for you. . . .'

'Oh,' exclaimed the curate's wife, 'you needn't be sorry for me. John and I are wonderfully happy—and I'd much rather ride *behind* him on a motor-bike than *beside* anybody else in a Bentley!'

365

She was a dear old lady, but rather shortsighted. Passing a newsvendor's board one day in 1943, she peered at the headlines in vain; so, turning to a soldier, she said: 'Excuse me, can you tell me what it says?'

'Certainly, madam,' was the reply. 'It says, *Enemy Driven Back in Tunisia.*'

'The very idea!' snapped the old lady indignantly. 'But *so* like the British! The Italians wouldn't have done *that* to our men.'

The soldier was mystified. 'Done *what*, madam?' he asked.

'Driven the enemy back,' replied the dear old lady. 'They'd have made them walk—and we ought to make the Italians walk, too.'

366

Some Chinese boys were playing a game with a ball when one of them chanced to kick it into the air so that it fell neatly on top of a tall, hollow wooden post. It dropped to the bottom and was lost to sight.

'There,' said his companions, 'you've done it *now*. We'll never get it out.'

They tried poking down the post with long sticks, but they could not reach the ball; and even if they had succeeded they could hardly have hoped to coax the ball to the top.

Meanwhile the boy who had done the mischief went off for a pail of water. When he came back he asked his companions to help him climb the post. Then he poured the water in; and the ball, floating to the surface, was easily regained.

367

We like this story of Lord Rosebery, the famous Archibald Philip Primrose who was born in 1847, and died in 1929 after a wonderfully brilliant career and a life of service.

The story has to do with his very early manhood when—as always—Rosebery was cool in judgment but instant in action, qualities which were to raise him above all party politics and give him an almost unrivalled place among our greatest statesmen.

While crossing from Liverpool to Dublin in company with one of the most faithful friends he ever had, he startled every one by an unexpected action. His friend, Mutton, was overboard—and Mutton was a dog.

'Stop the ship!' cried his lordship.

The captain said he was sorry, but it was against the regulations to stop the steamer for a dog. Had it been a man it would have been different.

'Oh, well, that can easily be arranged,' replied Lord Rosebery, and immediately plunged overboard.

The steamer was stopped—the man and his dog rescued.

368

A newspaper reporter was on his way home in a north of England city one evening when he was stopped by a schoolboy. 'Would you mind telling me the time, sir, please?' asked the schoolboy.

Glancing at his watch, the reporter said: 'Ten past ten, sonny.'

'Gosh!' exclaimed the schoolboy. 'As late as that! My, there'll be trouble when I get back. I dunno *what* Mum'll have to say!'

The reporter was amused. He liked the look of the boy—his knees were grubby; his hair was tousled; he carried a jar of tadpoles, and he had a frank, open face.

'Gosh!' exclaimed the schoolboy again, 'maybe your watch is fast, or the sun went down with a bump. Funny how time flies out of school, isn't it? I just went to get some taddies after tea—only it was a bit further than I'd thought; and there were such a lot of flowers, and the trees and things were full of birds, and I found a nest with eggs in, but I didn't touch 'em. . . . Gosh, time *does* fly, doesn't it?'

It was evident to the reporter that the schoolboy was between two fires—in haste to get home, but afraid of what would happen when he turned up. 'Do you live far from here?' he inquired.

'Just up the next street,' was the reply.

'Tell you what,' volunteered the reporter, 'I'll come along with you.'

'Gosh!' exclaimed the schoolboy. 'That's smashing—Mum'll be nice to you!'

So the reporter accompanied the schoolboy, asked that he might be forgiven, and added: 'I expect, madam, you're proud of a son who loves birds and things?'

'He's a scamp,' replied the prodigal's mother, smiling. 'But I'll let him off just this once.'

369

Oliver Cromwell once suffered a crazy Quaker to insult him in the gallery of Whitehall—and revenged himself by liberating him and giving him a dinner.

370

The ice on the lake was thronged with skaters—a merry crowd whirling and gliding this way and that in the frosty air of a sunny winter's day. Close to the edge of the lake, however, was a small boy clinging desperately to the branches of some overhanging willows. He was much too proud to ask for help, but every time he attempted to skate he slipped and fell.

Eventually an expert on skates took pity on the gallant little fellow who had been trying so persistently for so long. 'Can I help?' he asked kindly.

'No, thank you,' was the reply. 'I'll keep on a bit longer.'

'But you'll be covered with bruises,' went on the grown-up, admiring the boy's pluck and independence. 'Why not give up for the time being, and watch the others?'

'Give up?' repeated the boy. 'No fear! My dad didn't buy me these skates to give up with. He got 'em for me to learn with.'

G. S. SANDILANDS.

371

We did a good stroke of business the other day.

Answering a loud knock at the door we found someone hawking Crown Derby in a wheelbarrow. We dislike hawkers, but we simply *had* to listen to *this* one, for he had golden hair and blue eyes, and a most disarming smile. 'Please do you want any pots today?' he asked.

We could have the cups, it seemed, for a penny; the plate was a penny, also. Without hesitation we bought the lot. It appeared to us that there was a sudden slump in Crown Derby.

'Thank you very much,' said the polite hawker. 'I'm trying to get pennies for my mummy. She says she has to go down on her bended knees to get a penny from my daddy.' Then off he went, a little chap of four, trundling his wheelbarrow and singing to himself.

Happily the Crown Derby was none the worse, and we were later able to return it to the hawker's mother—and very glad she was to get the *pots* safely back in her china cupboard.

THE PILGRIM.

372

Once upon a time there was a wicked baron who hated a little cobbler because he was a cheery soul, and *would* keep on singing all day long while mending boots and shoes in his wretched shop. So the wicked baron threw the cobbler into prison, but there the little man sang as merrily as ever, for he said: 'I'm delighted not to have any work to do!'

Then the wicked baron sent the little cobbler into the castle yard, where he was made to chop wood all day; but he still sang like a bird, for he said: 'It's fine getting all this exercise!'

After that the wicked baron flung the cobbler into a cell as dark as midnight, but the prisoner went on singing, for he said: 'This is just the sort of place I like—nothing to distract one's attention, and all my thoughts on God and His goodness!'

Then the wicked baron had a fit, and died, after which the little cobbler went back to his shop, where he sang, as before, while mending boots and shoes.

373

It is possible that in all the history of the Reformation no moment stands out with such striking splendour as that in which brave Martin Luther—Europe's sixteenth-century Elijah—gave his answer to the Council of Worms.

The trouble began, as all the world knows, over the question of the Pope's right to come between men and salvation. It was brought to a head about 1519 with reference to the sale of indulgences. Luther, that bold, rugged figure standing alone in Europe, was summoned to the Council of Worms. He knew he had every chance of being burnt as John Huss had been burnt at the stake, but he went fearlessly. 'Though there should be as many devils in Worms as tiles on the roofs, yet will I go,' said he.

He went. He was called before an august assembly including the six Electors of the German Empire, eighty dukes, rulers of large territories, thirty archbishops, many Roman prelates, princes, barons, counts, and knights, seven ambassadors (among them those of France and England), the Pope's nuncios, the Archduke Ferdinand, Frederick the Wise and the Emperor Charles the Fifth, a mighty company indeed for one man to face.

'Will you, or will you not, recant?' he was asked.

Without hesitation, Luther replied, 'Since your Most Serene Majesty and your Mightinesses require a simple, clear and direct answer, I will give one. It is that I cannot submit either to the Pope or to the Council, because it is clear as noonday that they have often fallen into error, and even into glaring inconsistencies with themselves. If, then, I am not convinced by proof from Holy Scripture, or by cogent reasons, I neither can nor will retract anything, for it cannot be right for a Christian to speak against his conscience.'

Having said this he looked round the illustrious assembly which held life and death in its hands. '*Here I stand,*' he declared. '*I cannot do otherwise. God help me!*'

374

From the days of sailing ships comes the story of a vessel making the crossing between Liverpool and New York when a storm of exceptional violence arose. Struck suddenly in the darkness by the gale, the ship suffered much damage, her masts being crippled, the vessel plunging so violently that the passengers expected to be drowned any moment.

Amid the tumult and panic, the captain's daughter, a child of eight, slept soundly till the crashing of an immense wave on the foredeck shook the vessel so terribly that she awoke in alarm. 'It's the storm, darling,' said her mother, trying to hide her own terror. 'We've run into a gale.'

'Where's Daddy?' the child asked.

'Daddy's quite all right,' replied the mother soothingly. 'He's at the helm.'

The child lay down again. 'Oh,' said she happily, 'if Daddy's at the helm I needn't worry.'

A minute later she was sound asleep, and sound asleep she remained till morning brought calmer seas.

375

Richard, who is eight, lives on the outskirts of Birmingham. His father thinks the world of him, and until recently he always contrived to meet Richard with the car if the weather were bad.

One lunchtime Richard ran out of school when the rain was coming down hard. Father was at the gate, and as Richard jumped into the car he said, 'Lucky chap, eh, having a car to meet you. . . .'

'I suppose so,' was the unenthusiastic reply.

'*Suppose* so?' Richard's father was nettled.

'Well, I mean,' Richard explained, 'it's nice of you, Dad, but really, you know, the other boys just laugh at me; and I'd much rather *walk* home in the rain!'

376

Talking with the oldest inhabitant of a village, a tourist learned that he was 102. 'Wonderful!' he exclaimed. 'That *is* something to be proud of!'

The oldest inhabitant was too deaf to hear this word of praise, but an acquaintance replied, 'Why, it just depends how you look at it. It's nowt to be proud of when you think he's never done anything else but grow old—and it's taken him a jolly long time to do even that.'

377

In 1943 a pretty girl in a garden gave a farmer a lovely smile.

She was Tini Wierings, and she was sweet seventeen. But the farmer at whom she smiled was old Polling, the ugliest and loneliest man in all the province of Gröningen, in north Holland. Everybody in the village shunned him, for he had a shockingly mutilated face, so repulsive that nobody cared to catch sight of him. That life for Farmer Polling was unutterably wretched we know because he told his solicitor so, adding that only once had anyone been good enough to smile at him. When he died he left Tini Wierings 100,000 guilders (about £10,000) because, passing him in his garden one day, *she had smiled.*

378

A year or two ago a Leeds business man was surprised to receive a Bible which was sent, not to his private address, but to his office, an upper room. After glancing at the gift the Yorkshireman put it on a shelf.

A few weeks later one of his workmen said: 'By the way, sir, I haven't seen you opening that Bible very often.'

'Well, no,' began the business man.

'Why not, sir?'

The owner of the Bible hesitated. At last he said: 'Look here, Joe, would you like to read a chapter with me?'

'I would that, sir,' replied Joe.

So they read one there and then—*and together they have read a chapter every morning since.*

379

When Robert Bruce, crowned King of Scotland at Scone in 1306, was defeated by the English, he took refuge in Rathlin Island, and there, while hiding in a cave, observed a spider trying to climb up the wall to the roof. Six times the spider climbed high but failed to reach the roof; and Bruce (so goes the old story) marvelled at her patience and determination. 'Now shall this spider teach me what I am to do,' said he, 'for I also have failed six times.'

So Bruce watched the spider. He saw her begin to climb for the seventh time, and rejoiced when she reached the roof, and was there able to spin her web. Thus encouraged, he left the coast of Ireland, gathered three hundred followers, landed at Carrick, surprised the English garrison at Turnberry Castle by attacking at midnight, defeated the Earl of Gloucester, and in two years won so much of the kingdom that Edward III eventually acknowledged Scotland's independence.

380

During World War II a report was received at a station of the R.A.F. Coastal Command that a large German bomb had fallen in a field some miles away. As it had failed to explode, an officer and a corporal set out to investigate.

'We'll approach it singly,' said the officer. The corporal

offered to lead the way, but the officer would not hear of it. Dusk was falling when they came to the field.

'Excuse me,' said the officer, 'are those bulls?'

'I believe they are,' was the reply.

'I tell you what,' the officer said nervously, '*you* lead the way past the bulls, and *I'll* lead the way up to the bomb.'

381

He's just an old cobbler in a small town in the north of England —his cobbler's shop nothing more than a wooden shed. He hasn't got on in the world, but he is honest and God-fearing, and what he lacks in education is more than made up by his mighty faith and his love of all things good.

It was this old cobbler who talked to Richard in such a way that a year or two ago he began to think about entering the Ministry. 'I cannot afford to go to College,' said Richard.

'God will find a way,' said the old cobbler.

'I'll never find time to prepare myself,' said Richard.

'I'll pray for you,' said the old cobbler.

'I'll never have courage to stand up in a pulpit,' said Richard.

'God will supply your need,' said the old cobbler.

Last year a way did open for Richard. The money he needed came unexpectedly. He studied and was accepted by the College authorities; he found courage to preach his trial sermon.

Just before he left home for his training for the Ministry, he visited the old cobbler, who said: 'You don't know how happy I am about this, Dick. You see, when I was young I wanted to enter the Ministry, but somehow things didn't work out that way. Maybe I wasn't meant to be in the limelight—just a scene-shifter in the wings. And now you're going to preach the Gospel I want you to promise me one thing. While you're in College —and afterwards, if I'm still here—I want you to let me mend your shoes for nothing. I'd like to think that when you're in the pulpit you're standing in shoes I've mended for love, and that when you visit the sick and needy, you're walking in shoes I've made strong with prayer.'

382

A teacher sent a note to ask why Tommy had not been to school for a week.

'Please, miss,' wrote Tommy's mother, 'he won't be fit to come for another day or two. He hasn't even been able to go to the pictures yet.'

383

Opening an exhibition of Rabindranath Tagore's drawings in London, Lord Zetland told how the famous Indian writer found, by accident, that he had a gift for making pictures. He had given up his best years to his pen, writing books and plays and verses, enriching the world with noble thoughts finely and beautifully expressed; but one day he made a blot.

A sheet of paper was apparently ruined by this unsightly circle of ink. Instead, however, of the blot being the end of a little piece of work, it became the beginning of a big piece, for the poet began to draw round the blot in order to change it from a blemish to a thing of beauty. In so doing he found his skill as an artist. Later he developed it.

384

Yvonne had mapped out her future with childish simplicity and certainty. 'When I am really old,' she told her mother, 'I shall have *two* husbands—one to work in the garden and get all messy, and one to keep himself nice and tidy, and sit in the lounge with me.'

385

I called to see a friend. He was not at home, though his wife expected him back almost any minute. So I went into the lounge and was there entertained by my friend's small son, Peter, aged five. Peter was playing with his model tractor. 'You like tractors?' I asked.

'Yes,' said Peter. 'And I like trains. I've got a clockwork train. And I like bricks. I build houses and stations and things.'

'Good,' said I. 'And what else do you like?'

'Oh, I like painting, and cutting things out with scissors, and sticking things—only I get messy.'

I nodded. 'Tell me,' I said, 'what do you like most of all?'

To my astonishment Peter looked up, smiled, and said in the

quaint and surprising way a child sometimes will, 'Oh, what I like best of all is *doing things for people and making them happy.*'

H. L. GEE: *Of Countless Price.*

386

The old lady lived in what used to be called a workhouse. She had gone there when she was twenty, and she had stayed in year after year, no relatives ever going to see her or talk to her or tell her the news; no one ever saying they loved her; no one calling to take her out for half a day. In fifty years she had never once had a visitor and had never once received a letter.

But one day she received a post card!

It was sent by one of the nurses who was then on holiday, and it reached the good old soul three days before she died. It was the most wonderful thing in her life—*a post card*! It cost a penny to buy and, in those days, a penny to send; and it made her happier than anything had ever done in all her seventy years. That post card was read to her over and over again. She held it in her hand as her life ebbed out. She clutched it as she died; and when they carried her to her grave, the post card went with her.

387

One day in March 1949 a mouse wished to cross Fenchurch Street, London. The mouse paused on the pavement, and when a policeman on point duty noticed it, he immediately raised his hand, thereby halting cars and buses until the timid little creature scurried across the busy road in safety.

388

There is a lovely story of a little incident which happened as John Constable travelled up from East Bergholt for the last time. He had been to see his native village, and was riding in a coach with two passengers. As they passed the vale of Dedham the artist said how beautiful it was.

'Yes, sir,' replied one of the two passengers. 'This is Constable's country.'

The words must have been like music in John Constable's ears.

Already Suffolk was being called *his* country. At last he had opened the eyes of the blind to the glory in their midst.

389

When King George V was a young naval lieutenant on board H.M.S. *Thrush*, with no thought of the future before him as King, he wrote in a friend's Bible:

The secret of life is not to do what one likes, but to try to like what one has to do.

It was a counsel he followed in his own life when duty called him to the heavy responsibilities of a throne.

390

Mazzini, founder of the Society of Young Italy, was thrown into prison, the guard being ordered to watch him closely. But the revolutionary gave no trouble and made no attempt to escape. Indeed, he spent all his time gazing at the blue Mediterranean, and making friends with a finch which came daily to his window.

Suspicious authorities assumed that the little bird was being used by the prisoner in order to send messages to his followers. Accordingly he was removed to a different cell; but still the tame finch hopped in at the window. Again he was removed, but again the finch followed. The authorities then determined to catch the finch and kill it. Luckily, however, Garibaldi rescued Mazzini, and thus saved the faithful bird from an untimely death.

To this day we may see Mazzini's finch in the Milan museum.

391

Now that our old art master has passed on, we remember the days when we attended his class twice a week. A very charming and talkative little man he was; and though some of us never learnt much about drawing we all learnt from this good man a few things about living.

'Here is our model for today,' he would tell us, mincing across the floor to a board resting on a cube. 'A vase, a little fruit, and this half-loaf. I group them so. Very good. But one thing I must see to with care. I will pull down this blind, and I will ask one of you young gentlemen to be kind enough to pull aside the curtain at the other window. That will do. Very good. You see, gentlemen, we must always have our model in the best light. It is one of the essentials of drawing; and it is also one of the essentials in life—always put the other person in the best light when examining him. Often hidden good will appear. And now we will begin our lesson.'

Stirling Observer

392

During World War I, Walter Hines Page, American Ambassador at St James's from 1913, saw much of England and of English life. He came to admire both. Writing to Washington in the darkest days between 1914 and 1918, he told this story:

I know a lady of title, very well to do, who for a year got up at five-thirty and drove herself in her own automobile from her home in London to Woolwich, where she worked all day long in a shell factory as a volunteer, and got home at eight o'clock every night. At the end of a year they wanted her to work in a London place where they kept the records of the Woolwich work. 'Think of it,' said she, shaking her enormous diamond ear-rings as I sat next to her at dinner one Sunday not long ago, 'think of it—what an easy time I have now. *I don't have to start till half-past seven, and I get home at half-past six.*'

393

The scene is a street in Edinburgh one quiet Sunday forenoon. Church bells are ringing, shops are closed; and, walking sedately, comes an elder of the kirk wearing morning coat, top-hat and gloves. He carries an umbrella. Here is respectability. Here is the decorous spirit of Presbyterian Scotland in all its Sabbath panoply.

But what now?

The elder of the kirk, advancing with reverent steps, halts, looks up, carefully lays his gloves and umbrella on the granite pavement, and without more ado begins climbing a lamp-post.

This is no fiction but indisputable fact. The elder of the kirk climbed a lamp-post, and for no freakish prank either—simply that this dour Scot, having scrambled to the top, might with one hand liberate a small bird which had somehow become trapped inside the lamp, and was vainly fluttering about in an effort to escape. Having liberated the captive, the elder brushed his clothes, picked up his umbrella and gloves, and—sedately as ever —proceeded on his way to morning service.

394

Looking from my window I saw young Peter Stuart arm in arm with Mary Ward. They were strolling by, their heads very close; and he was whispering something to her, and she was listening with parted lips, and they never saw me spying on them, and I'm blessed if they would have cared two hoots if they had, for I know Peter very well—he has a limp earned in the last days of the late war—and I know Mary very well also and have almost fallen in love with her myself; and I'm delighted these two have found each other, and I wish them happiness; and what sort of a world would this be, I wonder, if there were no romance in it to keep life sweet and fresh and full of enchantment?

I apologize for having written so much without a full stop—but when I see Peter and Mary walking by the window . . . well, I just can't be bothered with punctuation and trivial things like that.

H. L. GEE.

395

There was a time when no one knew anything of Alexandre Dumas, except that although he had lived twenty years he had apparently learned nothing.

Tired of Villers-Cotterets, he determined to go to Paris and earn his living. He would call on some of his father's friends, and ask for work. Full of confidence he paid a visit to a general.

'What can you do?' asked the general.

'Nothing very wonderful, sir.'

'Mathematics?'

'Very little, sir.'

'Algebra, trigonometry, physics?'

'Hardly anything, sir.'

'The law, then?'

With burning cheeks the young man, realizing his ap
ignorance and thoroughly ashamed of it, burst out, 'Oh,
education is shocking, and I am ashamed that until today
not know it. I will make up for lost time, sir. I will soon answer all your questions with a *yes.*'

The general nodded. 'In the meantime you have to live. Give me your address. Write it down here.'

Dumas—the unknown Dumas—wrote his address. 'Ah!' exclaimed the general. 'Here's something at last! *Your handwriting is good!*'

396

She nestled very close to him. 'Dearest,' she murmured, 'nothing can ever separate us. We are two people with the world before us. I shall love to share all your joys and sorrows.'

'But, darling,' he said, 'I haven't any sorrows.'

'I know you haven't *now,*' she whispered, 'but I mean when we're married!'

397

It was Luther who wrote:

> A safe stronghold our God is still,
> A trusty shield and weapon;
> He'll help us clear from all the ill
> That hath us now o'ertaken.

No man ever lived to find his own verse come true so startlingly.

Though released from Worms, where he had expected to die at the stake, Luther was not out of the hands of his enemies. Countless plots were afoot to silence this daring mouthpiece of the people's thought. From Worms, where he had defied the Pope, he rode out by the Thuringian Forest, glad and thankful that he had triumphed gloriously, but aware that his very triumph would multiply his enemies.

A few miles only separated him from Worms when he was surprised by a band of men. Wearing masks and cloaks, they set upon him and his followers, taking Luther prisoner. These horsemen were daring fellows indeed, and Luther must have thought his last moment near at hand when they rode off with him to the great castle of Wartburg.

But life was strange for Martin, and he soon found that he had been carried off, *not by his enemies, but by his friends*, and that what appeared to be his prison in Wartburg was really his place of refuge from the infuriated Roman Catholics who were searching everywhere for him. Thus, what had seemed his worst turned best, and he found indeed that, *A safe stronghold our God is still.*

398

A Blackpool man had a delightful surprise in a busy Manchester street one day in 1938. Meeting an old fellow who looked down and out, he gave him twopence for a cup of tea, and was not a little startled when the 'down-and-out' asked him to accept a pound note for his kindness.

399

'My dear,' said a monkey to his wife one day, 'what's the matter with so many of our friends? They seem extremely sad.'

'They've been meeting trouble,' replied the monkey's wife.

'Dear me,' commented the monkey. 'I wish I could meet him. I wonder what he's like?'

After that the monkey worried so much that at last he went to the Wise One of the forest, and asked his advice.

'Oh,' said the Wise One, 'you can meet trouble any day. You see this sack? Well, carry it to the middle of the forest clearing —the *middle*, mark you, not the edge—and open it. You'll meet trouble sure enough.'

So the monkey carried the sack to the middle of the clearing, and opened it. Out sprang a great dog, terrifying the monkey so much that he ran as fast as he could. Unfortunately it was a long way to the nearest tree, and the dog gained on him, its breath hot at the back of the monkey's head, its fangs very near his legs. At last the monkey sprang to a branch and whisked himself far out of harm's way, the dog barking below. 'Well,' gasped the monkey, 'I'd no idea I should meet trouble so quickly.'

Later he told his wife about his experience, but she merely said, 'It serves you right. *Only stupid people go in search of trouble.*'

400

An amusing story from the musical North concerns two ladies who were attending a celebrity concert in Huddersfield. One had a soul for music, the other had not. While a famous pianist was playing one of the classics, the first woman turned to the second and whispered: 'You *are* enjoying it, aren't you?'

The other grunted. 'T' music's all right,' she said in a grudging undertone, 'but just look at dust on t' piano legs!'

401

The family note was always strong and moving at the Royal occasions I witnessed. I saw one formal, glittering ceremonial after another relax the moment the Royal Family entered and took their places, and I think I first became aware of the *family* when I attended the wedding of the late Duke of Kent to Princess Marina. King George V was so enchanted by the picture the bride and bridegroom made that his hymn-sheet drooped in his hands until Queen Mary, within sight of the distinguished congregation, nudged him vigorously with her elbow, and pointed to the line of the hymn that was being sung.

'Just like your wife—and mine!' whispered an enraptured man next to me.

JOE ILLINGWORTH: *Yorkshire Post.*

402

Left, right, left, right—the sentry marched backwards and forwards that June night before the battle of Waterloo. One of the famous Old Guard, he was a veteran who had seen much fighting, a Frenchman who not only honoured the Emperor but loved him, and would gladly have died for him.

Only a short distance across the fields he could see the English camp fires glowing like torches, for Marshal Ney had posted this trusted corporal at a strategic point. Left, right, left, right, the sentry marched up and down his beat that summer night. Summer—yes, but how cold it was; and rain fell pitilessly.

He had been tired before the watch began—tired and hungry and, perhaps, apprehensive, too. He was wet to the skin. His limbs ached. He did not know how to keep his eyes open. Five minutes' rest would do wonders—not that he would sleep, of course; he would merely close his eyes. Well, perhaps not five minutes, say *two* minutes. He would rise refreshed and more alert. . . .

So the sentry lay down, stretched himself, and closed his eyes for what seemed to him a few moments.

Suddenly he started to his feet. With the instinct of the old campaigner he *felt* he was not alone. Snatching up his musket, he was ready to fire. 'Who goes there?' he called. Then he staggered back a pace for even in that half light he recognized the stooping figure before him, the familiar cape enveloping the broad shoulders, the massive head with the square jaw; those piercing eyes.

'The Emperor!' he gasped. 'My God, sir, I have betrayed you. Take my bayonet, and honour me by killing me here and now!'

For a moment there was silence. Napoleon, whose armies had thundered across Europe, had a deep affection for the Old Guard; and with a compassion that some might have found strange, he replied: 'Corporal, I have kept watch for you. Resume guard.'

403

Rupert Brooke, one of the most promising of the soldier poets of World War I, lives for all time in his famous sonnet:

> If I should die, think only this of me
> That there's some corner of a foreign field
> That is for ever England.

He died not long after writing these words, passing on gallantly on St George's Day, 1915.

Shortly before his end he sailed for the Dardanelles, leaving Liverpool on what must have been one of the saddest days of his life, for there was no one to see him off.

Most of us at some time or other have known the bitterness of setting out on a voyage without a friend at hand, and Rupert Brooke felt the loneliness intensely. He felt it so terribly that after he had gone on board the ship which was to carry him to a foreign field, he went back to the landing stage, found a little ragged boy called William, and gave him sixpence to wave to him as the ship sailed.

It was the last thing Rupert Brooke did in the England he loved.

The Children's Newspaper, 1937.

404

Times were bad in Warsaw. The poor were suffering terribly, and when winter came they suffered still more. It was to raise funds to relieve distress that a great concert was given, all Poland's noblest and richest attending. The Grand Duke Constantine himself sat in the place of honour, lords and ladies in dazzling array on either side. Only famous musicians and singers appeared before that distinguished gathering; and at last came an item which everyone had been anxiously waiting for—the Wonder Child of Warsaw. A boy of nine, though he looked no more than six, he walked confidently across the stage. He wore a fine velvet suit with a marvellous lace collar, richer and more beautiful than any collar he had ever worn before. When he bowed there was a flutter of excitement. Fine ladies whispered that he looked charming. Gentlemen of noble blood noted that he walked with assurance before sitting at the piano.

After the applause the Wonder Child struck a few chords rather hesitantly. Finding, however, that the piano had the tone of the one he was used to at home, he began playing happily, almost carelessly, quickly forgetting his audience, distinguished though it was. On and on he ran, his fingers drawing music at the slightest touch; and when at last he slipped off the stool and bowed again, the theatre was shaken by tumultous applause, even the Grand Duke (always slow to praise) declaring it had been well done.

Little Frederick Chopin bowed and smiled—and when he reached his mother's arms he cried, 'Mummy! They clapped like anything *when they saw my new collar*!'

405

It was a surprise to the people in Duke's Place—hardly the most salubrious of neighbourhoods. They had never *meant* to give themselves a treat.

The idea was first mentioned by Mrs Waddington, wife of the grocer at the corner. As Mr Waddington thought it a good idea, ɔned it to Mr Cartwright, a kind of jobbing joiner and ı. Mr Cartwright thought he could do a little thing ɔut the wood would cost a bob or two.

ıe notion had gone so far, Mrs Waddington 'got cracking' in fine style. She went from house to house, and everybody agreed to help. Not that anybody had much money, but they all thought the world of Miss Riley, bless her.

Miss Riley, of course, was the little elderly lady who had kept on so gallantly until at last she was compelled to take to her bed, remaining there day and night. Her room was reached by a dingy staircase; and one might have expected her to be lonely. But she was never lonely. She had a Sunday School class in her bedroom once a week; and once a week the women of Duke's Place—*most* of them, anyhow—gathered in that upper room, and had a cup of tea, a chat, a sing-song, and a little prayer. There was never a morning or an afternoon or an evening when somebody didn't look in and tell Miss Riley their troubles or ask for advice or at any rate receive comfort and blessing and encouragement from the invalid who had time to think about everyone, and time to pray for those who never prayed for themselves.

And so, when Mrs Waddington went from door to door and explained about the window-box, why, everybody thought it a marvellous idea. They said it was kind of Mr Cartwright to make it free of charge, except for the price of the wood; and such a happy thing for everybody to club together to buy geraniums; why, that window-box would brighten Miss Riley's room no end.

And so it did.

But what surprised everybody was that Miss Riley's window-box made such a cheery splash of colour in Duke's Place.

406

When the body of King George V was lying in state, the Lord Mayor of Manchester sent two wreaths. One was the city's tribute, a noble and worthy mass of flowers; the other a little green cross with four artificial carnations, delivered at the Town Hall in a brown paper bag.

The Lord Mayor despatched both wreaths, the big wreath in the name of the city of Manchester, and the little one in the name of an old widowed pensioner whose message was, *To a good King who was kind to old people.*

407

Shortly before Christmas 1952 a prim and very fastidious elderly lady spent nearly an hour at one counter in a big West of London store. She was choosing gloves—gloves for her two married daughters, gloves for her three granddaughters, gloves for her sister who lived in Ruislip. The small blonde at the counter had a very busy time indeed, and she must have brought out dozens, if not scores, of gloves, all of which, of course, she had to pack away afterwards.

Then, when the gloves had at last been wrapped in individual parcels, when the bill had been made out and the amount paid and the change given, at the moment when the elderly lady ought to have vanished in the crowd, how the blonde wilted, for the elderly lady exclaimed: 'Oh, I was forgetting . . .'

'Anything further, modom?' murmured the blonde, finding a little smile, and putting it on.

'Well, yes, dear,' said the elderly lady. 'I'm in a fix, my dear. I don't know what'd suit her, really. She's not very big, but modern girls have such notions, haven't they? What do you think a girl of about your age would like in gloves?'

The assistant did not know; but eventually she thought up something, and showed the elderly lady another dozen pairs of gloves. 'They're all very dazzling, aren't they?' ventured the elderly lady, a trifle disapprovingly.

The blonde agreed. 'But young people like them,' she pointed out. 'Now, *this* pair, modom, if the right size . . . I'd say *any* young lady would just love them.'

'They certainly look attractive. I'll take your word for it,' said the elderly lady crisply.

So the assistant removed the ticket, wrapped up the gloves, took the money, and gave the change. How graciously the elderly lady smiled as she said: 'There now, dear, these are for *you*—and thank you for being so patient. I *do* hope you have a happy Christmas!'

408

'Uncle Joe,' said an author, meeting an old darky who was always good-humoured in spite of having had more than his share of life's troubles, 'how do you manage to remain so cheerful and calm?'

'Well, I'll tell yo',' replied Uncle Joe. 'I'se jus' learned to co-operate wid de inevitable.'

409

The Rev. Dr Leslie F. Church had to make a sea trip when a gale was increasing in fury. The friend who went to see him off remarked, 'It's blowing hard. I'm afraid you're in for a bad passage.'

With unusual pessimism Dr Church said, after looking at the small and rather ancient vessel, 'This isn't exactly one of the finest boats, is it?'

'No,' his friend agreed promptly. 'As a matter of fact, she's the worst boat in the line *—but she has the best captain.*'

410

Long ago a farmer went to market at the time of the 'hirings' and looked about for a lad to work on his farm. Chatting with one, he said, 'Well, my lad, what can *you* do?'

'I can plough and reap,' was the reply.

Another said: 'I can milk cows and tend sheep.'

A third said he could groom horses.

Then the farmer met a fourth boy. 'Now, my lad,' said he, 'what do *you* do on a farm?'

'I sleep well on windy nights,' replied the lad, touching his cap.

The farmer was so struck with this unexpected answer that he engaged the youth at once, and soon found he had made a good bargain, for everything the lad did, he did well.

One wild night the wind reached gale force, and the farmer never had a wink of sleep. He was sure that daylight would show him an empty stackyard—or, at any rate, half his stacks would be scattered far and wide. When he went down to the kitchen and found the lad there he asked if he had been able to sleep.

'Like a top,' said the lad.

This nettled the farmer. 'You wouldn't have slept like a top if they'd been *your* stacks,' he retorted. 'I've been awake all night wondering what would happen to them.'

'Oh,' said the lad quietly, 'I didn't worry about them. *I thatched the stacks myself—so I knew they'd be safe.*'

411

They still tell this story in Scotland. Though very simple, it is not without its dramatic touch.

Years ago, workmen blasting rock in the Stirling quarries used to make a bore in the rock, fill it with gunpowder, attach a fuse, and when all was in readiness give the alarm to retire to a safe distance. One day the unexpected happened. The fuse was alight, the workmen had withdrawn, the explosion was expected any moment, when, to their horror, a child of about three began wandering across the open space near the quarry.

Every second death was rushing on him. The workmen did the only thing they could think of, calling to him and waving their arms, but the child only stood looking at them, amused by their queer antics. No man dare run forward, for the explosion was bound to occur within a breathing space; and though they shouted frantically the little chap never thought of moving. Deliverance came only just in time.

The child must surely have been killed had not his mother appeared. Taking in the situation at a glance, she did the one thing a mother *would* do in such circumstances. To have run towards the child might have sent him to his death. To have called might have frightened him. What she did was to kneel down and open her arms. Instantly the child ran towards her, and when the air shook with the explosion he was safe.

412

It is reported of a bold French knight that when he was told the enemy was at the door of his house, battering it down, he laughed. 'God be praised,' he cried. 'No more waiting! Now to fight! When the worst comes He is ever a friend!'

413

The house in Ohrdruf is silent. Everyone is in bed, and there is peace.

But not everyone is asleep, for the boy of ten is wide awake, and presently he goes noiselessly down the stairs.

There is a latticed cupboard in one of the rooms, and in the cupboard is a book of famous examples of organ music. The boy's slim fingers creep under the locked door (for brother Christopher, who is a noted organist, will not allow the boy to play these pieces as yet) and by dint of much manœuvring the 'thief' moves the book till it can be drawn out without the door being unlocked.

Then, like a phantom, he glides upstairs to his own room. As he dare not light a candle, he stands at the window and copies the scores by moonlight. This he does night after night whenever there is light enough. For six months the boy runs off with the precious book, no one knowing anything of it, no one knowing anything of the hunger for music in the 'thief's' soul. One day, however, brother Christopher finds the copied music, and confiscates it.

It was little Johann Sebastian Bach who stole that he might play—the boy who was to grow up to be one of the greatest of all musical composers. Often, in later years, he used to say with a wry smile that stolen music was sweetest.

414

Lord Shaftesbury once said:

In one of the worst parts of London there is an institution which I often visited; and once I found in one room there about thirty-five men listening to the teachings of the daughter of a small shopkeeper. She was one of the prettiest women I ever saw in my life. I noticed no one was present except that young woman and these rough men, so I said to the superintendent: 'Are you not afraid to leave my dear little friend alone with all those men?'

He replied: 'I am.'

'Then why don't you go to her?' I inquired.

'You mistake my fear,' said the superintendent. 'I am not afraid of *their* doing her any harm—they love her so much they would lick the ground on which she walks; but I *am* afraid some person may step in one day, and, not being under authority, or not knowing the manners of the place, may say something impertinent to her. If he did, he would not leave this place alive.'

415

From World War II comes the story of a soldier who had been severely wounded and was visited in hospital by a padre.

When the padre asked if there was anything he could do, the dying man whispered, 'Yes. Be good enough to write to my mother and tell her I loved her to the end; and write to my Sunday School teacher, and tell him I've never forgotten what he taught me.'

The padre did as he was asked. Shortly afterwards he received two letters. One was a letter of thanks from the proud but broken-hearted mother. The other was from a man who wrote: '. . . God forgive me, I gave up teaching in Sunday School years ago. I felt sure I was wasting my time.'

416

They used to tell this story in the East Indies:

While a company of British soldiers were camped in the Province of Bojepore, a horse belonging to one of the officers was stolen, but the thief, mistaking his way among the tents, was detected and brought back.

The officer, highly pleased at recovering the horse, and much surprised at the dexterity of the thief who had carried off the steed while six or seven grooms had looked on helplessly, was more inclined to admire his address and expertness than to punish him. Next morning, therefore, having ordered the fellow to be brought before him, the officer inquired by what contrivance he had effected his purpose.

The thief replied that he could not easily *tell* His Honour; but that, if he pleased, he would *show* him. 'Well then,' replied the officer, 'since you are so bad at description, we'll see how you did it.'

'Now, sir,' said the artful culprit, 'pray take notice: This is the way I crawled over the grooms. The next thing was to loosen the ropes, which I did thus. I then clapped a halter—observe, sir, if you please—over the neck, thus.'

'Admirably clever!' exclaimed the officer, rubbing his hands.

'In this manner,' continued the fellow, 'I jumped upon his back—and once I am mounted, I give anyone leave to catch me *if he can*!'

Thereupon the thief gave the horse a smart blow, pushed him through the gaping crowd, put him to his full speed and carried him clear away to the great mortification of the astonished owner.

417

One Monday morning a lively, rather bantering young man, called to see an old lady. 'Good morning,' he said briskly. 'Fine morning. How are you?'

'Nicely, thank you, Jim.'

'You'd be at church yesterday, no doubt?'

'Yes, Jim—morning and evening.'

'Ah, a saint in a white apron! Well, what was the text in the morning service?'

'The text, Jim. Well, let me see . . .'

'Forgotten it already, eh?'

'It was a very good sermon.'

Jim chuckled. 'Never mind about the morning service,' he went on. 'What about the *evening* service? You'll remember the text, of course?'

'No, I just can't say *what* it was. I think it was in St John's Gospel—but it's slipped my mind.'

'Queer,' remarked Jim, evidently much amused. 'It beats me. What's the use of going to church on Sunday if you've forgotten the text by Monday? If you don't bring anything home, why in the world . . . ?'

'Jim,' said the old lady quietly, 'will you do me a favour? Just take this old clothes-basket to the pump and bring it back full of water.'

How Jim laughed. 'You don't catch me with *that*,' said he. 'Thank heaven I'm not *quite* brainless. Why, there wouldn't be a drop of water in the basket by the time I got back!'

The old lady smiled. 'Ah, well, perhaps you're right, Jim,' she said gently. 'Perhaps you're right. *But the basket might be a bit cleaner*.'

418

A day or two before Christmas, Miss Stott received a letter which disturbed her a good deal.

Her only sister had died some weeks before, and somehow Miss Stott dreaded that first Christmas alone. She dreaded being alone without the joy of attending the invalid she had loved so long, but she shrank even more from being with others, feeling she simply *couldn't* join in the merrymaking.

The letter was from Mr Crawshaw, a neighbour who had gone up to London early in December, he and his wife intending to be home again long before the twenty-fifth. But Mrs Crawshaw had unfortunately caught a chill, so they wouldn't be home until the New Year; and (so ran the letter) please would Miss Stott do them a favour. 'I enclose two pounds,' went on Mr Crawshaw. 'You see, every year since the War we've called on Christmas Eve to see these two dear Old Age Pensioners, and I rather think they'll be expecting us. We wondered if *you* would go this year instead of us?'

No, she wouldn't! She couldn't! Miss Stott passed a thin, nervous hand through her greying hair. She didn't want to be unfriendly, of course; and the Crawshaws were very nice people, and she would willingly have obliged, but it was much too soon after Cissie's passing. Well then, she would sit down at once and write to Mr Crawshaw explaining everything. . . .

But there wasn't much time for the Crawshaws to ask somebody else to go—and it would be a thousand pities if the two Old Age Pensioners were disappointed. So Miss Stott changed her mind. She bit her lip. She dabbed her eyes with a very small hanky—and went shopping.

If only her poor dear sister had been with her! Christmas, to be sure, meant nothing to Miss Stott that year . . . but the shops certainly *did* look attractive; and there was excitement and hope and wonder in the air; and, really, it *was* rather jolly spending somebody else's money, and taking your time over buying a chicken in the big store with its pretty decorations, and the good humoured crowd jostling on all sides; and it was no use pretending that she didn't enjoy buying the sausages and the small cake and the boiled sweets and the magazines and an ounce of tobacco . . . fancy Miss Stott buying tobacco, of all things! What *would* Cissie have said?

And so, on Christmas Eve, towards dusk, Miss Stott set out for the little house; and after knocking timidly she found herself being ushered into the sitting-room with its friendly fire. There she sat between a perfectly delightful Darby and Joan, both of whom were *so* pleased to see her. They were very grateful for the good things she displayed. They thanked her in a way which touched her heart. They *made* her remove her hat. They insisted on her unbuttoning her coat. While the old lady brought out mincepies, the old gentleman put the kettle on; and so the three sat drinking tea by the fire, the shadows behind them, the spirit of Christmas upon them; and they talked of days gone by. The old folk told Miss Stott about their wonderful daughter who had died so suddenly and left them desolate; and Miss Stott told them about her sister, and her sister's patience and her glorious faith.

Presently the two Old Age Pensioners sang *Holy Night*. In spite of their years their voices were remarkably sweet and tuneful; and as they sang there in the firelight, tears coursed down Miss Stott's cheeks—hot tears; and yet . . . Miss Stott never quite understood how or why . . . oh, the joy and comfort and peace that somehow took possession of her, as if the very spirit of Christmas had broken through the darkness and had lit a little candle in her heart!

419

When a Leicestershire farmer retired in July 1928, a crowd attended the sale of cattle, machinery and vehicles. Everything was sold except one brightly-painted farm wagon. 'What's the idea, George?' asked many of the visitors. 'Aren't you selling the wagon?'

'No,' replied the farmer. 'I reckon I'll keep the wagon a bit. I'd feel sort of queer if I'd nothing to lend a neighbour in harvest time.'

420

On one occasion William Wilberforce and his four sons planned a holiday together. It was agreed among them that each was to bring a *new* book with him so that each might read five books and discuss them while on their travels. It was a happy idea; but when all five were assembled, each pulled from his baggage a copy of *The Christian Year*, by John Keble. Published in 1827, it has been described by Bishop Barry as a book that leads the soul to God, not through one but through *all* the various faculties implanted in man.

421

I had always thought of him as the man who read the meter. From time to time he came to the back door and asked to see the electric meter—a little man in a shabby coat; a rather ordinary looking man who had never anything to say except that the weather was colder or milder.

One day, happening to meet him on the garden path, I chatted with him; learning that he had a delicate child, and a wife who had been in a bus accident three years before, and had never walked again. He told me he never went to the cinema in the evening, preferring to stay at home and either read to his wife or help her to make scrapbooks which she sent to boys and girls in hospital. He had had the opportunity of securing a job where he would have made an extra two pounds a week, but it would have meant moving to another neighbourhood, thus depriving his wife of the friends who often looked in to see her.

Today I think of him as the *hero* who reads the meter.

H. L. GEE.

422

Once upon a time there was a little man who travelled in buttons. He represented a Birmingham firm, and though his salary was a modest two hundred a year, he put his heart and soul into his work, and was highly esteemed by his employers.

It happened that in 1815 this little man was in Brussels on business for his firm, and on that June day when the fate of Europe was decided by the battle of Waterloo, what must he do but hire a small horse and go riding off, as he put it, 'to see the fun'? More than once, when looking through his telescope, the Duke of Wellington observed this little man in plain clothes trotting about the battlefield, sometimes on the very fringe of the fiercest fighting; so, during a lull in one section of the field, His Grace beckoned the little man, inquiring of him his business. 'Oh,' said the traveller in buttons, 'I just happened to be in Brussels, and as I've never seen a battle, I thought I would make of the opportunity.'

'You are in grave danger,' warned the Duke.

'Not more than Your Grace,' replied the little man.

Then he rode off.

An hour or two later the Duke wished to send a message to a regiment on his left, and as there was no one whom he could well spare from his staff, he again beckoned the little man, asking him to ride over to the officer in charge. The little man galloped off without delay, and very soon afterwards the Duke noted with satisfaction that the regiment moved forward according to the orders its officer had received.

After the battle of Waterloo had been fought and won, and when the victorious Duke of Wellington was visiting Birmingham he made inquiries about the traveller in buttons. Later still, having invited the little man to visit him, His Grace said: 'There is a vacancy at the Mint worth eight hundred a year. It has to do with making up the accounts. Would it be any use to you?'

'It would indeed,' replied the little man gratefully. So he ceased to be a traveller in buttons, and found himself a man of means.

423

There was a curious little comedy in a Scottish town in 1937.

One of the town's firemen was sitting comfortably in his own but and ben, taking his ease and warming his toes, when a summons came. Jumping up, he ran to the fire station, took his place on the engine, and dashed off with the brigade. Then the engine stopped *at his own door.*

It was *his* chimney which was blazing!

424

Tradition says that Sir Walter Raleigh scratched on a window in Greenwich Palace the words:

Fain would I climb
Yet fear I to fall;

and that when Queen Elizabeth read the couplet she wrote with a diamond:

If thy heart fail thee,
Climb not at all.

425

In 1934 Mayor La Guardia of New York addressed (through a translator who talked with his hands) a congress of deaf and dumb people who were bright and responsive. Said the Mayor: 'I am very glad to find an audience which can understand though it cannot hear. I spend most of my time addressing people who hear but cannot understand.'

426

When Jean Baptiste Lully, the famous French composer, was seriously ill, his friends sent for a confessor who refused absolution unless the patient promised to burn the opera he had just completed. Lully pleaded in vain. His friends remonstrated, but to no purpose. So the script of the unpublished opera was there and then consigned to the flames.

As it happened, however, Lully recovered. One day a nobleman, who had long been the musician's patron, called to see the composer. Having heard the sad story of the lost opera he roundly upbraided Lully for destroying anything so precious, even though it had been done to ease his conscience. 'I hear you have burnt your papers,' declared the nobleman. 'You are a blockhead!'

'Ah,' murmured Lully, 'I was feverish at the time, and tormented with pain, and death seemed very near. But, my friend, I knew what I was doing . . . you see, although I allowed them to burn *one* copy of the opera, I kept the other! *And here it is!*'

427

The story is told of a foolish Irish woman who repeated tales about her neighbours. One day she found that something she had said had made trouble for another woman. She was sorry; so, going to the priest, she confessed, asking what she must do as a penance.

'Go to market tomorrow,' ordered the priest, 'buy two chickens, and pluck them as you are coming home. When you have done that, come and tell me.'

So the woman went to market, bought two chickens, plucked them as she trudged home, and then went to tell the priest.

'Now,' said the priest, 'there remains only one thing to do: *Go back and gather up all the feathers.*'

428

He was a little chap of eleven. Nobody thought much of him, and most of the other boys laughed at him, making fun of his clothes, for he wore a rough grey suit with nothing pleasing about it—indeed nothing could be said in its favour except that it was made to wear a long time. *And he wore spectacles!* They cracked jokes about him. It was stupid sending *him* as a candidate to the Choir School attached to the Court Chapel at Vienna—he hadn't a chance, not 'Goggles'.

The boy in spectacles was the son of a Moravian peasant who had worked his way up until he had become a teacher at a village school. Born in 1797, the boy—one of a big family—had had a pretty hard time of it at home, though he had early learned to play the fiddle. As he had grown out of childhood into boyhood he had surprised the family by the beauty of his voice, and it was in the hope that he might be lucky enough to win a scholarship to the Choir School that he had come up to the Court Chapel for a few days to see if he would be chosen. He might as well have stayed at home. All the other boys knew he never would be chosen—not 'Goggles'.

But they were wrong, for two or three days later the boy in the grey suit was dressed in a gold-laced uniform. He was to sing in the choir! The boys who had laughed at him were sent home—but not 'Goggles'.

Thus began the musical career of Franz Schubert, the short-lived genius whose songs delight millions today.

429

Some of us have treasures of countless price, and don't know it.

Take Mrs Henshall, for example.

'George,' said she one evening, 'I'm fed up with this house. We've *got to move*! It's handy for you going to business, and for the children going to school, but I've to live in it morning, noon and night, and I'm sick of it. Do you hear? It's getting on my nerves.'

So said Mrs Henshall.

Next morning came Mrs Swan—anything but swanlike. She did the chores. She also talked. 'Eh, you know, Mum,' said Mrs

Swan, 'there's seven of us at home now, and we've only three bedrooms, one of 'em too small to swing a cat in, and it's somethink awful. I was saying to my old man only last night, "Eh," I says, "*if only we'd a house like Mrs Henshall's, or half as good I'd be happy ever after*." That's what I said, Mum; and I never cleans up here without thinking as how this here's a little palace. It kind of makes me feel envious.'

430

His mother had given him a new velvet hat, and very proud he was of it, this little Spanish boy whom everyone loved for his bright eyes and taking ways. He marched up and down the streets of Seville wearing his fine hat, and then ran indoors to keep house while his mother went off to church. His Aunt Eulalia was expected any time, and the doors of the house were not to be shut in her face, so Bartolomé must look out for her, and be a good boy.

Bartolomé found doing nothing very difficult, so he wandered from room to room, and came to one where he looked up at a picture he knew well, a picture of a little boy with a sheep in his arms. The boy had no fine hat, and a sheep was a silly thing to nurse, so Bartolomé felt sorry for him. Presently he found a bit of charcoal, climbed on a table, and began giving the boy in the picture a fine velvet hat. Then he changed the sheep to a pert little dog. After that he stood back to look at his work—and there was his mother, astonished, shocked, grieved.

The picture was ruined, she said, and Bartolomé was a naughty boy who was never to be trusted. Down into the cellar he must go.

Aunt Eulalia came, but Bartolomé did not see her. Instead he sat in the dark, whimpering. It was a cruel world, he thought, for he had not meant to be wicked. Later, Padre Pedro called, a wise old man whom everyone respected. 'Where is Bartolomé?' he asked.

'Where is Bartolomé?' his mother repeated. 'In the cellar, where he deserves to be; he has ruined my treasured picture of John the Baptist, ruined it! Come, I will show you what he has done.'

So they went into the room, and Padre Pedro looked up at the picture. For a whole long minute he stared, saying nothing.

When he did speak he said something to the angry mother which amazed her. He did not say, 'Bartolomé *is* a bad boy.' He did not say, 'You ought to have whipped him.' He did not say, 'What a pity.' He said, 'You must send him to an artist to learn painting.'

So Bartolomé was brought out of the cellar, and set on the road which led to his becoming one of the greatest Spanish artists of the seventeenth century—Bartolomé Murillo.

431

The teacher asked the class to name some long words.

'Procrastination,' said one boy.

'Elastic,' called out his companion.

'But *that's* not a long word,' snapped the teacher.

'No, Miss,' replied Jimmy, 'but you can stretch it.'

432

Two business men met in Leicester one day. Said the first: 'I hear your brother has just made a cool three thousand in a retail deal at Nottingham.'

'That's interesting,' replied the second. 'But you haven't got the story *quite* right. The deal wasn't in Nottingham—it was here in Leicester. It wasn't a retail transaction, it was wholesale; and actually the sum involved was not three thousand pounds but thirty thousand. Oh, and by the way, he didn't make it, he *lost* it . . . and, in point of fact, old chap, it wasn't my brother, it was *me*.'

433

When Anaxagoras, the famous Greek philosopher who taught in school, was dying, he was asked if there was anything he wanted. With his last breath he whispered, 'Give the boys a holiday.'

434

The late Stanley Twidle, a successful man of business with a rare humour, once told the compiler of an experience of his early years. 'It was the time when I dared to make a speech in a crowded hall in Hull,' he said in his own whimsical way. 'It was a political speech, for I knew no better then. It was impromptu. I warmed to my theme. Convinced of the justice of the cause I was defending, I felt inspired to employ wit and metaphor, argument and appeal. I roused my audience. I sat down amid tremendous applause.

'Then I went home—but not to sleep. I had the impression that a turning-point in my career had been reached that night and I was eager to see the newspaper in the morning, expecting my name to be in the headlines on the front page, and rather hoping that my day and generation would immediately recognize in me the most brilliant orator of the century. My speech, I was sure, would occupy two columns. Actually, however, it did not occupy all that space. It did not take up half a column. In point of fact, the front page did not carry my speech at all—but on page five I discovered a brief notice of the meeting I had attended. The insignificant paragraph ended with the words: *Mr Twidle also spoke.*'

435

President Coolidge bore many burdens of State, but never lost his sense of humour. On one occasion he took a nap in the middle of the day—forty winks between arduous executive duties—and when he awoke he grinned as he remarked to a friend: 'Say, is the old country *still* here?'

436

A man who had suffered much and had come very near to losing his faith, found himself one day in a lonely Scottish glen. He watched a shepherd guiding his flock into a field, and noted how amazingly quick and intelligent the dog was—instantly interpreting a whistle given by its master.

Presently the tourist got into conversation with the shepherd, who proved to be so kindly and understanding and sympathetic that at last the troubled man told him of his doubts. 'I *used* to believe,' said the man. 'But now—well, I never hear God speaking to me. I don't believe there *is* a God to pray to.'

To this the old shepherd made no reply, but he did a curious thing. He removed his scarf, tied it round the dog's head, walked on twenty yards or so, and then whistled. But the sheep dog which before had responded so swiftly to each note, remained lying in the rough path.

'You see,' went on the old shepherd, 'not even God Himself can make us hear if we won't listen. He's aye guiding us all the time . . . but we've to wait patiently on Him to hear His voice.'

437

'When I was *your* age, my boy,' declared father, 'I was thankful to get even dry bread to eat.'

The son pondered. Then he said brightly, 'Say, Dad, you're much better off now you've come to live with us, aren't you?'

438

Hardly anywhere in the world is there a lovelier spot than Molokai, the Pacific island always bathed in sunshine, always fanned by soft and sweet airs. Yet this was once one of the world's saddest places, a place where hope was abandoned, where suffering was intense, and where loneliness was almost unbearable, for Molokai was the island to which lepers were sent, there to linger unloved until death brought release.

But the wretchedness of its exiles came to the ears of Joseph de Veuster, a Belgian born at Tremeloo, near Louvain. Becoming a monk at eighteen, he took the now famous and honoured name of Father Damien. Of his own free will he turned his back on home and kindred, sailed for Molokai, and there became a father of the people.

He was one with them in their distresses. He loved those whom all men loathed. He served the outcasts day and night, ministered to their souls, and did what he could for their bodies. After some years his glorious act of sacrifice won wide recognition, and a medical station was established so that Father Damien could give at least some treatment and ease pain a little.

The kind of life Father Damien lived would have been altogether impossible had he not loved, and loved passionately.

There came a day which many regarded as tragic—that day

when Father Damien accidentally overturned a kettle of boiling water. To his astonishment he discovered that although his arm was scalded *it did not hurt*. He told a medical missionary what had happened, and the missionary looked Father Damien steadily in the eyes but remained silent.

'Well?' asked the hero and saint of Molokai. 'Am I a leper?'

'You are,' was the reply.

Many a man would have been stunned, but Father Damien *smiled*. 'Ah,' said he, 'now I am not only *with* them, *I am one of them*!'

439

'The Head wants to see you.'

The words were addressed to a lively schoolboy at Harrow, and they must have sounded ominous indeed. Obediently the pupil presented himself, receiving a lecture. Finally the Head trusted that as a result of what had occurred on that occasion the young scamp would apply himself more diligently to his lessons, and possibly make better progress.

It is good to know the culprit did. His name was Winston Churchill.

440

Miss Barbara Stone died in 1948. For many years before she retired to a cottage at Bury St Edmunds she had been a charwoman in London where her life had been one of constant drudgery and unremitting toil, though there had scarcely ever been a day without its redeeming feature, namely, a pleasant chat with somebody. In her cottage she at last found a peace she had never known before; and her greatest joy in retirement was to talk with other elderly folk about what, strangely enough, she called the good old days. Miss Stone had been in service in a number of big houses and had seen, if only from a distance, some important people. To recall former experiences was her never-ending delight.

Simple, humble body that she was, Miss Stone came to realize that old folk love nothing quite so much as recalling their yesterdays. In her last illness she told a neighbour she had eighty pounds hidden away in a chest of drawers, and she went on: 'I'd like it to be used to provide a meeting-place for my neighbours and friends, so that they can go on chatting about old times.'

She passed on at seventy-nine, and soon afterwards the Mayor of Bury St Edmunds opened the Barbara Stone Room at the Town Hall—a comfortable spot where elderly folk now meet to enrich the present with memories of the past.

441

There are tracts of Yorkshire where a man may lose his way even in these days of sign-posts, but two hundred years ago it was easier still.

One evening in the eighteenth century a man was riding slowly through the streets of York, giving his horse its head, when the landlord of an inn hailed him. 'Hi!' he shouted, 'I've a stranger here who wants to get to Harrogate tonight. Will you guide him, Jack?'

Jack said he would.

A few minutes later the stranger mounted his horse, and the two travellers set off. Apart from the fact that his guide was an unusually big fellow, the stranger saw nothing odd about him. All that concerned him was that Jack seemed to know every turn in the road and every inch of the way, seeing, one might have thought, in the dark.

There were moors and fens to steer clear of in those days, and there was treacherous bogland where man and horse might easily stick fast, but the two went on through the darkness, and only once did the guide hesitate. That was when he fumbled at the wrong side of a gate for the latch.

Presently the guide asked the stranger if he saw two lights ahead and was told he saw only one. 'That will do very well,' said Jack. 'We'll be there presently.'

So they were. But a surprise was in store for the stranger. Entering the lighted inn he discovered to his amazement that he had been guided by a *blind man*—famous John Metcalfe, better known as Blind Jack of Knaresborough.

'I would not have set off with you for a hundred pounds, had I *known* you were blind,' exclaimed the stranger.

'And I couldn't have lost my way for a thousand,' Jack replied.

442

'Do you know, Daddy,' said little Jane, looking up from her book, 'a baby fed on elephant's milk gained twenty pounds in five weeks!'

'Impossible!' exclaimed her father. 'Whose baby was it?'

'The elephant's,' said Jane.

443

One morning during World War II the new probationer nurse brought the morning cup of tea into a ward in a Caithness hospital, and an aged patient, who happened to be in a chatty mood even at that early hour, asked kindly: 'An' what's *your* name, lassie?'

'Elizabeth Sinclair.'

'An hev ye ony brithers an' sisters?' the old woman went on.

'Oh, yes.'

'An' what do *they* work at?'

'Well,' explained the nurse, 'ma sister, she's milkin' the coos at the castle; and ma brither, he's driving a lorry at Todhall. Ma mither's serving in the canteen at Thurso.'

'My,' remarked the patient, 'isn't that fine? An' what does your feyther do?'

'Oh, him? *He's the Air Minister.*'

444

Nobody knows much about Mrs Walker—the Mrs Walker who was born in 1700 and died when she was ninety. She was the wife of a well-to-do yeoman farmer in North Yorkshire—that's just about all anybody can tell us. She never won fame as a traveller. She never wrote poetry—as far as we know. She never sang before large audiences. She was a motherly soul who kept house, and liked to chat with her neighbours.

Oh, and she made broth for a little boy; and often, across the dinner-hour, she'd take him on her knee and teach him his letters from the family Bible.

The little boy was not *her* little boy. He was the son of a poor labourer at Marton-in-Cleveland. When the labourer moved to Great Ayton, his son soon showed that he was able to read better than most boys of his age. He liked school. He learned to write as well as to read. Later he went to sea. He became a captain, and made three memorable voyages to southern seas. Today we regard him as one of the greatest of all English navigators, for he was Captain James Cook.

There came a time when everybody was reading Captain Cook's *Journal*—one of the most famous books ever written, and a best-seller in the eighteenth century.

Did Mrs Walker read the *Journal*, we wonder? Nothing is more likely, for she was alive long after the famous navigator was dead. Perhaps Mrs Walker not only read the *Journal*, but was tempted now and again, when a neighbour popped in, to say with pardonable pride: 'Yes, I've been reading the *Journal*, and I was just thinking that if I hadn't taken little James on my knee when he was nowhere as high as this table, and if I hadn't taught him his letters, why, he might never have learnt to read—and then he'd never have learnt to write, and so we'd never have had the *Journal*.'

Surely Mrs Walker—simple, loving, but unimportant kindly body that she was—had a hand in putting Australia on the map?

445

Charles Lamb was never bitter. His quick wit was usually more like gentle humour than sarcasm, though he could be superbly crushing when necessary. He thought it necessary on one occasion when he happened to meet a snob.

The snob, anxious to impress Lamb with the dignity of breeding and the worth of culture, argued that all the best men—the men who were really worth notice—had attended a public school. Lamb listened as patiently and politely as he could. 'In support of my contention,' said the snob loftily, 'there was Byron, for example. He, of course, was a Harrow boy.'

'Yes,' said Charles Lamb drily. 'And there was also Robert Burns. He was a plough-boy.'

446

Lord Henry Cavendish, who died in 1810, lived strangely indeed. Caring nothing for his money, he was content to allow it to accumulate in the bank while he continued his experiments at home. The greatest scientist of his day, he was the shyest of men—so shy that when he had given London a noble library he dare not let the librarian know who he was. Punctiliously he took a ticket for every book he borrowed, pretending he was an ordinary member. He was so odd that he lived in only three rooms of his large house, and would never see any visitors except one or two scientific friends. He never married. No woman ever came into his life. Terrified of most men, he would have fainted if he had been compelled to remain more than a minute or two in the society of a woman.

He died immensely rich but alone, not even his servant with him. He died as a pauper might have done, no hand to hold his, no friend to speak a word.

But this is the odd and thrilling thing! After his death a friend went through his papers and rummaged among his effects. He found journals and scientific notes, letters on abstruse problems, valuable calculations, *and something else*. It was something which amused him though it brought tears to his eyes—a chest in which lay tattered scraps of a woman's dresses, some of them richly embroidered, one or two with precious jewels.

What were *they* doing in the dark house of the shy millionaire? Had he loved once, and lost?

447

A coloured gentleman once asked the pastor of a noted church in New York if he might have a sitting. The pastor fenced. 'Well,' he said, 'I'm not sure, Mr Jones, if our people would—er—care to have a coloured gentleman. I suggest you go home and pray about it, and see what the Almighty has to say.'

The coloured gentleman acted on the pastor's advice, and a few days later these two met again, whereupon Mr Jones made bold to say: 'Pastor, I took you at your word. I prayed about the matter we were discussing the other day, and the Almighty said, "Mistah Jones, you go careful about that very exclusive church. You aren't likely to get in—I've been trying to manage it somehow myself for fifteen years, and haven't pulled it off yet." '

448

In the darkest days of World War I Britain came to know something of hunger. Food kitchens were opened up and down the land, and almost invariably there was a long queue by the time the hot meal was ready to serve.

A story of those days is of the man who went back. He was an elderly man, a poor man. One day he turned up at a food kitchen in London and presented his plate to a very gracious lady who was serving at a window. When she handed him his plate again, he smiled as he went off with a polite, 'Thank you.'

After pausing to cover his plate with a sheet of newspaper, he shuffled out of the food kitchen, and hurried homewards as quickly as he could, for he was very anxious to eat his dinner before it became cold. But someone who stopped him asked if he knew *who* had served him. The man shook his head, and hurried along. After all, it mattered little *who* served dinner as long as there was plenty of it—and it was *hot*.

'Well,' said his friend, 'you've been served by the Queen of England. It was Her Majesty Queen Mary who put the meat and vegetables on your plate!'

'You don't say,' exclaimed the old man, coming to a standstill. '*The Queen?*'

Anxious as he was to enjoy his dinner, the old man turned about, joined the queue, and patiently moved up bit by bit. It was a slow business, and he was twenty minutes before at last he reached the window again. By that time his dinner was stone cold.

But his turn came at last, and the Queen was still there. With his plate in his left hand, the old man solemnly removed his cap, waved it three times, bowed—and then went home to dinner.

449

The great German reformer, Martin Luther, had an unhappy childhood; and as his parents were too poor to keep him long at school he was sent from home, when still young, to beg his way as best he could.

Wishing to be a scholar, he trudged along with a bag in which all his worldly possessions were packed, singing every night for food and shelter. One day he was taken into the house of a woman who gave him all the help he needed. Working hard at his studies, he was later able to go to the University, where he took his degree when he was twenty-two.

His one desire was to acquire more learning, for he had then no dream of changing the minds and hearts of men, though his nobler passion was to come soon, and to come dramatically.

We are told that one day he was walking with a friend when the sun was lost behind a heavy cloud. Thunder rumbled in the distance, the sky became darker, and presently a storm broke. The two friends went on side by side, walking and talking, and now and then looking up at the threatening sky. Then it was that a lightning flash struck Luther's friend dead.

It was this experience which turned the Reformer's thoughts to deeper things, prompting him to vow that a life, so narrowly spared, should be dedicated to God's service.

450

A Coventry workman sat down to eat his lunch one day. Opening a parcel, he took out his sandwiches one by one, reading the newspaper in which they had been wrapped as he munched away contentedly. While doing so his eye fell on a legal notice, and to his astonishment he saw the name of one of his mates. 'Here, William,' he said, turning to the man sitting by him, 'you'd better look into this.'

William looked into it, and the result was that he found himself heir to £20,000. He was Mr William Seddon, and the money was left to him by his uncle, brother of a former New Zealand Prime Minister.

451

Said the sightseer: 'This cliff is dangerous. There ought to be a warning notice.'

'There *was*,' replied the local inhabitant, 'but no one had an accident, so we took it down.'

452

They all loved her, of course.

A mixed crowd they were, men from South Wales and Tyneside, and anywhere between, all billeted next door to the little white-haired lady whose cottage overlooked the village green. They were a rowdy lot, and war had not made saints of any of them; but bit by bit, as summer gave place to autumn and the evenings were colder, they got into the habit of looking in to see Mother Megson. Their billets were cheerless at best—but Mother Megson always had a roaring fire in her kitchen, and nothing gave her more pleasure than making tea or cocoa and handing round pieces of apple pie.

She never had too many soldiers, and she made them all welcome. Rough and uncouth as some of them were at first, they seemed gradually to shout less and to look more and more admiringly at the little old lady with the placid face and the serene smile. Surreptitiously they would do little things for her—chop firewood or bring in logs or even, with much laughter, wash up; and now and again she would read a passage of scripture to them before bedtime. When they had to leave she would smile, and say, 'Well, off you go, boys. Be good.'

And how Mother Megson loved her boys! How fervently—though they never knew it—she prayed for them! Nothing was ever too much trouble. All were welcome.

But Mother Megson was not so well one day, and a week or two later she took to her bed in the downstairs front room. The soldiers were shy, but they looked in to see her now and then until that windy afternoon when a whisper went round the billets that Mother Megson was nearing the end. 'She'd like to see us all,' said the corporal huskily.

So they went in quietly. She looked radiantly happy, and the crimson light of a winter sunset lit up her room. They had never thought of her as being brave, but how brave she was at the end. Into their minds and hearts flashed a new vision of what real goodness means. Losing Mother Megson was like losing the best of yourself. 'Nice to see you,' murmured Mother Megson. 'I'm sorry . . . sorry I can't give you any apple pie.' A pause, and then a glorious smile. 'Off you go, boys,' she said. 'Be good.'

453

At a time—shortly before World War II—when the weather in New York was exceptionally cold, the city began to run short of coal, owing to a strike. The position became serious, but Mayor La Guardia settled the dispute in record time. He invited representatives of the trade to meet him in the City Hall. They did so, only to find that the hall was unheated. When all were in the doors were locked, and it was not long before the strike was over.

454

The introduction of the potato to France was long delayed because the French would not take the new vegetable to their hearts, as one might say. It is said that at last the King, by a curious stratagem, succeeded in giving his subjects a liking for potatoes.

He did it—so runs the tale—by having an immense potato-pie built outside Paris. After a strong guard had been placed round the pie, a royal decree went forth that no one was to steal even one potato. Terrible punishment, it seemed, was in store for anyone caught running off with the King's potatoes. For all that, the guards were secretly informed that if they saw a thief they were to look the other way.

On the principle that stolen milk is sweetest, the peasants in the neighbourhood made bold, under cover of darkness, to run off with a potato, then with two potatoes, then with a barrowful of potatoes; and because they imagined they were not supposed to do this, the 'stolen' potatoes tasted singularly delicious. Before long the great heap of potatoes had vanished, and all over France people were boiling, frying, or roasting potatoes—and thus, so they say, the new vegetable won its way to the menu.

455

Among the stories said to have been told by the Buddha is one with a moral for greedy people.

There was once a king who determined to make war on a region where few people lived, and where there was little worth having even if the kingdom became his.

On the way to the frontier the king halted his army near a forest. Wandering among the trees, with a minister or two for company, he was amused to see a monkey drop from a branch, steal a handful of boiled peas from a pan in which a soldier had cooked them, and scamper back to safety among the leaves. While eating the peas, however, the monkey happened to drop one, and instantly it climbed down for that one, was frightened by the soldier before it could grab the pea, and in its haste to get out of harm's way lost all the peas it had stolen.

The king laughed.

Then said a minister: 'You see, Sire, how easy it is to lose much for something small.'

After that the king gave orders that his army was to be disbanded.

456

After the irate father had chastised his son he stood back breathless. 'Now,' he gasped, 'tell me *why* I spanked you.'

'What,' moaned the small boy, 'don't *you* know either?'

457

In Lloyd George's *War Memoirs* is this story of a song that saved the Allies in October 1917.

There was strong feeling among the Welsh miners when they heard that more recruits for the Army were to be taken from their ranks, and they were even ready to go on strike. It was then that General Smuts was asked by Mr Lloyd George to go down to Wales and speak to them.

From Cardiff the General went to the coalfields. When he reached Tonypandy, where a great meeting was held, he saw thousands of angry men. He said: 'I have heard in my country that the Welsh are among the greatest singers in the world and, before I start, I want you first of all to sing to me some of the songs of your people.'

Like a flash somebody in that huge crowd struck up *Land of My Fathers*. The song ended, and the speaker began. He did not say more than a few words. He told them that their friends and comrades were defending the Land of their Fathers, and he was sure that *they* also would defend it.

On the General went to other meetings, and everywhere the same thing happened. The song was sung, and the hearts of the Welshmen were moved.

That night, after all his speeches, General Smuts took train to London, and next day he was in the Cabinet.

They said to him: 'What has happened? All the men are at work. How did you settle it?'

The General replied: 'Well, it is news to me that the men are at work.'

A song was the secret. The hour was an hour when much depended upon the action of the miners. The Navy had reserves of coal for only a week. If a strike had taken place the Navy would have been paralysed. The strike did *not* take place. The song, *Land of My Fathers*, saved us.

458

Many years before Stanley Baldwin became Prime Minister he had an office boy who used to plague an old clerk whenever he could, teasing him mercilessly, shying bits of blotting-paper at him, making his life a misery.

One day when this mischievous lad had been up to his tricks and had roused the old clerk's anger so that he chased him across the room, the boy flung open a door, dashed out of the old man's way, and ran headlong into Mr Baldwin.

Shortly afterwards Mr Baldwin sent for the culprit. 'My lad,' he said, 'I want to say that if I were in an office with an old clerk I think I should treat him much as you do. But I think if I were your age, and someone asked me *not* to treat him as you do (asking because they appreciated the services of this old servant) I should promise not to do it, and I should keep my promise.'

It proved to be an irresistible appeal.

459

A Hindu once praised a boy for saving a girl from drowning. When asked why he himself had not rushed into the water, the Hindu replied: 'I could not. I was saying my prayers.'

460

'Now, Andrew,' said the teacher, 'suppose you had four shillings in one pocket of your trousers and three shillings in the other, what would *that* be?'

'Somebody else's trousers, Miss,' was the unexpected reply.

461

One exceptionally dark night in World War II, a Scottish airman, one of nearly a thousand drafted to a town on the east coast of Yorkshire, was at a loss which way to take. He stood irresolute, waiting.

Presently he heard someone approaching on the other side of the road, and called out: 'Excuse me, can you direct me to Trinity Avenue?'

'With pleasure,' responded a pleasant voice. 'Cross the road, and we'll go along together.'

Having groped his way in the blackout, the Scotsman fell into step with his companion. The two men could not do more than see blurred shapes of each other, and for safety they linked arms. 'I say,' remarked the airman, 'I don't want you to go out of your way on *my* account.'

The other chuckled. 'Oh, that's all right,' he said. 'I live hereabouts and can find my way anywhere. It's easier to take you where you want to go than to tell you how to get there a night like this.' He paused. Then he added: 'By the way, you're Scotch?'

'Yes—Glasgow.'

'I thought so. It's good to hear a bit of music like that.'

'Oh? You're not Scotch, too, are you?'

'No. I'm Yorkshire—that's the next best thing. But I've lots of friends in Scotland. Funny you should mention Glasgow, though.'

'How do you mean?'

'Well, here am I trying to help you to get where you want to be, and the last time I was in Glasgow there was a Scotsman who went out of his way to save me from getting lost.'

'I'm glad to hear you say so.'

'Yes, I'd have fared badly but for him. It was Port Dundas Street I wanted, and I'm hanged if I'd have found it if he hadn't walked along with me.'

'Indeed? When was this?'

'Oh, it would be last October, or early in November.'

The airman stood still. 'Mon, mon,' said he excitedly, 'that was the time you talked of angling in the Tweed, wasn't it now—and about a holiday you'd spent at Kelso?'

'It was,' replied the astonished Yorkshireman.

'Aye,' said the Scot. 'I remember it well. Ye ken, *I was the chap that took you to Port Dundas Street that night*.'

462

She was appealing to members to supply refreshments for the church social.

'And so,' she ended, 'what we need are not abstract promises but concrete cakes.'

463

All of us are criticized behind our back, or made fun of to our face. It is never pleasant, as one of our most distinguished statesmen realized very fully some years ago.

Every statesman is, of course, used to opposition—it is part and parcel of his life. Often he is grateful for criticism from able politicians or editors whose judgments he values, and many a statesman has turned such fault-finding to good account. But on this occasion the distinguished statesman was being continually criticized by a very incapable and conceited politician, a Member of Parliament who never hesitated to be abusive. In spite of this the statesman refused to hit back. No matter what the conceited Member might say, he took not the slightest notice of the bitter attacks.

One day a friend asked the statesman how in the world he could keep his temper and remain so calm, and why he did not crush this particular critic with a sledge-hammer retort. 'Oh,' replied the statesman, 'that is best answered by a little story. You see, when I was quite a small boy we lived next door to a man who had a dog, and whenever the moon was shining, the dog used to get angry and bark—sometimes for an hour or two. It was very disturbing for everybody, except the owner of the dog, who was deaf.'

The statesman paused, consulted his diary, and added: 'Well, I must hurry along. I'll see you in committee.'

'Just a minute,' said his friend. 'You can't leave the story unfinished in that fashion. What happened?'

'Oh,' murmured the statesman with an odd smile, 'there's really nothing more to the story. The moon kept on shining, and after a while the dog got tired of barking.'

464

From Persia comes this tale of a man who found wealth and was sorry.

Travelling through the desert, he somehow strayed from the caravan and found himself alone in a wilderness of sand. For a whole night he plodded on, and when the hot sun rose he was so thirsty that he hardly knew how to endure. All that day he longed for water, and all the following night, but his search was in vain.

Next day, hardly able to drag himself along on all fours, he suddenly spied what seemed to him a water skin. Managing to crawl towards it, he tore it open, finding to his great disappointment that it was only a bag of pearls.

465

In the heart of the busy Yorkshire town of Selby rises the noble abbey where prayers have been said and praises have been sung since the eleventh century. Here many treasures are to be seen, but perhaps the greatest—and certainly the most romantic—is the Abbey seal.

One day in 1293 William Aslakeby, then Abbot of Selby, sat at his desk examining a document. Presently one of the monks dropped hot wax on the parchment—an indenture of some importance—and Abbot Aslakeby pressed on it the abbey's official seal, which bore an embossed portrait of himself. This done, the seal was put away.

The strange thing is that it was never seen or handled again by Abbot Aslakeby. When next he wanted it, the seal was missing. Search was made, but not a trace of it could be found, and in the end it had to be given up for lost.

Time marched on. Abbot Aslakeby went the way of all the earth. The Hundred Years' War was fought to a finish. Henry the Fifth triumphed gloriously at Agincourt. Caxton printed books. Columbus discovered America. The first Tudor was crowned and the last Tudor passed on in a blaze of splendour. Shakespeare wrote his plays. The *Mayflower* sailed. Marlborough won resounding victories. Napoleon thundered across Europe . . . and all this time not a soul anywhere gave a thought to the lost seal of Selby Abbey.

Then, as two fishermen of Yarmouth were drawing in their nets one day this century they came upon an odd-looking stone. At least, they *thought* it was a stone dragged up from the bed of the North Sea, miles from land. As it seemed to be rather a curiosity, the fishermen gave it to the Rector of Gorleston, *who discovered that it was the lost seal of Selby Abbey*.

So, after more than 600 years, what had been long lost was found; and there came a day when the Dean of Selby took the old seal and made with it a wax impression identical with the one made by William Aslakeby twenty-five generations earlier.

466

When her small daughter was busy with a book, her mother asked: 'What are you reading about, dear?'

'I don't know, Mummy,' replied the child.

'But you were reading aloud.'

'Yes, but I wasn't listening.'

467

It is said that Balzac had a high opinion of himself as an expert in reading character as revealed by handwriting. One day an elderly woman brought him a few lines of a child's scribble, and asked if he would tell her what he thought of it.

Studying the writing for a minute or two, Balzac said: 'Madam, I will tell you frankly that this child is stupid and careless. I'm afraid he will never achieve anything in life.'

'Very interesting,' murmured the woman. 'This is a page torn from one of the books you used as a very little boy at school.'

468

From a remote fishing village on the rocky coast of Scotland comes this story of the Minister who did his duty.

He did it because he felt he *must*. The calm winter's day had given place to one of the wildest nights of the year, yet the Minister prepared to plod uphill to the wee kirk high on the cliff. His wife urged him to stay at home, saying that a night like that would keep everybody indoors.

She was right. After muffling himself against the cold, after struggling against the furious gale and the driving hail and sleet, the Minister, lantern in hand, reached the kirk, opened the door, placed his lantern on the window-sill, and waited *in vain* for a congregation to appear.

How could he blame them for not coming to the week-night service? Well then, he would *pray* for them—and so, meekly upon his knees, the devout Minister offered his petitions to Almighty God; and having asked forgiveness for his own sins, he took his lantern once more, closed the church door, and went home to bed.

But that is not the end of the story, for it so happened that a fishing vessel, already delayed, was trying to make the harbour that night. So continuous, however, was the 'wall' of high-flung spray above the stone pier, that the harbour light was invisible, and the vessel must certainly have been wrecked a mile to the south had not the skipper recognized the light high on the cliff as coming from a window of the kirk. Steering by that light, and by that light only, he brought his vessel and his crew safely into port.

469

Some years ago a solicitor and his client were discussing business when a clerk entered the room quietly, put some papers on the desk, and withdrew.

'I've seen *him* once or twice,' remarked the client. 'I guess he's been with you a good many years.'

'He *has*,' replied the solicitor. 'Certainly more than twenty. Bob's the best clerk I've ever had—but I nearly lost him.'

'Oh?' murmured the client.

The solicitor toyed with the papers in front of him. 'We *ought* to get on with the business in hand,' he said, smiling. 'But I don't mind telling you that Bob came to me straight from school, and that he was the most stupid fellow imaginable. Even at fifteen he couldn't address an envelope properly; and as for adding up figures—he was hopeless. I'm afraid I gave him rather a bad time—he exasperated me.

'Eventually I decided to be rid of him. He'd been clumsier than ever, but I felt I ought to give him one more chance, so I handed him a column of figures, and ordered him to tot them up, and to be quick about it.

'I wasn't surprised when I checked his total to find he'd got the pounds and shillings wrong, though he'd managed to get the pence column right. In my anger and disgust I said sarcastically: "Wonderful! Congratulations! The pence are correct!"

'I meant it witheringly, but the silly boy thought I was praising him. His face shone. "Oh, sir," he gasped, "I'm *so* glad. I'll have another go at the pounds and shillings!"

'And, bless me, if from that moment Bob didn't turn over a new leaf. He worked. He tried. And from that day to this he's never once looked back.'

470

Isaac Watts, writer of evangelical hymns, had, even as a child, a natural genius for rhyme, and it was this genius which (oddly enough) got him into serious trouble. Often quite unintentionally he would talk in rhyme at home, this always annoying his father who thought he was doing it for fun. Time after time little Isaac would reply in rhyme, and his father would threaten to punish him. On one occasion—so we are told—his father lost all patience. Taking the boy by the collar, he twisted him under his arm, and was about to administer punishment with a heavy hand when the little fellow sobbed:

> 'Pray, father, do some pity take,
> And I no more will verses make!'

It saved him.

471

Born in 1832, Charles Dodgson was an Oxford mathematical professor who knew all about facts and figures, and might have been forgiven for knowing nothing about Wonderland. Yet it was his *Alice in Wonderland*, published in 1865, that made him famous. We know of no exceedingly dramatic moment in his life, but there was one which was certainly astonishing.

An odd trait of this clever Oxford lecturer was his pretence that Charles Dodgson and Lewis Carroll were two people. One day, when all the world was laughing at Alice and her amazing adventures, the author found himself in a railway carriage with a lady and her daughter. The girl was reading a book—a very funny book. It made her laugh, which was not surprising, for it was none other than *Alice in Wonderland*. She and the author had a pleasant conversation, and presently the girl's mother joined in, surprising Charles Dodgson by saying, 'Isn't it sad about poor Mr Lewis Carroll?'

'Is it?' asked the author.

'He's mad, quite mad, poor man,' declared the lady.

'I've never heard *that*,' Charles Dodgson replied.

The lady sighed. 'It's true,' she said, 'quite true. I have it on the best authority!'

472

A Highland shepherd met a botanist on the hills.

'Just look through this magnifying glass,' said the botanist, putting a tiny flower into the shepherd's hand.

'Mon, mon,' exclaimed the shepherd, 'to think I've been treading down rare wee bits o' loveliness like this a' the time!'

473

The story of Jamie Logan was often told during the American Civil War. He was a boy of twelve, and he had hoped to enlist, but no officer would take such a little fellow. They said they did not need any more drummer-boys; so Jamie asked if he might carry water to the wounded, and one of the officers, seeing how anxious he was, said he might do that.

All the next day Jamie Logan went to and fro among the dead and dying, carrying water in a tin mug, cheering a man here and easing another there until a bullet found him out, and his work of glory was done. At sunset they buried him in a shallow grave, firing over him as many shots as they would have accorded a general.

474

A legend which Sir James Barrie loved is of Father Anselm, a monk who, having wandered into the fields one summer morning, stood still to hear a lark sing. He was entranced.

Looking up, he watched the singing speck soaring into the blue, and having delighted in the song, he returned to the monastery.

But when he would have entered, a door-keeper he did not know ordered him to wait outside. He asked the monk's name, and when Father Anselm told him, he shook his head, saying no monk of that name belonged to the monastery. Other monks came, all strangers to Father Anselm. At last, having consulted their records, they discovered that a certain Father Anselm had been a member of that fraternity *a hundred years before.*

Time, it seems, had been blotted out while Father Anselm had listened to the lark.

475

Ronnie was a typical English schoolboy, a bright, intense laddie, and above all a cricket enthusiast. He knew almost everything there was to know about cricket, and he had, of course, his hero—Roy Kilner, the Yorkshire batsman now almost forgotten, but immensely popular in his day. It was hardly too much to say that Ron worshipped the ground Kilner walked on.

One day Ron came home with his school report; and as it proved to be a very good report, his father said: 'Ron, you and I are going to see a bit of real cricket tomorrow. We'll run over to Leeds, and watch Yorkshire play.'

A trip round the world would not have been more to Ron's liking. 'Why, Dad,' he exclaimed, 'that means I'll see Roy Kilner batting!'

None knew better than his father how Ron followed his hero's fortunes; and it was, therefore, a very happy pair who set off for Leeds. Once inside the enclosure, Ron slipped from his seat and —schoolboy-like—squatted on the grass close to the pavilion gate. There, almost too excited to speak, he waited and watched. Presently the opposing team took the field, and then, amid wild cheers from the crowd, out came two of the Yorkshire batsmen, one of them Roy Kilner himself. Bat in hand he came down the steps and strode easily towards the pitch, swinging a glove as he did so.

A moment later Ron slipped back to the seat by his father, who declared afterwards that he would never forget the look on his son's face, or the light in his eyes. 'Dad,' whispered the boy, 'did you see it, Dad? *One of his gloves touched me!*'

476

Every year the church had had its Gift Day—a luncheon, a sale of work, and an evening concert. The evening concert had long been the concern of the young people of the congregation, and proud they had been to make their contribution. But in 1941 things were different. At the best of times the congregation had never been very large, and during the first months of the war nearly forty young folk had left for the Forces or for war work. When a committee was called to organize the Gift Day someone said: 'As for the evening concert, that will have to be dropped. We've no young people left—we just cannot do *this* year what we did in other years.'

'Why not?' someone else inquired. 'Even if so many young folk are serving their country, there are the old folks at home.'

Though lightly said, it led to a gallant effort on the part of many men and women who had little desire for the limelight. Accepting the challenge of new and hard conditions, they planned a concert and carried it through to a triumphant conclusion.

477

The Persian poet, Sa'adi, tells us that a very powerful athlete was one day seen foaming at the mouth in the market place. A wise man inquiring the cause was told that the athlete was disputing with people who had insulted him.

'What?' exclaimed the wise man. 'Do you mean to say this poor fellow who can lift and carry huge stones is unable to support the weight of an unpleasant word?'

478

From Yorkshire comes this story of a Private who happened one day to pay a visit to the church of St Mary and Good Shepherd in Leeds.

The Private, a very young man, walked into the church and began looking round. His interest and reverent demeanour attracted the notice of a churchwarden who noticed him standing before the carved oak lectern, a memorial to Studdert-Kennedy, the famous Woodbine Willie of World War I.

The young soldier read the inscription which tells how Studdert-Kennedy, poet, prophet and ardent advocate of Christian fellowship, was for a time curate of the church, and that he was born in Leeds in 1885.

Presently the churchwarden said, 'Yes, this lectern is a memorial to a man who was very dear to us.'

The young soldier listened intently. 'Tell me more about him,' he begged.

The churchwarden was only too glad to talk of one much honoured in Leeds—the friendly, great-hearted chaplain who wore himself out in the service of others. 'But you are too young to remember him,' he added. 'He was before *your* time.'

The Private smiled. 'I'm always glad to hear people talk about him,' he replied. 'You see, *I am his son*.'

479

One snowy morning two boys determined to see who could make the straightest line across the village green to the school. The first walked very carefully and slowly, keeping watchful eyes on his feet as he tramped through the snow, but long before he was half way across the common he discovered, when he looked back, that his footprints were (as he put it) all over the place.

But the second boy, fixing his gaze on the school gate, strode manfully along, his eyes always on his goal, and not once did he look back until he reached the school. His tracks across the snow made a straight line.

480

A vivid imagination came to Mozart's rescue in his last days. *The Magic Flute* was not only his 'farewell' to the world but the composition of which he himself was most proud, and his passion for it remained to the end. The masterpiece was first performed in Vienna, and Mozart was able to attend the first ten performances. After that, however, he became so feeble that he was compelled to remain in bed at home.

Even then he contrived to conquer the cruel circumstances in which he found himself. Taking out his watch, he calculated the time between the raising of the curtain in the theatre and the playing of his masterpiece. From the moment when he assumed the orchestra would begin performing *The Magic Flute*, he lay back on his pillows, and *in imagination* enjoyed the whole performance—*hearing* every note as distinctly and with the same exquisite appreciation as he would have done had he actually been present.

481

The lady regarded the tramp severely. 'Have you ever been offered work?' she asked.

'Only once, ma'am,' he replied. 'Apart from that I've been shown nothing but kindness.'

482

Writing of the Queen Mother (widow of King George VI), Joe Illingworth said in the *Yorkshire Post* (7 February 1952): The Queen, whenever I have seen her, has always been at her ease with people, and nowhere was this more apparent than in the billiards room at the Ministry of Pensions Hospital, Leeds, before the war. She walked round the room talking to the wounded warriors, and then she saw a *Yorkshire Post* photographer.

'Would you like a picture *here*?' she asked him.

The photographer indicated that he would, and she at once beckoned the wounded about her. Some of them were a little shy, and as she stood among them, waiting for the picture to be taken, she noticed their diffidence and solemnity. After all, a picture with the Queen in it—with *them*!

A gleam entered the Queen's blue eyes. She turned. 'I mustn't blush *now*, must I?' she asked.

I recall that it was a very smiling picture the *Yorkshire Post* published next morning.

483

It is recorded that Edward FitzGerald never went into Woodbridge, in Suffolk, without dining at the *Bull Hotel*, where his host was honest John Grout who had a very high regard for Mr FitzGerald, though he had never heard even a murmur of *Omar Khayyam*. One day FitzGerald took a tall, bearded man to the *Bull Hotel*, and asked John Grout to put him up for the night, which John did. Landlord and guest had only a brief conversation—mostly about horses.

When the tall, bearded gentleman had gone, FitzGerald told John Grout that his friend's name was Alfred Tennyson. Seeing this made no impression on his host, he went on to explain that Queen Victoria had made him Poet Laureate; whereupon John Grout stared in amazement. 'What!' said he. 'Does the Queen think *such* a lot of a man who knows next to nothing about horses?'

484

One of the strangest and loneliest literary geniuses of France was Alfred de Musset, whose forty-seven years began and ended last century. Much that he did was shameful, but he was by no means wholly bad; and the spark of divinity never quite went out after that illness in which he was nursed by a Sister of Mercy.

We know almost nothing of her except that she preached goodness by being good. We do not know her name, but we know that her influence remained to the end.

All she did was to attend the patient. She talked to him as she sat by his bed; and, rather than be idle, this Sister of Mercy whiled away the hours by making two little trinkets—stupid little things, we might almost call them, namely, a small piece of worsted work knitted during his convalescence, and a pen-holder of coloured silks. On the pen-holder she embroidered the words: *Remember your promise.*

In time the poet and author fought his way back to a measure of health and strength. We may wonder, if we choose, what the saintly and lovely-spirited nurse had made Alfred de Musset promise, but we shall never know, though we know very well that he did not keep his promise, and that his moral life degenerated even more after she had gone.

But the strange thing is this—that when, though still comparatively young, this French genius came to his end, it was the calm and beautiful face of that woman which haunted him, and it was her quiet words that spoke to him like the voice of conscience. Much in his life had been bad, yet his soul longed for what was pure and good; and in his dying hours he whispered: 'Bring me the Sister of Mercy's presents, and bury them with me.'

485

Though still young, David Petch is an exceptionally experienced and capable farmer. He is the son of Methodist parents who live near Middlesbrough; and in 1953 he was chosen, along with two other young men, to spend four months in Australia in connection with exchange visits arranged by the Junior Farmers' Clubs of Australia. He returned from his travels with no end of stories, always attributing his good fortune to anything except its real cause—his own charm of manner.

David relates that towards the end of his tour of Australia he had to spend a night in Melbourne. Arriving late in the afternoon, he discovered to his consternation that he had no loose money with him. As the banks were closed he was unable to cash his travellers' cheques, and he was very well aware that no hotel proprietor would accept cheques as payment, especially from someone they had never seen before, and someone who wished to be on his journey again early next morning.

What was he to do?

With two shillings and sevenpence in his pocket—all the loose money he possessed—David walked into a café in Little Collins Street. It looked as if he had hit his unlucky day, for not only was he financially embarrassed, but there wasn't one chair vacant in the crowded room. No place to sit down and drink a cup of tea and think. All the tables were filled . . . all except one!

David made a bee-line for the small table in the corner—the table which had an empty chair. Others made a bee-line for that one vacant chair, but David got there first and sat down wearily. He found himself facing a middle-aged gentleman, at whom David nodded and smiled, for it is second nature to this Yorkshire farmer to be friendly. He made some casual remark, and in thus opening his mouth advertised his origin. 'You sound as if you haven't been down this way very long,' remarked the middle-aged gentleman.

David pleaded guilty, adding that he came from Great Ayton, near Middlesbrough, in Yorkshire. . . .

'Why,' exclaimed the middle-aged gentleman, 'Middlesbrough's only next door to Darlington, the town I lived in years ago when I was a boy. I've never been back since I came out here, but I remember . . .'

Elbows on the table in the crowded, noisy café, the two strangers compared notes and talked away as if they were old friends. In a few minutes the middle-aged gentleman knew just what had brought David to Australia, and David was informed that the middle-aged gentleman was proprietor of a photographic store, President of the Melbourne Camera Club, and—as luck would have it—a Methodist!

So the temporarily embarrassed traveller attended a meeting of the Camera Club before going on with his 'friend' to a meeting in Melbourne's Central Methodist Mission. Finally, he went to his hotel jingling all the money he needed, for the man from Darlington had been delighted to cash a traveller's cheque into Australian currency—yes, delighted to do anything he could for a fellow from Middlesbrough, which is only next door to Darlington, you know!

'There was only one seat in that crowded café,' David related, 'and I sat in it!'

486

In the days when animals could speak there lived in India, near the sacred city of Benares, four very pious creatures, a jackal, a monkey, an otter and a hare. Like hermits they dwelt apart, thought not of worldly pleasures, and kept the feast days, as do all good Brahmins.

One evening there came through the wood a poor old man. Finding the jackal crouching on a log, and deep in holy meditation, he said: 'Good beast, pray give me a little food.'

'Certainly,' replied the jackal. 'I have meat in my cave. I will bring you some.'

'I do not eat meat,' said the old man, and passed on.

Presently the beggar saw the otter on a rock in the stream. The otter was deep in meditation, but when the old man asked for food, he dived into the water, caught a fish, and offered it. 'I do not eat fish,' said the old man.

By and by he drew near the monkey as he swung from a branch by his tail, concentrating all his thoughts on immortality. When the old man asked for food, the obliging monkey gathered mangoes, and laid them at the beggar's feet. 'I do not eat fruit,' said the old man.

Lastly, when night had fallen and the moon was high in the cloudless sky, the old man found the hare crouching in the grass, the dew silvered on her thick fur. She, too, was deep in meditation. 'Of your charity,' pleaded the old man, 'give me to eat, for I am hungry.'

But the little hare had nothing to give except the lush grass to be found in the forest glade, and she knew men do not eat grass. So she thought: *I have nothing to give except myself. I will be his evening meal.*

Then, aloud, she replied: 'Sir, kindle a fire.'

So the old man kindled a fire, and when it was blazing fiercely, the little hare closed her eyes and took a leap into the flames. She expected to suffer before death brought release, but the flames did not scorch. Instead, she felt as if she were lying among cool lotus flowers; so she opened her eyes. Gazing at the beggar, she said, 'Kindle your fire again. I do not burn!' But even as she spoke, behold, the old man became young. He shot up taller than the highest trees, standing there arrayed in magnificent and regal apparel.

'Oh, little hare, little hare,' he whispered in tones softer and gentler than the sweetest music, 'I sought to test your charity. Truly it is boundless. It shall remain for all time an example and a challenge to men, for I will draw your portrait on the moon, and all who see it there shall remember your love.'

As he spoke he tore up a huge boulder, crushing it till it flowed like ink. Then, using a pine-tree as his pen, he drew a portrait of the little hare on the full moon.

487

John had worked for nearly sixty years on a Yorkshire farm. One day his employer ventured, gently, to suggest that it was time he retired.

The old man was indignant. 'Soa it's cummed ti *this*, 'as it?'

he asked. 'Ah'm not wanted neer longer? Ah worked for thi grandfather and for thi father, an' Ah tell thi, if Ah'd known this here job warn't going to be permanent, Ah'd nivver 'ave takken it on!'

488

Sir Wilfred Grenfell of Labrador used to tell the story of how a young Eskimo once went to him with a dislocated shoulder. He was able to put the shoulder right.

It was two years before Grenfell again called at that spot on the bleak shores of Labrador, but no sooner did the ship tie up than the Eskimo appeared with a pair of beautifully ornamented boots. As he presented them to Grenfell he pointed to his shoulder.

489

We always think of Blackpool as the home of fun and entertainment, the holiday place where everybody is happy all day long. But in 1953 there was a man in Blackpool who felt that he could not keep on keeping on much longer.

His wife was ill and in hospital. His own health was indifferent. He was in business for himself, but things were not going well, and he felt unable to make improvements. Somehow, worry and frustration had got him down, and he knew that he had been poor company for his wife even when she had been at home. He worried, and worrying made things worse.

One bright evening he called at the hospital, saw his wife, and learnt that, after all, the surgeon was going to operate. Feeling he could not return home there and then, he walked along the promenade towards Norbreck, unaware of the magnificent sunset, wrapped only in his own dark thoughts and fears.

Then he walked wearily back. Suddenly he stood still.

A party of cyclists—perhaps twenty-five or thirty of them—had been eating fish and chips. They'd been laughing and joking. They were girls and young men with gay spirits; but as the worried man approached they formed a circle on the sea-front, and had a sing-song. They sang: *Jesu, Lover of my soul.*

The worried man removed his hat, and listened as one

spellbound. The voices were strong yet sweet, and there were one or two tenors who ran off with the high notes. And as they sang:

> Thou, O Christ, art all I want,
> More than all in Thee I find;
> Raise the fallen, cheer the faint,
> Heal the sick, and lead the blind,

he found not only peace and strength and hope and faith but courage enough to keep on bravely until his wife was restored to health, and until—with new vigour—he made his business pay and found in his home the happiness he had lost.

490

Canadian history has many stirring tales of brave deeds and narrow escapes, but the story of Madeleine stands alone.

Madeleine de Vercheres was fourteen, the daughter of a French settler. Startled one day by a warning cry, 'The Indians!' she looked up to see the Iroquois running to the settlement. Back she flew from the river to the fort—if the settlement, a mere handful of cabins grouped together and protected by a rough stockade, might be called a fort. The menfolk were all away in the fields or woods; and, though at that moment Madeleine did not know it, most of them had been killed.

Strange as it may seem, the generalship fell naturally upon Madeleine, slip of a girl though she was. Slamming the doors of the compound, she gathered the entire personnel of the fort—two soldiers, an old man, some women and children, and her own brothers, the eldest only twelve. Had the Indians known how small were the numbers of the defenders they would have attacked instantly. Happily they did not know—and Madeleine had wit enough to see that they *must* not know. She determined that they never should know.

The two soldiers were so frightened that they ran off, and Madeleine found them preparing to blow up the magazine as the quickest way of ending their troubles. Girl though she was, she took command, posting the soldiers by the stockade, setting her brothers at two points, and pushing a gun into the old man's hands. Some of the women took guns also, and the single cannon was fired as a signal of distress, the signal to be sent on from fort to fort until it reached Montreal. Thus, in a few minutes, Madeleine put up a stout defence, contriving that shots should be continually ringing out from every quarter, a ruse which made the Indians believe the settlement was strongly defended.

All that night Madeleine moved about the fort, and all the next day. Now and then the Iroquois showed themselves, but the small hail of bullets routed them, and the apparent activities deceived them. So a week dragged by, the longest week in Madeleine's life, and still she held the fort, and still the Indians held back, hoping to starve out the garrison and make a dash when they weakened.

Then relief came from Montreal. The Iroquois were scattered, and General Madeleine's task was finished!

491

Once upon a time, long ago, an old lady lived in a vinegar bottle. How she got in, nobody knows; but in the vinegar bottle she was—cramped and stiff and miserable, for somebody had pushed the cork well down, and it pressed tightly on her head.

So she asked a fairy to get her out of the vinegar bottle, and give her a cottage to live in—just a little cottage in the country . . . two rooms and a tiny garden; that would be perfect. She'd be happy there a thousand years. Well, no sooner did she wish, than her wish came true—and you never saw a prettier country cottage.

After a few weeks, however, the old lady grew tired of having to polish the brass knocker and fetch water from the well; so she asked the fairy to do some fresh magic, and give her a more convenient residence.

And the fairy did. In the twinkling of an eye the old lady found herself in a mansion with no end of servants, and a fine carriage, and four white horses and a red-faced coachman. It was all perfectly marvellous until first one servant gave notice and then another. At last the old lady called for the fairy, and said: 'Look here, I want to be queen—then I can cut their heads off if they don't do as they're told!'

And, believe it or not, before she could turn round she *was* queen, with a heavy golden crown, and levees to attend. It's not surprising she was soon bored to death; so she shouted for the fairy, and said: 'Listen! What I *really* want . . .'

But the fairy vanished in a puff of smoke; and when the old lady got over the shock—why, you've guessed, of course . . . she was in the vinegar bottle again, *with the cork right down*!

492

Mrs Barker, who lives in a back street, has had a hard life, and it is harder now than ever. All along, Mr Barker has been a good-for-nothing, and for over thirty years it has been Mrs Barker who has somehow kept the home going, brought up a family of six, and done it all with little help and no praise from her shiftless husband.

When her youngest son was married Mrs Barker heaved a sigh of relief, and confided in her neighbour, Mrs Wentworth, that the last of her brood was off the nest, and maybe life would be a bit easier.

But things didn't work out that way, for her daughter, Tessa, died soon afterwards, leaving two small boys. Their father wanted to put them in an institution, but Mrs Barker (as perhaps you have guessed) wouldn't hear of it. So Alfred and Peter came to live with her.

It was like having a family all over again. It meant cooking for four instead of two. It meant washing and mending and cleaning and baking. It meant weariness and worry.

One evening Mrs Wentworth looked in to ask Mrs Barker how she was getting along. She knew Mr Barker would have shuffled off to the pub, and that she wouldn't have to stand any of *his* nonsense. And she was right. Mrs Barker was sitting by the fire, darning socks and looking the very picture of content. Peter had gone to bed, but Alfred was sitting on a stool by the fender, a book in his hand.

'Eh, come in, come in, dearie,' said Mrs Barker as the back door opened. 'Bring a chair up to the fire. Eh, I was just thinking how lucky I am—I can't see to read these days, but Alfie, *he* reads beautiful, and I do like listening.'

493

When an eighteenth-century headmaster of Plympton Grammar School died, his widow did her best to make a living by opening a girls' school. Her husband had not been rich, but she was now so poor that although she managed somehow she hadn't a penny left over for luxuries.

Among her pupils was a little girl who happened to hear some local gossip never intended for such small ears. She learnt that the widow never appeared at local functions simply because she couldn't afford a new dress.

For weeks this piece of information troubled the schoolgirl, whose one desire was to see her schoolmistress arrayed in finery. Could she help? Dare she try? She remembered that Sir Joshua Reynolds had once been a scholar at the Plympton Grammar School; and so, with truly feminine intuition, she stole back to the schoolroom after the other girls had gone home one day, and composed a letter to the famous artist. Her penmanship was indifferent. Her fingers became very inky, but the love in her heart overflowed as she begged the great man in London to provide the widow in Devon with a beautiful dress.

We know that Sir Joshua—as generous as he was rich—was deeply touched by this appeal, for one day two wonderful silk gowns arrived in Plympton.

We are sure the widow was delighted with her unexpected bit of good fortune, but we suspect that the little maid with the loving heart was even more so.

494

A Roman Catholic writing to the *Church Times* with charity and a rare touch of humour gives us a quaint peep of heaven. While being shown round he was told by his guide: 'Over there you see the Wesleyans. Yonder the Anglicans; and that noisy crowd is the Salvation Army.'

The visitor wished to know who were behind the high wall, whereupon the guide said: 'Ssh! Those are the Roman Catholics. They think they're the only people here.'

495

A man who had lost his only son was so distressed that he shut himself in a dark room, and wept day and night. At last

Demonax, the Greek philosopher, visited him, saying: 'My friend, I feel quite sure that I can restore your dear boy to you if only . . .'

'If *what*?' demanded the mourner passionately.

'If you can tell me the names of three people who have never had occasion to mourn,' replied Demonax.

The bereaved father sank back, as in despair; but presently, reflecting that death comes to all, and that every mourner is one of a vast company, he dried his tears and walked calmly out of his darkened room into the sunshine.

496

Three hundred years ago there lived in the Yorkshire town of Bridlington a Quaker named Robert Fowler. Strange though it may sound, he built a ship not knowing why he did so, but sure that God had need of her. An inner voice had said, 'Build!' So Robert built.

Robert named his ship the *Woodhouse*; and when she was finished he sailed her south along the coast to the Thames, and berthed in the Port of London. Then he came ashore, and the first person he happened to meet was another Quaker who, that very afternoon, had attended a meeting at which he and nine Friends had prayed that God would provide a ship to take them all to America. When he told Robert about this, the Yorkshire Quaker replied: 'Friend, thy prayer is answered.'

So the matter was concluded there and then; and within a few weeks the ten Quakers and their families, accompanied by Robert, set sail for America.

Their adventure was perilous indeed—a kind of seventeenth-century Kon-Tiki expedition. Not one of the Quakers knew anything of ocean navigation. Their vessel was so small and so heavily laden that no seaman would sail in her. They had no chart. But with sublime faith they hoisted sail, steered steadily westwards, and met together for prayer whenever they did not know what to do. They ran into storms. They were buffeted by contrary winds. They were chased by a French privateer. They were becalmed for days together.

But the amazing thing is that they reached North America safely, *landing at Long Island within two miles of the spot they had hoped to reach.*

497

The writer gave up his seat in the bus to a little harassed woman one day in 1942. 'Eh, thanks very much,' she murmured, as she sat down. 'I'm dead beat! Do you know, Sunday's the only day I don't go out to scrub other people's floors, and the only day I cook a dinner. And now, with Jim being in hospital, I've to leave home at one, and walk two miles to catch a bus, and maybe stand in a queue, and then stand all the way to the hospital; and going home I've to fight to get on, and it's a struggle and a harass from beginning to end.'

She paused for breath. 'And it's all so that I can see Jim for a few minutes,' she added. '*But it's worth it.*'

498

John Bradshaw, who sentenced Charles the First to death, wore an iron hat, and William Murdock wore a wooden hat, without which we might never have heard of him.

The story is told that he applied for a post with Boulton and Watt of Birmingham in the days when they were making the first steam-engines. The interview was not going well for Murdock, and Boulton was about to dismiss the blunt Scotsman, who seemed ill at ease, when something dropped. It was Murdock's hat. Murdock snatched it up at once, but it had made such a clatter that Boulton remarked, 'That's a hard hat of yours.'

'Yes, sir,' stammered Murdock, more nervous than ever. 'It's timmer, sir.'

'Timber? Do you mean to say it's a *wooden* hat?'

'Yes, sir. I made it myself; turned it on a lathe I made myself, sir.'

'You'll do,' said Boulton.

It was the beginning of Murdock's long and glorious association with the firm.

499

We sometimes wish the critics would be less vigilant. They say this story is untrue, that it can never have happened, and that Beethoven's immortal *Moonlight Sonata* was born much less romantically than tradition would have us believe. Well, perhaps they are right, but for all that it is a story worth telling again:

One moonlight night (says the tale the critics laugh at) Beethoven and a friend were walking in the streets when the great musician stopped. 'Listen,' he said, 'someone is playing one of my compositions.'

The music came from a little house in a poor street. Beethoven peered into a room where a man repaired shoes while a girl played to him. As the musician watched, the girl burst into tears, saying: 'Oh, it is so beautiful that I cannot do it justice.' When she turned from the piano, he saw that she was blind.

Beethoven then knocked at the door, and when the two friends were admitted he told the girl he was a musician, and asked if he might play to her. She was delighted. Taking his seat at the piano, the immortal genius played as only he *could* play. For an hour he entertained father and daughter. The candle went out. The cobbler left his shoes unmended, and still Beethoven played on.

'Wonderful!' exclaimed the girl. 'Who are you?'

For answer Beethoven struck the first chords of the sonata she had been trying to play, and at once she ran forward and kissed his hands. 'You are Beethoven, Beethoven!' she exclaimed. 'Oh, it is wonderful, wonderful! Play again!'

And the story goes on to tell that there in the moonlight, in that poor house, Beethoven, inspired, composed the *Moonlight Sonata*.

500

Long years ago the Red Indians of North America trained their boys and youths with the greatest possible care. Every Red Indian boy dreamed of the day when he would be acknowledged by his tribe as a *brave*, that is, a fully accredited warrior—one who had proved himself efficient in peace and war, resourceful, reliable, and above all courageous.

The long and severe period of training began early; and one of the very first ordeals was that of the vigil.

A time came when a boy who had already passed some of the easiest tests was taken by his father deep into the forest. The two followed familiar paths until they entered a region the boy did not know. The wigwam was miles behind; everything about him was strange and—to a boy nurtured in the terrifying superstitions of his tribe—full of sinister loneliness. Towards sunset father and son shared a meal; then, as darkness fell, the father said, 'Good-bye,' turned his back on the lad, and left him to spend the night alone in the forest.

It was an experience which might well have frightened a full-grown man, and we may be sure that such a night-long vigil would intimidate even the son of a brave.

There, hour after hour, the Redskin boy had to keep watch alone—alone in the impenetrable darkness, alone with wild animals prowling round, alone with his fears of ghosts and evil spirits. How long that night must have seemed!

But even the longest night wears to morning; and when at last the dawn broke, the Red Indian boy made the glorious discovery that actually he had *not* been alone, for in the pale light he saw, standing close by him, his father who, unknown to him, had shared the vigil, and had kept watch through all the hours of darkness.

ACKNOWLEDGMENTS

THE compiler gratefully acknowledges his indebtedness to the following:

Mr James Barnes and Appleton-Century-Crofts Inc. for permission to quote *From Then Till Now*; Mr Ross L. Holman and the Editor of *Good Business* for the story numbered 309; the Marchesa Stella Vitelleschi and Messrs Hurst and Blackett Ltd. for a quotation from *Out of My Coffin*; the Executors of David Lloyd George and Messrs Ivor Nicholson and Watson Ltd. for the item from Lloyd George's *War Memoirs*; Messrs William Heinemann Ltd., and also but separately Doubleday and Co. Inc. for the extract from *Madame Curie*, by Eve Curie (copyright, 1937); Messrs Arthur Barker Ltd. for the story of Churchill, Hitler and Mussolini from Colonel Rémy's book, *The Silent Company*; the Editor of *The Children's Newspaper* for many items, including one or two from *My Magazine*; the Editor of the *Christian Science Monitor*; the Editor of *The Church Times* for the story numbered 494; Messrs William Heinemann Ltd. for the quotation from J. B. Priestley's *English Journey*; Messrs Hodder and Stoughton Ltd. for permission to use a story from *A Labrador Doctor*, by Sir Wilfred Grenfell, and the same publishers and Mr Hugh Redwood for an item from *God in the Slums*; Mr A. Tilney Bassett and the Editor of *The Listener* for a story of W. E. Gladstone; Messrs Methuen and Co. Ltd. for several items; the Manager of Reader's Digest Association Ltd. for unfailing co-operation and permission to include a number of selections from *Reader's Digest*; Messrs Williams and Norgate Ltd. for a story adapted from Mark Hambourg's *The Eighth Octave*; Messrs Jonathan Cape Ltd. for an item from *The Summer Game* by Neville Cardus; G. S. Sandilands and Messrs A. R. Mowbray for a quotation from *Stories and Prayers at Five to Ten*; my friend, Rev. Dr Leslie F. Church, the Editors of the *Stirling Observer*, *Paisley Daily Express*, *Newcastle Journal*, *Hexham Courant* and *Cornish Guardian*, and Mr F. Austin Hyde, Mr H. E. Walter and Sir W. L. Andrews, Editor of the *Yorkshire Post*, for generously allowing me to use their stories. I am also deeply appreciative of the help and encouragement given by Mrs Southwick, Mr Maurice Horspool, Mr A. P. Masser and especially Mr E. P. L. Dixon.

INDEX

Note: Numbers refer to the stories, *not* to pages; s. indicates *story* or *stories*.